ROYAL HISTORICAL SOCIETY
STUDIES IN HISTORY
New Series

GENDER AND SPACE
IN EARLY MODERN ENGLAND

GENDER AND SPACE
IN EARLY MODERN ENGLAND

Amanda Flather

THE ROYAL HISTORICAL SOCIETY
THE BOYDELL PRESS

First published 2007

Transferred to digital printing

A Royal Historical Society publication
Published by The Boydell Press
an imprint of Boydell & Brewer Ltd
PO Box 9, Woodbridge, Suffolk IP12 3DF, UK
and of Boydell & Brewer Inc.
668 Mt Hope Avenue, Rochester, NY 14620, USA
website: www.boydellandbrewer.com

ISBN 9780861932863

ISSN 0269-2244

A CiP catalogue record for this book is available
from the British Library

This publication is printed on acid-free paper

Contents

List of Tables

Acknowledgements

I have incurred many debts of gratitude in writing this book. The greatest is to John Walter, for his patient, generous, insightful and good-humoured supervision of my PhD thesis. Thanks are also due for his continued enthusiasm for this project. I should also like to thank Alison Rowlands and Joan Davies, who were involved in supervising parts of the thesis and from whom I have learnt a great deal. I am also extremely grateful to the staff of the Essex Record Office for the time spent helping me to get to grips with the records of the church courts.

The final shape of the project owes an enormous amount to Alex Walsham who, as my advisory editor for the RHS Studies in History series, has been immensely helpful and encouraging during the process of reworking and expanding my PhD into this book. I wish to thank her for her vigilance, generosity, unstinting insight and encouragement. I have been aided by the critical comments of my examiners, Bernard Capp and Laura Gowing. I am also indebted to the RHS anonymous reader for his suggestions. I have benefited enormously from discussion with fellow students and staff in the Department of History at the University of Essex. David Borg-Muscat, Lisa Smith, Rachel Rich, Julie Gammon, Deirdre Heavens, Jane Pearson and Janet Guyford, in particular, have been very generous with ideas. I am also grateful to Clodagh Tait and Wendy Gagen who read some, or all, of the final draft.

I am indebted to the Arts and Humanities Research Board for a three-year postgraduate studentship and to the staff of the Department of History at Essex for providing continued support, which enabled me to redraft the manuscript. Finally, I would like to thank my family, John, Edward and Charlie Flather, Daphne and Phillip Stovin and Madeleine Flather for the numerous ways in which they have given me support.

Amanda Flather
January 2007

Abbreviations

BL   British Library
C&C   *Continuity and Change*
CSPD   *Calendar of state papers, domestic series, of the reign of Charles I,*
              1625–1649, ed. J. Bruce and W. D. Hamilton, Nendeln 1967
EcHR   *Economic History Review*
ERO (Ch.)   Essex Record Office, Chelmsford
ERO (Col.)   Essex Record Office, Colchester
ESRO   East Suffolk Record Office, Ipswich
G&H   *Gender and History*
GL   Guildhall Library, London
HJ   *Historical Journal*
HWJ   *History Workshop Journal*
JEH   *Journal of Ecclesiastical History*
LMA   London Metropolitan Archive
P&P   *Past and Present*
PRO   Public Record Office
TNA   The National Archive
VCH   *The Victoria county history of Essex*, 1903–

Note on the Text

Quotations from manuscript sources retain the original spelling and punctuation. U/v and i/j have been distinguished. Abbreviations and contractions have been expanded. Dates follow old style, but the year is taken to begin on 1 January.

Introduction

Writers of domestic manuals, sermons and educational tracts defined the spaces within which daily life unfolded in seventeenth-century English society in gendered terms. Dod and Cleaver's *Godlie forme of householde government* (1612) offered the most comprehensive version of this commonplace theme of classical origins that asserted:

> The dutie of the Husband is to get goods: and of the Wife to gather them together, and save them. The dutie of the Husband is to travell abroad, to seeke living: and the Wives dutie is to keepe the house. The dutie of the husband is to get money and provision: and of the Wives, not vainely to spend it. The dutie of the husband is to deale with many men: and of the Wives to talke with few. The dutie of the Husband is to be entermedling and of the wife, to be solitary and withdrawne. The dutie of the man is, to be skilfull in talke; and of the wife, to boast of silence. ... The dutie of the Husband is to bee lorde of all: and of the wife, to give account of all: The dutie of the husband is, to dispatch all things without dore: and of the wife, to oversee and give order for all things within the house.[1]

According to early modern male moralists, these principles provided people with a divinely ordained and natural spatial system through which human experience should be organised; yet it was hardly successful. Space could be theoretically defined but male and female experience of it could not be so ordered. People lived space as social beings, and the way they did so could not be organised in so orderly a pattern.

Thus we encounter the dual themes of this book. On the one hand the theories about gender and space that formed part of the ideological framework for men's and women's lives; on the other the way people experienced space and imposed their own meanings upon it. Far from being simply the structure that determined how gender relations developed, space was the basis for the formation of gender identities, which were constantly contested and reconstructed. Where people lived, worked and worshipped in early modern England are all questions rich in symbolism and social meanings. In this book the gendering of space is not just about how the location of the activities of men and women was determined, but also how spaces for these activities were used by men and women and given social and cultural meanings. It is also not simply about men and women but different categories of men and women. It is about the complexities created in the way people experienced and gave meaning to space through the way gender intersected with other categories

---

[1]   J. Dod and R. Cleaver, *A godlie forme of householde government: for the ordering of private families, according to the direction of Gods word*, London 1612, 167–8.

of social identity such as age, social and marital status. Space had different meanings not only for men and women, but also for different types of men and women.

This book shows that by focusing upon the issue of space it is possible to illuminate aspects of the often opaque constructions and workings of gender in early modern England. The links between space, social relations and power are a well-established field of enquiry amongst scholars of disciplines other than history. The geographer Doreen Massey has argued that 'the spatial organisation of society ... is integral to the production of the social and not merely its result. It is fully implicated in both history and politics.'[2]

Similarly, the anthropologist Shirley Ardener has argued that 'space reflects social organisation, but of course, once space has been bounded and shaped, it is no longer a neutral background; it exerts its own influence'.[3] The organisation of space is not then just a reflection of society and its values, it is a medium through which society is reproduced, since it provides the context in which social and power relations are negotiated. Space, as Massey has asserted, 'both reflects and has effects back on the ways in which gender is constructed and understood in the societies in which we live'.[4]

Central to these arguments, therefore, and to the analytical focus of this book, is the conceptualisation of the complex and 'malleable' term space in terms of social relations. A space is more than, and different from, a physical location or place. A space is an arena of social action. Natt Alcock explains that 'space is a practised place. Thus the street geometrically defined by urban planning is transformed into a space by walkers.'[5] Similarly, Hannah More has argued that 'meanings are not inherent in the organisation of ... space, but must be invoked through the activities of social actors'.[6] A place is transformed into a space by the social actors who constitute it through everyday use.

This analytical recognition of human agency overcomes two main criticisms of attempts to combine the study of space with historical analysis. First of all, recognition of the role of the subjects who give meaning to space through everyday use counters the charge that the study of space is 'unhistorical' in the sense that it studies static structures at the expense of change over time. Space conceptualised in terms of social relations has temporal dimensions. As Doreen Massey has argued, space is 'inherently dynamic', since social actors

---

[2] D. Massey, *Space, place and gender*, Cambridge 1994, 4.

[3] S. Ardener, 'Ground rules and social maps for women: an introduction', in S. Ardener (ed.), *Women and space*, London 1981, 12.

[4] Massey, *Space, place and gender*, 186.

[5] N. Alcock, 'Physical space and social space', in M. Locock (ed.), *Meaningful architecture: social interpretations of buildings*, Aldershot 1994, 207–30.

[6] H. Moore, *Space, text and gender: an anthropological study of the Marakwet of Kenya*, Cambridge 1986, 8.

attribute different meanings to space at different times.[7] Such a conceptualisation of space, moreover, acknowledges differential and temporal experience
and use of space by distinct individuals or groups, whether the distinction is
based on gender, age, social status or some other factor.[8]

Second, the recognition that the use and organisation of space both
constructs and is constructed by social relations, allows the historian to move
beyond debates about an apparent opposition between structure and agency
to explore the relationship between them. As various theorists have argued,
subjects are simultaneously subject and active in what Anthony Giddens has
termed the process of 'structuration' of institutions that characterise society.[9]
Structures do not exist as an abstract, mechanistic set of rules, acting as a coer-
cive force on helpless human subjects. But, at the same time, the strategies
and intentions of social actors are regulated.

The micro-sociology of Pierre Bourdieu is helpful here. His concept of
habitus can help explain how individual agents ascribe cultural meanings
– in our case to spaces. The *habitus* is a set of deeply internalised dispositions
that limit, without determining, the possibilities of individual agency. The
habitus is learned through a slow process of inculcation. Patterns and norms
of behaviour and ways of thinking about the world gradually become internalised and naturalised through training in mind and body. Mechanisms of
inculcation include factors which arrange the physical disposition of subjects,
such as the learning of table manners and ways of walking, the use of material objects, the time and location of practices, the ease and constraint of
access to architectural settings. They also include factors such as reading and
hearing, which shape the mind. All these form media by which an individual
becomes socialised into the performance of a social role within the culture of
the group. Bourdieu emphasises that the *habitus* is flexible and, in a limited
way, enabling: it is defined as 'a set of schemes enabling agents to generate an
infinity of practices adapted to endlessly changing situations'.[10] Constructing
the parameters set by the *habitus* therefore does not preclude the possibility
of agency or change. The *habitus* sets boundaries, to both the conceptual
and practical options available to a person, but it does not wholly determine
them.

The *habitus* operates in relation to what Bourdieu has described as a 'social
field' – in our case a space. A social field is inhabited by several different
habituses placed in differential power relations. This helps to explain why and

7 Massey, *Space, place and gender*, 2–3.
8 Ibid. 3; More, *Space, text and gender*, 7; S. Kent, *Domestic architecture and the use of space:
an inter-disciplinary cross-cultural study*, Cambridge 1990, 3.
9 A. Giddens, *Central problems in social theory*, London 1979, and *The constitution of
society*, Cambridge 1984; P. Burke, *History and social theory*, Cambridge 1992, 113, 161.
10 P. Bourdieu, *Outline of a theory of practice*, Cambridge 1977, 16, 78–87; Burke, *History
and social theory*, 120.

how different social actors can ascribe different meanings to the same space or field. Those meanings are shaped and limited by a person's *habitus*.[11]

Drawing on these theoretical approaches, this book embarks upon a systematic analysis of how spaces were socially used by men and women in early modern England and the meanings that they attached to them. A historian of gender has much to gain from a study structured in this way. Gender is recognised by historians not as a natural given but as an inculcated social construction.[12] It is not used to describe the sexual differences ascribed to bodies. It refers to a complex process of social construction and reassertion through continual performance, a process that changes over time.[13] Since space is not simply the product of social relations, but also a ground of social construction, space lies at the heart of our concerns.

Gender history is also a history of power relations. Recent work on early modern gender has offered a corrective to the assumption that all men were confident, autonomous patriarchs and women were always and simply passive victims of absolute male dominance. Scholarly attention is now paid to the complex, varied, uneven and changing articulation of patriarchal authority and the different positions of different men and women within the early modern social system. Bernard Capp, for example, has explored the agency of older married women within the household and the neighbourhood, focusing in particular on the role of plebeian married women's social networks; Laura Gowing's study of the early modern body has highlighted the power exercised by older married women and midwives over the young and the single.[14] In addition, Alex Shepard's path-breaking study of early modern masculinity has shown that men were not uniformly powerful, that access to 'patriarchal dividends' depended upon age, marital and social status as well as gender.[15] Taken together this work has exposed the ways that contradictions and tensions between the ideal model of gender relations disseminated through the pulpit and prescriptive literature and the practices of everyday life, as well as the intersection of gender with other social factors such as age, social and marital status, created arenas for female agency. It has been emphasised that this agency can best be seen not in occasional acts of resistance, but in the continual negotiation of everyday interactions. Michael Braddick and John Walter have called recently for a search for 'sources and spaces' in which the historian can see these informal, often opaque and complex aspects of

[11] Bourdieu, *Outline of a theory of practice*, 16, 78–87, and 'Social space and the genesis of classes', in his *Language and symbolic power*, Cambridge 1991, 230; Burke, *History and social theory*, 110–14, 118–26.

[12] J. W. Scott, 'Gender: a useful category for historical analysis', *American Historical Review* xcii (1986), 1053–76.

[13] J. Butler, *Gender trouble: feminism and the subversion of identity*, London 1991, 139–41.

[14] B. Capp, '*When gossips meet*': *women, family, and neighbourhood in early modern England*, Oxford 2003; L. Gowing, *Common bodies: women, touch and power in seventeenth-century England*, London 2003.

[15] A. Shepard, *Meanings of manhood in early modern England*, Oxford 2003.

the everyday politics of gender in process.[16] In similar vein, Alex Shepard has argued forcefully that 'to understand the social practice of patriarchy in early modern England, we need to be far more aware of precisely which men stood to gain, which women stood to lose, and in which *contexts*'.[17] Yet while we have large numbers of *thematic* studies in print, remarkably little work has been done on the contexts in which social relationships were negotiated. Since space is the context in which these power relations were played out, and the organisation of space influenced how and when interactions occurred, the usefulness of spatial analysis becomes apparent. It provides us with a highly contextualised, dynamic picture of how gender relations were constructed, maintained, manipulated, negotiated, contested or changed by daily human encounters and through the medium of space.

The relationship between gender and space has been a consistent theme in histories of women and of gender over many years, even if not always explicitly stated. One of the most influential master narratives about the status of women is a story of decline from the early modern to the Victorian age. Historians who support this theory argue that, with the advent of capitalism and the rise of a class society, female marginalisation was reflected in, and reinforced by, progressive loss of access to public space by women. The earliest articulations of this approach came in the field of economic history. Alice Clark's classic *Working lives of women in the seventeenth century* (1919) and Ivy Pinchbeck's *Women workers in the industrial revolution* (1930) both argue that the decline in women's economic status came about as a result of the separation of work from home, even if they differed as to when they thought these changes in the spatial organisation of labour took place.[18] Other historians have argued that, as the division between domestic space and workspace became more distinct, the household became more sharply identified as private, domestic and feminine, in opposition to the public and masculine spaces of work and politics, from which women were progressively excluded. The most important and influential of these arguments about the emergence of 'separate spheres' has been made by Laura Davidoff and Catherine Hall in their *Family fortunes: men and women of the English middle class, 1780–1850* (1987). They argue for, and trace, an evolution of separate spheres during the period and they link the separation of male and female worlds to the formation of middle-class identity. The outcome of this sharpening of spatial and social distinctions was to produce a more rigidly hierarchical and patriarchal society.

---

16 M. J. Braddick and J. Walter, 'Grids of power: order, hierarchy and subordination in early modern society', in M. J. Braddick and J. Walter (eds), *Negotiating power in early modern society: order, hierarchy and subordination in Britain and Ireland*, Cambridge 2001, 39.
17 Shepard, *Meanings of manhood*, 4.
18 Clark saw the allegedly rapid advance in capitalism at the end of the seventeenth century as the pivotal period of change, while Pinchbeck argued that fundamental changes in the spatial and social organisation of labour did not occur until the 'industrial revolution' in the nineteenth century.

The separate spheres paradigm remains influential. But there is a mounting body of literature, which challenges many of its assumptions. Work on masculinity, for example, has drawn attention to the 'private' and domestic aspects of the lives of men as well as women.[19] The 'public' aspects of the family have also been addressed in terms of its relationship to the community, to political institutions, public policy, and in terms of its economic role.[20] Studies have begun to stress continuity in the spheres and status of women. Historians of women's work in particular have argued that during the pre-industrial era of domestic production, women's economic status was already low and opportunities for work were constrained. Amanda Vickery takes arguments for continuity still further by stressing that normative notions of a basic separation of spheres in which women were associated with home and children, while men controlled 'public institutions', was not a creation of the nineteenth century, but could be 'applied to almost any century and any culture'; it was an idea 'at least as old as Aristotle'. She calls for detailed studies to find out 'how women accepted, negotiated, contested or simply ignored the much quoted precepts of proper female behaviour' in different times and in different places.[21]

Vickery's work points to the need to extend study of the ways in which ideologies about gender and space and practices of gender roles intersect back into the seventeenth century, but to date most research has focused on the period after 1750. While it has been acknowledged that the gender order of early modern England was often defined in spatial terms, for the most part historians of the early modern period have implicitly or explicitly rejected the applicability of the separate spheres' paradigm for the pre-modern past.[22] Research has concentrated on recovering the 'public' aspects of women's lives and the ways in which the worlds of men and women were integrated rather than separated, especially in arenas of work and worship.[23] Work on the early

[19] For studies that emphasise the 'private' and 'domestic' aspects of men's lives see J. Tosh, *Men at home: domesticity and the Victorian middle class*, London 1999, and R. B. Shoemaker, *Gender in English society, 1650–1850: the emergence of separate spheres?*, London 1998. For a discussion of the relationship between men's 'private' behaviour and their 'public' reputation see E. A. Foyster, *Manhood in early modern England: honour, sex and marriage*, London 1999.

[20] K. Lynch, 'The family and the history of public life', *Journal of Interdisciplinary History* xxiv (1994), 665–84.

[21] A. Vickery, 'Golden age to separate spheres? A review of the categories and chronology of English women's history', *HJ* xxxvi (1993), 413, 414, and *The gentleman's daughter: women's lives in Georgian England*, London 1998, 6.

[22] For studies that outline the patriarchal model of gendered space see S. D. Amussen, *An ordered society: gender and class in early modern England*, Oxford 1988, 68–9; A. Fletcher, *Gender, sex and subordination in England, 1500–1800*, London 1995, 120–1; and L. Gowing, *Domestic dangers: women, words and sex in early modern London*, Oxford 1996, 86–7. Studies that explicitly reject the 'separate spheres' paradigm include M. Hunt, *The middling sort: commerce, gender, and the family in England, 1680–1780*, London 1996, and J. Smail, *The origins of middle-class culture: Halifax, Yorkshire, 1660–1780*, New York 1994.

[23] Detailed bibliographies of this research are given as they relate to each chapter.

modern family has argued that pre-modern households were not 'areas of privacy' but 'public political institutions'.[24] Keith Wrightson in particular has stressed that early modern marriage was an economic if unequal, partnership, and other studies have highlighted the ways in which the tasks and spaces of men and women overlapped in a society in which there was not the sharp division between work and home that later generations experienced.[25]

Influenced by the insights and accomplishments of the social history of the 1970s, more recent work has been keen to make distinctions between prescription and practice, to recover the material circumstances of the lives of men and women in early modern society. Yet while this research enormously enriches our knowledge of female and male experience and emphasises that prescription and practice should not be confused with one another, in other ways it shrinks the scope of analysis of gender and space. First, it presents an uncritical picture of a heterosocial world, and conceals the degree of segregation that obtained in early modern society. Universities and formal institutions of local and national government were exclusively male arenas.[26] More important, it overlooks more recent developments in gender history that, influenced in part by the linguistic turn, have complicated our understanding of how prescription and practice relate to one another. While prescription tells us how people were supposed or told to act, it does not provide evidence of how people actually behaved. But 'ideal' prescription and 'real' practice were not wholly distinct. The content of conduct literature was a product of the interests and concerns of its readership, just as 'real' lives were shaped by the texts that formed part of the culture. People might revise or reject normative notions, but the two are not wholly separable. Laura Gowing, for example, in her study of early modern gender relations, has stressed that relationships within 'real' households were shaped by prescriptive and popular literature, just as imaginative and informative descriptions of marriage drew on stories of 'real' lives. The language of insult and the examinations and informations of witnesses in marital disputes were informed by familiar printed fictions and prescriptions. At the same time, women manipulated normative notions and texts telling tales of female weakness and dependence to pursue their own interests, in particular if they wished to extricate themselves from an

---

[24] P. Collinson, 'The Protestant family', in his The birthpangs of Protestant England: religious and cultural change in the sixteenth and seventeenth centuries, London 1998, 60–1.
[25] K. Wrightson, English society, 1580–1680, London 1982, 93. For studies that stress patterns of gender-mixing within early modern society see Hunt, The middling sort; Shoemaker, Gender in English society; and M. Ingram, Church courts, sex and marriage in England, 1570–1640, Cambridge 1987, 241–2.
[26] For studies that highlight more segregated aspects of the early modern social world see B. Capp, 'Separate domains? Women and authority in early modern England', in P. Griffiths, A. Fox and S. Hindle (eds), The experience of authority in early modern England, London 1996, 117–45, and 'When gossips meet'; Gowing, Common bodies; and S. Mendelson and P. Crawford, Women in early modern England, Oxford 1998, 202–55.

unattractive marriage agreement.[27] Experiences and discourses are not the same thing, but they intersect and overlap. Gender roles as actually lived were a product of complex interactions of ideas and material circumstances.

With these developments in mind, the following analysis of the social effect of gender on the use of space in the early modern period will examine normative notions and practice in relation to one another rather than viewing them as prescription on the one hand and practice on the other. There is an important difference between this analytical focus and the various strands of the 'separate spheres' literature. The analytical framework of this study is not constructed around a male/public and female/private or domestic dichotomy, which runs the risk of an unhistorical, contextually insensitive application of those terms. By contrast, the analysis heeds Vickery's advice that 'we should take care to discover whether our interpretation of public and private marries with that of historical actors themselves'.[28] The focus of this study is not 'spheres' but the spaces themselves, how historical actors defined and described them and how normative ideas and practice intersected to shape gendered use and experience of those spaces. This allows us to move discussion of gender relations away from arid arguments about 'prescription versus practice' or 'representational versus real' and to attend to the complex interactions between them.[29] It is the argument of this book that normative notions shaped individual perception and experience of space in early modern society, but the links between them were far from straightforward. Men and women might accept, negotiate, manipulate or even ignore normative boundaries, just as they do today (though the distribution of power meant that some were more able to do so than others).

Studies of different spaces in modern societies have discussed the extent to which individual understandings of them, and behaviour within them, are influenced by a host of cultural clues, enabling individuals to create their own 'mental maps' to help them to use spaces, and to let them know when spaces might be difficult or dangerous to enter.[30] These different perceptions and experiences are determined in large measure by the different degrees of power wielded by individuals or groups over how the space is accessed, used and given social and cultural meanings. As Massey has argued, spaces can be gendered in 'a myriad of ways', even when they are shared.[31]

This study is concerned principally with the idea that spaces can be

---

[27] Gowing, *Domestic dangers*, 54–5, 232–9.
[28] Vickery, 'Golden age to separate spheres?', 412.
[29] For studies that explore the interaction between ideologies and practices of gender roles see O. Hufton, *The prospect before her: a history of women in western Europe*, I: 1500–1800, London 1995; Shoemaker, *Gender in English society*; and Shepard, *Meanings of manhood*.
[30] D. Stea, *Landscape*, London 1967, 17, 27–8; P. Gould and R. White, *Mental maps*, London 1986, 108; Massey, *Space, place and gender*, 185–6.
[31] Moore, *Space, text and gender*, 8; Massey, *Space, place and gender*, 185–6.

gendered, even when they are not exclusively used by men or women through perception, experience and use. This does not imply a lack of interest in or investigation into spaces in early modern society that were organised around systems of sexual segregation, as the chapter on sacred space will show. But it does allow for a more sophisticated and nuanced analysis of gendered power relations within spaces that until recently have simply been classified as 'mixed'.[32]

We already know a great deal about the layout, appearance, form and content of the spaces that form the focus of this study, from detailed empirical examinations of material culture by archaeologists and some historians. Without such research this book could not have been undertaken. Scholars have used this material evidence to explore how the material world was given social and cultural meaning. Pamela Graves, for example, has used plans of parish churches, 'with the aim to develop an understanding of the architectural space of the later medieval parish church in England, based on social practice'.[33] Roberta Gilchrist has used archaeological and architectural evidence to provide a nuanced and complex account of the gendering of space in medieval monasteries.[34] Andy Boddington has analysed the material remains of Anglo-Saxon churchyards to trace links between burial sites and social status,[35] while Brown has used house plans to determine changes in layout and use of houses in seventeenth-century London. Lorna Weatherill has studied household inventories to map room use and to look at the way objects take on cultural meanings in different contexts. Rachel Garrard's work on household inventories has focused on the significance of the varying quality of objects such as beds or chairs assigned to individuals within the household as symbols of power and status. More generally, Matthew Johnson has used a variety of forms of material and documentary evidence to argue that changes in the spatial organisation of fields, churches and houses, associated with the 'rise of rural capitalism' between the fifteenth and eighteenth

[32] For studies that conceptualise and define 'gendered space' in terms of sexual segregation see A. T. Friedman, *House and household in Elizabethan England*, London 1989, and C. Wall, 'Gendering rooms: domestic architecture and literary arts', *Eighteenth Century Fiction* v (1993), 349–72. For socio-anthropological studies that discuss the links between female power and status and systems of sexual and spatial segregation see Massey, *Space, place and gender*; Moore, *Space, text and gender*; R. R. Reiter, 'Men and women in the south of France: public and private domains', in R. R. Reiter (ed.), *Towards an anthropology of women*, New York 1975, 21–49; L. Roubin, 'Male space and female space within the Provençal community', in R. Forster and O. Ranum (eds), *Rural society in France: selections from the Annales, economies, sociétés, civilisations*, London 1977, 252–82; and D. Spain, *Gendered spaces*, London 1992.

[33] C. P. Graves, 'Social space in the medieval parish church', *Economy and Society* xviii (1989), 297–322.

[34] R. Gilchrist, *Gender and material culture: an archaeology of religious women*, New York 1994.

[35] A. Boddington, 'Raunds, Northamptonshire: an analysis of a country churchyard', *World Archaeology* xviii (1987), 411–25.

centuries, reflected and reinforced a growing social and spatial segregation of society along class and gender lines.[36]

Although these studies have added considerably to our understanding of how space was organised, reconstruction of social practice from documentary evidence such as floor plans and inventories raises certain problems. In the first place, even when augmented by the material record, written documents such as plans and inventories can only tell us about prescriptive patterns of use: they do not allow us to see space as actually lived. In the second place, plans and inventories are static documents. They do not allow us to develop an analysis sensitive to short- or long-term shifts in the social use and social meaning of space. To determine how spaces were gendered we require sources that provide a dynamic picture of the activities of men and women within space, in which it is possible to see how prescriptive ideas interacted with social practice to shape experience.

For this reason the study moves away from material evidence and turns to the methodology adopted by Jennifer Melville in her pioneering analysis of the use and organisation of domestic space in seventeenth-century London, to which this study owes a great debt in terms of its concepts, methods and organisation.[37] Chapter 1 explores prescriptive texts about gender and space. Those that follow rely on narrative descriptions of the ways people used and experienced their houses, churches, markets, streets and fields, provided by presentments, depositions, informations, examinations and confessions from the ecclesiastical and secular courts, supplemented in places by evidence derived from chapbooks, ballads and diaries.[38]

---

[36] F. Brown, 'Continuity and change in the urban house: developments in domestic space organisation in seventeenth-century London', *Comparative Studies in Society and History* xxviii (1986), 558–90; L. Weatherill, *Consumer behaviour and material culture, 1660–1715*, London 1988; R. Garrard, 'English probate inventories and their use in studying the significance of the domestic interior, 1500–1700', *AAG Bijdragen*, xxiii (1980), 53–77; M. Johnson, *An archaeology of capitalism*, Oxford 1996. See also A. Yentsch, 'The symbolic division of pottery: sex related attributes of English and Anglo-American household pots', in R. M. McGuire and R. Paynter (eds), *The archaeology of inequality*, Oxford, 1991, 192–230; H. Glassie, *Folk housing in middle America: a structural analysis of historic artefacts*, Knoxville 1975; and J. Deetz, *In small things forgotten: the archaeology of early American life*, New York 1977.

[37] J. D. Melville, 'The use and organisation of domestic space in late seventeenth-century London', unpubl. PhD diss. Cambridge 1999.

[38] The core sources of the thesis were all extant presentments and witnesses' depositions made at the archdeaconry courts of Essex, Colchester, and the bishop of London's commissary in Essex and Hertfordshire between 1580 and c. 1720. All extant Essex witnesses' depositions made at the bishop of London's consistory court between 1580 and 1720 were also examined, together with a sample of presentments. In addition all extant witnesses' informations, examinations and confessions made between 1580 and 1689 at the Essex court of quarter sessions were looked at, together with all extant examinations made between 1573 and 1687 at the borough court of Colchester. The Maldon borough court books were sampled for the period 1557–1623. In addition, Essex witnesses' depositions made at the equity court of Star Chamber were sampled and a preliminary survey was undertaken of

Judicial evidence is not unproblematic. Historians have long recognised the complex mediations through which these records were composed. Some attention to the circumstances surrounding their production is necessary to make sense of them as sources. First of all, it must be emphasised that these documents vary both in content and in tone, being produced for different reasons in different jurisdictions. The depositions of the church courts were the end product of a complex series of legal procedures. The testimonies of witnesses were usually given in private to a clerk and in answer to questions posed by the plaintiff's statement of the case, technically known as a 'libel', constructed under the direction of lawyers known as proctors. Unlike other courts, there was no jury to interpret the testimonies of witnesses or litigants. Material went straight to the judge.[39] The examinations and depositions surviving for the borough courts and court of quarter sessions were slightly different. They were essentially 'verbatim' accounts of evidence given by plaintiffs, defendants and witnesses, recorded by the examining magistrate before committing suspected felons or witnesses to bail, or suspected felons to prison.[40]

Thus, all these documents are in some way edited and re-worked versions of the original oral testimony. This generates some problems of interpretation. In the case of the church courts, the information is filtered and potentially distorted, first by the questions constructed by the lawyers, to which witnesses responded, and second, by the clerk who wrote them down. Not all witnesses', plaintiff's or defendant's words were necessarily recorded, and their testimonies were framed in legal language.[41] Equally, the magistrates who recorded the examinations and depositions of the quarter sessions and borough courts would identify which elements of the testimony were important and would prioritise information according to legal requirements. Any unnecessary details might be eliminated.[42] The pioneering work of Natalie Zemon Davis and Laura Gowing has also drawn our attention to the ways litigants themselves shaped their testimony by including some details, excluding others, emphasising some points, suppressing others – to gain legal advantage.[43]

These problems of distortion can be exaggerated. In the first place, censorship is not thought to have been widespread, and while testimonies cannot be taken as absolutely accurate transcriptions, many are notably individual in

Essex witnesses' depositions made at the courts of Exchequer and Requests. While the issues addressed in the thesis relate to the time-frame 1580 to 1720 and evidence has been used wherever possible to examine trends within this broad chronological framework, detailed archival work has had to focus on the years from 1580 to 1680, since depositional evidence is less plentiful after 1680.

[39] Ingram, Church courts, sex and marriage, 48; Gowing, Domestic dangers, 42–7.
[40] J. A. Sharpe, Crime in early modern England, 1550–1750, London 1984, 35.
[41] Gowing, Domestic dangers, 47.
[42] J. M. Beattie, Crime and the courts in England, 1660–1800, Oxford 1986, 268–71.
[43] N. Z. Davis, Fiction in the archives, Oxford 1987; Gowing, Domestic dangers, 232–9.

content, vocabulary and tone. Some depositions are clearly redrafted versions of statements provided by the plaintiff or witnesses where the description of events is ordered and repetition and inconsistencies are largely eliminated. More typically, many contain disorderly, repetitious and confused accounts of events, with additions added in the margin or at the end that look as if they were written down rapidly as they were heard. In the second place it is important to stress that while the judicial context was important its effect on witness statements varied. The way that a plaintiff or defendant described his or her own behaviour or that of the legal opponent can hardly be seen in the same way as a passing reference to social behaviour made by a witness more to set the scene than to impress the judge. The last chapter of this book relies on pew cases that are directly about space but other parts make use of this wealth of spatial detail that was often incidental to the crux of the matter before the court. These casual remarks recount seemingly trivial actions, words and gestures that provide very useful insights into how people used space as well as popular attitudes to social behaviour.

Most important for the purposes of this study, what Natalie Zemon Davis meant when she argued that she had found fiction in the archives was that she had found evidence that 'authors shape the events of a crime into a story' and that the purpose of this shaping was to provide a testimony that would be believable to their readers, because the activities and patterns of behaviour were unremarkable and conventional.[44] The fictive aspects of these records actually help to bridge the gap between prescription and practice. The records are not about social realities; they are about how people presented those realities in a plausible manner that would be believable to the authorities – refracted through contemporary expectations about behaviour appropriate to the gender, social and age hierarchies.

The extent to which the records are representative in terms of sex and social status is clearly an important issue. The variety of these documents, drawn from the ecclesiastical and secular courts, and dealing with marriage, moral, family and neighbourhood disputes, as well as criminal matters, means that they introduce people from a wide social range. Some cases in the courts of quarter sessions concerned members of the gentry, although they rarely appeared in church courts business. The poorest members of society, paupers and day labourers, were equally unlikely to appear before the archdeacon, but they feature regularly before the justices as defendants in cases of petty crime or vagrancy. Servants and apprentices appear as witnesses, defendants and occasionally as plaintiffs in both courts. However the members of society best represented in the records of both jurisdictions were men and women of middling status – tradesmen, craftsmen, husbandmen or yeomen and their wives.[45] For this reason, and to provide a more coherent study of the use and organisation of space, the study will focus primarily on the social practices of

44 Davis, *Fiction in the archives*, 2.
45 Gowing, *Domestic dangers* 48–53; Sharpe, *Crime in England*, 94–120.

social groups below the level of the elite – with emphasis on the middling-sort broadly defined.[46] This of course creates problems of meaning. The picture of attitudes, habits and spatial experience might be very different if we looked at the upper ranks or the poor.

The proportion of female litigants at the court of quarter sessions was very low due to the numerous disincentives to litigation, primarily the law of *coverture*. There is also the possibility that women's testimony at court was less likely to be taken as seriously as men's and so women witnesses may have been called less often than men. However, at the inferior borough courts and, above all, in the ecclesiastical courts, which were outside the common law, female participation was much higher.[47] Thus, although women appeared less often than men, they are reasonably represented in this range of documentation. Recognising that gender is a relational concept the book focuses upon one particular pole, women, but includes evidence about men wherever possible and draws on existing work on men, which illuminates gendered spatial analysis.

The book concentrates on the county of Essex. It does so for three main reasons. First of all archival evidence is rich, since depositions are extant for all jurisdictions for the period. Second, little work has been undertaken to date on the rich church court depositions which survive for the county. Third, the distinctions of the local regional economy and culture, in terms of the dominance of the cloth trade and proximity to the economic and intellectual influences of London, meant that the well-attested social, economic, religious and cultural changes of the period were especially pronounced in Essex.[48] By concentrating on this county, the study is able to offer an analysis of different aspects of the gendering of space, especially sensitive to the influence of these social, economic and cultural forces.

The time-frame of the study encompasses what Sara Mendelson and Patricia Crawford have termed the 'long seventeenth century', from 1580 to 1720.[49] Where possible, broad patterns of continuity and change are traced as they relate to each field or space, but close attention is also paid to short-term shifts in social meaning and social use according to time of day or season of the year.

This book explores the spatial patterns within which men and women lived their lives in seventeenth-century England. It aims to show that, despite the immense force of patriarchal spatial ideology within early modern society,

---

[46] Articles by Keith Wrightson discuss the problems in assessing social structuring in early modern England: 'The social order of early modern England: three approaches', in L. Bonfield, R. M. Smith and K. Wrightson (eds), *The world we have gained: histories of population and social structure*, Oxford 1986, 177–202, and 'Estates, degrees and sorts: changing perceptions of society in Tudor and Stuart England', in P. Corfield (ed.), *Language, history and class*, Oxford 1991, 28–51.

[47] Shoemaker, *Gender in English society*, 293–4.

[48] For the classic account of these changes see Wrightson, *English society*.

[49] Mendelson and Crawford, *Women in early modern England*, 11.

the dichotomies that it sought to impose between male/ female and outside/ inside were complicated and undermined by inconsistencies within as well as between prescription and practice, age, status, context and time. Chapter 1 examines why the classical model of 'separate spheres' was so important for early modern rhetorical constructions of gender order. It then explores the inconsistencies and outright contradictions within this rhetoric, which created space for female agency. The chapters that follow explore how these complexities were interpreted and manipulated in the ways in which men and women lived and gave meaning to space.

Chapter 2 focuses upon the influence of gender on aspects of the organisation of domestic space. It examines the distribution of authority between household members with regard to control over access to the house and use of its spaces, and looks in detail at the organisation of space for eating and sleeping. It shows that the everyday organisation of the house and use of its rooms reflected the tensions within a married woman's role as subordinate and domestic governor. Both household heads, mistresses and masters, used space to assert authority and married women had a significant amount of power and control over the use and organisation of their own homes, in sharp contrast to the servants and children who lived under the same roof. The organisation of space for eating and sleeping also reflected and reinforced the superior position of the mistress in relation to other subordinates. In contexts of conflict between husband and wife over control of the house, however, her subordinate role is made manifest. None the less, at all times, assertion of patriarchal authority had to be balanced against the economic and practical demands of running a complex multifunctional household, which often rendered doctrines of male dominance irrelevant. The organisation of domestic space was highly dynamic and, at any given moment, it could be used to assert authority or to signify commonality, depending upon the context.

Chapter 3 develops this theme through exploration of the links between gender and the organisation of space for work. It examines tensions between ideological constructs of appropriate spatial relationships between men and women and how people lived and constructed space within the specific circumstances of a particular family and the regional economy in which it participated. It shows that while there was a sexual division of labour, how individuals used space for work was determined more by practical than hierarchical considerations and less attention was paid to defining relationships in a rigid manner. Chapter 4 explores how gender influenced the way that men and women lived and gave meaning to space for sociability within and beyond the house. It shows that the social character of space was shaped but not determined by patriarchal norms. Social spatial maps were very fluid, altering according to context and to the ways in which other social factors competed to define order. Gender was a very prominent determinant of access to and use of drinking houses, for example. It also shaped and constrained experience of the street and aspects of domestic sociability. At every turn, however, experience was complicated by time, context and competing claims of age and status that determined different experiences, and degrees of power between different types of women as well as between different types of men.

Chapter 5 looks at the parish church, the most important social arena in early modern local society, in which hierarchy was spatially, visibly and materially displayed. It shows that within the church, seating arrangements represented and reinforced the secondary status of women within the hierarchy of gender. The orderly arrangement of pews according to rank, on the other hand, meant that, as wives, married women had an important public role in the representation and defence of the superior symbolic position of their households within the hierarchy of status. More generally, their accepted role as parishioners gave married women, especially the godly, a continuous role in local negotiations and confrontations with official ecclesiastical authority over the ordering and meaning of space within the local parish church.

The organisation of space was thus highly dynamic and enormously varied in early modern England. A patriarchal ideology that sought to confine women within the domestic sphere had immense structural force, but its impact upon the everyday organisation of space, and consequently gender relations, was very uneven. It was complicated and undermined by inconsistencies within its rhetoric, short-term shifts in use of space, and the way that gender intersected with other categories of social identity. It is the contention of this book that spaces should be understood and read as social fields in which individual actors are placed in differential power relations. In early modern society the relative position of any person within the field or space was determined by the place they occupied within the various hierarchies that competed to determine the ordering of society – gender, age, social and marital status. Analysis of space allows us to see that women as well as men occupied different positions within these different hierarchies. They therefore performed a variety of social roles within a multiplicity of arenas that variously empowered or constrained them.[50] Close attention to the points of connection between the various hierarchies, that is the contexts or spaces where these complex, competing and unstable gender identities were negotiated on a daily basis, allows us to explore the intricacies of these changing dynamics of gendered power. It broadens and deepens our understanding of the role of gender in the structuring of social relations within early modern society. It emphasises the inadequacy of analysis of gendered power relations framed around a binary model of male domination and female subordination or resistance that fails to address such complexities within the construction and experience of gender and authority.

What follows is an exploration of how individual women and men interpreted normative definitions of gender roles and gendered space in the course of daily life. It is the argument of the book that space in early modern England was gendered in complex ways, reflecting and reproducing varied

[50] Ibid. 11–13.

and changing articulations of gendered power, depending on the context. Space had a range of gendered meanings that were fluid rather than fixed. A patriarchal discourse existed side by side with other codes of behaviour to which men and women could appeal and that allowed them to assert a more complex gendered spatial identity. While moralists established the irrational, inferior character of femininity that rendered women unfit for activities outside the home, advice manuals acknowledged the impracticality of this patriarchal model for the practice of marital roles. It was accepted that men worked at home and women were expected to work outside when necessary, to be competent assistants in their husbands' businesses, to buy and sell produce at the market, to be good neighbours and dutiful parishioners. These tensions and inconsistencies between competing expectations of female and male behaviour, as well as between prescription and practice, meant that the gendered meanings of space were constantly being contested and redefined and that they were invested with many contradictions. The book argues for the inadequacy of the explanatory power of the separate spheres paradigm for early modern gendered spatial relations where, in most contexts, the worlds of men and women consistently intersected and overlapped. Complex and contradictory gendered meanings were ascribed to space that were not wholly determined by patriarchal prescription.

1

Prescriptive Space

'For *Admonition*, to admonish every Christian woman to learne to know her place and her part; and to fashion her minde and her will, her disposition and her practice accordingly thereunto.'[1]

'God hath appointed their station to them both, the one, without, the other within.'[2]

Space and gender were intimately linked in early modern theoretical constructions of patriarchal order. The classical doctrine that order in families, and by extension within the wider commonwealth, required adherence to a spatial system that assigned a public role to men and confined women within the domestic sphere was restated repeatedly in sermons, conduct literature and educational tracts throughout the period. The principle was summarised simply by William Whately in his wedding sermon *A bride-bush*, when he said that the husband should be 'without door, she within; he abroad, she at home', and by the Puritan preacher Henry Smith in 1591 when he declared that husbands and wives should see themselves as like the cock and the dam: 'the cock flyeth abroad to bring in and the dam sitteth upon the nest to keep all at home'.[3] The purpose of this chapter is to outline briefly why this spatial system was believed to be so important for the gender system in early modern England. It then explores the inconsistencies, complexities and ambiguities that arose when male moralists tried to delineate in detail what the recommendation that women should stay at home actually meant.

The principle that the home was the proper sphere for women, and that they were unsuited to activities outside it, rested on the widely held conviction, hardly ever debated in early modern England, that the female of the species was inferior to the male in several important respects. According to most early modern male writers and political thinkers, women's intelligence, physical strength and ability to reason were secondary to those of men. The consequence was that they should be subject to the male and remain within

---

[1] T. Gataker, *Marriage duties briefely couched togither*, London 1620, 10.
[2] D. Rogers, *Matrimoniall honour*, London 1642, 270.
[3] H. Smith, *A preparative to marriage*, London 1591, 43; W. Whately, *A bride-bush or a wedding sermon: compendiously describing the duties of married persons: by performing whereof, marriage shall be to them a great helpe, which now finde it a little hell*, London 1617, 14.

the home. Three main sources of authority were used to provide justification for these widely held beliefs – biblical, medical and classical.[4]

The Bible, and particularly the creation account and narrative of the Fall in the first chapters of Genesis, were revisited again and again by writers of sermons, conduct books and household manuals to explain the divine origin of the gender hierarchy that insisted on women's subordination to men. The order and manner of creation was believed to be of great significance in this respect. The first chapter of Genesis describes the creation of woman after Adam, 'the man was first created and not the woman', for Adam, as 'an help-meet' for him, and of Adam, 'taken from the side', the rib of the man.[5] For some early modern commentators who defended women's nature, these texts suggested that woman was cast as man's spiritual equal.[6] But for most male moralists the fact that woman was an addendum to the divine plan confirmed to them that the female was lesser and secondary to the male even before Eve succumbed to temptation, ate the ill-fated apple of the tree of knowl-edge and banished mankind forever from the Garden of Eden.[7] That 'woman was former in transgression' provided final and incorrigible proof of female inferiority and the necessity for them to be assigned a subject and domestic role. Eve's transgressions established that women were governed by pride and passion rather than reason, that they succumbed easily to temptation and that they might use their sexuality to lure men into sin. Daniel Rogers summarised Eve's responsibilities and its consequences for her sex succinctly when he reminded his female audience to 'remember thy sex is crazy ever since Eve sinned'.[8] The inescapable conclusion, confirmed in the New Testament by the prescriptions of the Apostles St Peter and St Paul, was that, as the 'weaker vessel', women should be subject and stay at home.[9] William Gouge clearly defined the position of women after the Fall in his lengthy treatise *Of domes-ticall duties* when he stated, 'she who first drew man into sin should now be subject to him lest by the like womanish weakness she fall again ... her nature will be more depraved, and her fault more increased'.[10]

---

4   These ideas have been fully analysed and will only briefly be rehearsed here. See Mendelson and Crawford, *Women in early modern England*, 15–74; Fletcher, *Gender, sex and subordination in England*, 60–82; Amussen, *An ordered society*, 34–66; M. Sommerville, *Sex and subjection: attitudes to women in early modern society*, London 1995, 8–39; and Shoe-maker, *Separate spheres*, 15–36.

5   Gataker, *Marriage duties*, 8; W. Gouge, *Of domesticall duties, eight treatises*, London 1622, 270; M. Griffith, *Bethel: or, a forme for families*, London 1663, 243–4.

6   E. C. McLaughlin, 'Equality of souls, inequality of sexes: women in medieval theology', in R. Reuther (ed.), *Religion and sexism: images of women in the Jewish and Christian tradi-tions*, New York 1974, 218–19.

7   Gouge, *Domesticall duties*, 268; Gataker, *Marriage duties*, 8.

8   Rogers, *Matrimoniall honour*, 281.

9   Dod and Cleaver, *Godlie forme of householde government*, 27; Gouge, *Domesticall duties*, 22.

10   Gouge, *Domesticall duties*, 268–9; Whately, *Bride-bush*, 36; T. Gataker, *A good wife's God's gift: and a wife indeed: two marriage sermons*, London 1623, 23.

The second authority that provided support for the belief that women were inferior to men and should remain within the domestic sphere was medical theory. Defects in women's intellectual ability, their physical strength and their ability to reason were explained by their physiology. Early modern medicine, based on the humoral theories of the classical Greek philosophers Aristotle and Galen, posited a hierarchical view of the sexes, in which women were regarded as imperfectly formed men who through a lack of vital heat had retained inside the body structures of sexual reproduction that in the male were visible outside it. According to this humoral theory, each body was governed by the four humours of yellow and black bile, blood and phlegm. Health and happiness depended on maintaining the proper balance between them. These humours were thought to correspond with the four elements – earth, air, fire and water – and with the qualities of hot, cold, wet and dry. Heat was viewed as the most positive of these qualities. It could change one kind of bodily fluid into another, and it rose naturally towards the heavens and towards the brain. The different balance of these humours within the male and female body explained the different temperaments and abilities of men and women. The male was, unsurprisingly, hotter and dryer and so his body was believed to be closer to perfection. His heat made him more rational and creative, active, energetic, brave and strong. The woman, by contrast, was more cold and moist. According to early modern medical thinking this meant that she was weak and passive and more suited to a sedentary life.[11] William Whateley alluded to this female physical incapacity in A bride-bush, when he explained that the female form was 'framed ... to tenderness, mens more to hardness'.[12] Richard Allestree also urged his readers in his lengthy exposition on The ladies calling to remember that 'nature hath befriende women with a

11 For the classic account of these theories see T. Laqueur, Making sex: the body and gender from the Greeks to Freud, Cambridge, MA. 1990. There is a large and growing literature that explores how medical discourse constructed female inferiority upon which the following discussion is based: Fletcher, Gender, sex and subordination, chs ii–iv; I. Maclean, The Renaissance notion of woman: a study in the fortunes of scholasticism and medical science in European intellectual life, Cambridge 1980; L. Macray Beier, Sufferers and healers: the experience of illness in seventeenth-century England, London 1987; L. Schiebinger, The mind has no sex? Women and the origins of modern science, Cambridge, MA. 1989; G. Paster, 'The unbearable coldness of female being: women's imperfections and the humoral economy', English Literary Renaissance xxviii (1998), 416–40; L. Jordonova, Sexual visions: images of gender in science and medicine between the eighteenth and twentieth centuries, London 1989, ch. ii. For an analysis of contemporary medical accounts of differences and divisions between male bodies according to age and status see Shepard, Meanings of manhood, 47–69. The extent to which medical discourses were broadly disseminated outside them is currently much debated. See, for example, R. Porter and M. Teich (eds), Sexual knowledge, sexual science: the history of attitudes to sexuality, Cambridge 1994; Gowing, Common bodies; and M. Fisssell, Vernacular bodies: the politics of reproduction in early modern England, London 2004.
12 Whately, Bride-bush, 36.

more cool and temperate constitution, put less of fire, and consequently of choler, in their compositions'.[13]

Woman's moist physiology was important in explaining her intellectual incapacity and lack of reason or, as Allestree put it, her 'natural imbecility, which renders [her] liable to seducement'.[14] Her moist and cold composition made her less healthy because her metabolism functioned less efficiently and it left her brain too soft and cold for rigorous thought. It made her changeable, deceptive, of a generally tricky temperament, governed not by her brain but by her lower parts. Her problems were compounded by the irrational influence of the uterus or womb, which created emotional disturbance through a superfluity of blood. In the sixteenth century the womb, along with several other organs in the body, was believed to have independent powers and could move around the body at will, causing emotional imbalance if it was not filled up regularly by sexual intercourse or reproduction. By the seventeenth century these ideas had faded but it was still believed that the womb was sufficiently potent to cause lust, irrational behaviour and mental instability.[15] Scripture and science were therefore mutually supportive of the conclusion that women were inferior to men in intellectual and physical capacity, sexual and emotional self-control and ability to reason. Thus, when the Puritan divine William Heales preached upon the theme of the unequal qualities and functions of the two sexes, he offered his audience 'natural' as well as metaphysical explanations. Men and women were:

> Both like and yet dislike, like in specifical nature, their bodies of the like feature ... dislike in the individual ... the one stronger, the one weaker ... the one laborious in the fields, the other mild and diligent within the doors: that what the one had painfully gotten abroad the other might carefully conserve at home. The one fairer and as a delightful picture of beauty: the other more stern and as a perfect mirror of manhood. The other more deeply wise, the other of pregnant wit.[16]

Over the course of the seventeenth and eighteenth centuries medical understandings developed and began to stress the physical differences between the sexes, and the considerable moral capacities of women, but this did not alter ideas about female inferiority or function. Women's brains were still believed to be smaller, so that women continued to be regarded as intellectually inferior. Their nerves were thought to be thinner so they were emotionally more fragile and they were still believed to be 'naturally' physically weaker.[17]

Developing emphasis upon human capacity for reason and attacks on patriarchy as a political system proved no more effective in dislodging the

---

13 R. Allestree, *The ladies calling*, Oxford 1693, 48.
14 Ibid. 36.
15 Maclean, *Renaissance notions of women*, 41; Lacqueur, *Making sex*, 108.
16 W. Heales, *An apologie for women*, London 1609, 23.
17 Schiebinger, *Mind has no sex?*, 190–210; Jordonova, *Sexual visions*, ch. ii.

entrenched belief that female inferiority was natural and that women were suited solely to domestic affairs. At the start of the eighteenth century the Whig contractarian William Fleetwood, bishop of Ely, espoused the opinion that the education of women 'would never fit them for the performance of the great businesses of trade and merchandize, and making wars abroad and executing justice at home'.[18] In similar vein the seventeenth-century anti-patriarchal English philosopher John Locke concluded that women's subjection and exclusion from the public sphere had 'foundation in nature', for 'generally the laws of mankind and customs of nature have ordered it so', because men were 'abler and stronger'. It was only men who possessed characteristics of free and equal beings.[19] The inescapable conclusion was that women were best suited to staying at home to care for children and to perform the essential but intellectually undemanding activities required for running the house. Throughout the period under discussion therefore it was widely believed that women's inferior intellectual and physical incapacities, together with their lack of reason, meant that they were unsuited to 'public' activities outside, where they would face forays upon their modesty and chastity that they might be unable to resist. As Dod and Cleaver reminded their readers in their lengthy treatise on A godlie forme of household government, 'a good wife keeps to her house', for the Apostles St Peter and St Paul reminded all good women that the home was 'chastities keeper'.[20]

Writers of treatises on marriage and conduct books agreed on the necessity for all families in early modern England to be governed according to these principles of gender and spatial order. The husband and master should have absolute dominion over the house and household and take charge of 'public' affairs. The wife had to be subject and obedient to him, focusing her attention solely upon the ordering of the house. This system was deemed to be of essential importance for the maintenance of a godly, ordered family, and by extension a stable commonwealth. If it were not adhered to, according to Dod and Cleaver, then chaos would ensue. Where the wife 'be not subject to her husband, to let him rule all the household, especially outward affaires; if she will make against him, and seeke to have her own wayes, there will be doing and undoing. Things will go backward, the house will come to ruine.'[21] The worrying thing for Puritan preachers was that so many women apparently fell short of the standards expected. William Gouge complained at the start of his treatise that 'wives for the most part are most backward in yielding subjection to their husbands' and throughout his text he referred to the problem of 'stout and rebellious' wives.[22] Bishop Hugh Latimer was appalled by the number of

---

[18] W. Fleetwood, The relative duties of parents and children, 2nd edn, London 1716, 133–5, cited in Sommerville, Sex and subjection, 21.

[19] J. Locke, Two treatises of government, ed. P. Laslett, Cambridge 1988, 174; C. Pateman, The sexual contract, Stanford 1988, 52–3.

[20] Dod and Cleaver, Godlie forme of householde government, 222.

[21] Ibid. 87–8; Gataker, Marriage duties, 10; Whately, Bride-bush, 36.

[22] Gouge, Domesticall duties, 26.

married women that he encountered for whom obedience to their husbands was 'made a trifle and a small matter' and William Whately bewailed the fact that 'the greater number of women' were at fault in habits of obedience.[23] That such anxiety was indicative of a 'crisis in gender relations' during the first half of the seventeenth century is difficult to establish from this evidence, given the lamentation at levels of female independence after the Restoration.[24] For male moralists throughout the period, female disobedience was believed to be a prevalent problem and a serious matter, not only because womankind's 'natural' tendency towards disorder was socially disruptive but more importantly because it was sinful.[25]

It was widely believed that female recalcitrance in necessary obedience could only be overcome by a rigorous programme of education and inculcation of the female mind and body into principles of subordination within the home. As Gataker put it, it was his duty to 'admonish every Christian woman to learne to know her place and her part; and to fashion her minde and her will, her disposition and her practice accordingly thereunto'.[26] For this reason close attention was given by male moralists not simply to the demarcation of separate 'spheres' for men and women but also to the detailed delineation of methods of enforcement of subordination through the everyday organisation of space.

The first and most important principle within these prescriptions was of course that the wife should stay at home. A plethora of sermons, conduct books and household manuals was produced throughout the period that emphasised to their readers that female chastity was a fragile state that was best maintained by confinement.[27] Proper government of the household demanded that the husband set and maintain strict social boundaries to the movement of his wife beyond the house. William Gouge warned women that it was an aberration 'to think their houses a prison, that cannot tarrie long at home' and advised wives that it was not part of their prerogative to 'journey abroad

---

[23] *Sermons by Hugh Latimer*, ed. G. E. Corrie (Parker Society xxii, 1844), 252–3; Whately, *Bride-bush*, 194.

[24] For the description of gender as a focus for 'crisis' between c.1560 and 1640 see D. Underdown, 'The taming of the scold: the enforcement of patriarchal authority in early modern England', in A. Fletcher and J. Stevenson (eds), *Order and disorder in early modern England*, Cambridge 1985, 116–36. For revisions of this argument see M. Ingram, ' "Scolding women cucked or washed": a crisis in gender relations in early modern England?', in J. Kermode and G. Walker (eds), *Women, crime and the courts in early modern England*, London 1994, 48–80. On anxiety about female liberty during the Restoration see Allestree, *Ladies calling*, 79, 167, 172–3.

[25] Capp, *'When gossips meet'*, 21.

[26] Gataker, *Marriage duties*, 10.

[27] On the printing and growing popularity of conduct literature from the beginning of the sixteenth century see Shepard, *Meanings of manhood*, 70–1; Fletcher, *Gender, sex and subordination*, 335; K. M. Davies, 'Continuity and change in literary advice on marriage', in R. B. Outhwaite (ed.), *Marriage and society: studies in the social history of marriage*, London 1981, 70–80.

without their husbands consent'.[28] Several writers recommended the snail or tortoise as a suitable emblem for women because these creatures carried their house upon their backs.[29] Dod and Cleaver reiterated these sentiments, repeatedly asserting that the ideal wife was like Sarah, the wife of the Old Testament prophet Abraham who kept 'within the tent'.[30]

Women were continually warned that the 'aberrant' wife was 'the woman that gaddeth from house to house to prate'.[31] Daniel Rogers bemoaned the tendency of women to 'gad' abroad, complaining that 'we now have meetings of women drinkers, tobacconists, and swaggerers, as well as men', regarding this behaviour as a portent of providential disaster.[32] Several male moralists reminded their female readers that in characterising the qualities of the whore Solomon 'setteth her at the doore now sitting upon her stall, now walking in the streets'.[33] Barnabe Rich memorably interpreted this particular passage in Proverbs to explain to his readers that 'The harlot is mooveable ... *now she is in the house, now in the streetes, now she lieth in waite in everie corner, she is still gadding from place to place, from company to company*'. Robert Cleaver proclaimed that it was the whore, whose 'whole property is to bee abroad in the streets to meet with companions and to entice men to follie by her looks and behaviour'.[34] The message was very plainly put. Too much time 'abroad', or indeed, gossiping with neighbours at home, led to distraction from domestic duties and encouraged idleness, or worse still immorality.

Moralists did not simply focus their attention upon confinement of women within the home however. Conduct writers were extremely concerned to offer advice about how the internal arrangements of households should be organised day to day. Protestantism was not simply a Sunday activity, according to these prelates, but a whole way of living that was to be ordered and directed by God's Word. Samuel Hieron, minister at Modbury in Devon, explained to his parishioners that the Scriptures were important to give man 'direction for his apparrell, his speech, his diet, his company, his disports, his labour, his buying and selling, yea and for his very sleepe'.[35] The godly, in particular, were renowned for their close attention to scriptural instruction on the details of

---

28 Gouge, *Domesticall duties*, 310, 314.
29 Gataker, *Marriage duties*, 20.
30 Dod and Cleaver, *Godlie forme of householde government*, 222.
31 Ibid.
32 Rogers, *Matrimoniall honour*, 290.
33 Dod and Cleaver, *Godlie forme of householde government*, 222.
34 B. Rich, *My ladies looking glasse: wherein may be discerned a wise man from a fool, a goode women from a bad*, London 1616, 43; R. Cleaver, *A briefe explanation of the whole booke of the proverbs of Saloman*, London 1615, 150.
35 S. Hieron, 'The dignitie of the Scripture, togither with the indignitie which the unthankfull world offereth thereunto', in *All the sermons of Samuel Hieron, minister of Gods word, at Modbury in Devon*, London 1614, 72.

daily life, carrying their Bibles to church, as well as taking down notes during sermons, to apply in private devotion at home.[36]

Puritan preachers advised male readers that their domestic spaces had to be structured as a type of 'school' or 'seminary' in which women were to be trained into appropriate habits of deference and obedience that provided an outward reflection of an inner awareness of the subject status of their sex.[37] The social formation of the female body was of great importance in this respect.[38] Husbands were to guide their wives daily into habits of bodily self-discipline that would contain their passions, protect their modesty and ensure obedience, submission and esteem.

It has to be understood that the principal way of acknowledging status in daily life in early modern England was through the medium of the body. There was a widespread expectation that clothing, modes of address, gesture and carriage had to be organised and performed properly to reflect a person's station in life. Differences in status were thereby marked out more easily and systems of hierarchy effectively maintained.[39] Gender was very similar to social rank in this respect. According to conduct writers the female form had to be 'fashioned' at home into habits of obedience and deference so that in her 'speech', in the 'ordering of her countenance, gesture and whole carriage before her husband', a married woman conveyed respect, obedience and awareness of her inferior 'place', physically, every moment of the day.[40] William Whately clearly defined the importance of the physical performance of female deference at home in his wedding sermon when he stated that 'The whole duty of the wife is referred to two heads. The first is to acknowledge her

---

[36] P. Collinson, 'Elizabethan and Jacobean Puritanism as forms of popular religious culture', in C. Durston and J. Eales (eds), *The culture of English Puritanism, 1560–1700*, Basingstoke 1996, 49.

[37] Gouge, *Domesticall duties*, 17.

[38] P. Stallybrass, 'Patriarchal territories: the body enclosed', in M. W. Ferguson, M. Quilligan and N. J. Vickers (eds), *Rewriting the Renaissance*, Chicago 1987, 126–7.

[39] Recent works that have explored the connections between bodily codes of behaviour and social relations include J. Wildeblood and P. Brinson, *The polite world: a guide to English manners and deportment from the thirteenth to the nineteenth century*, London 1965; R. Chartier (ed.), *A history of private life, III: Passions of the Renaissance*, London 1989; J. Bremmer and H. Roodenburg (eds), *A cultural history of gesture*, Oxford 1991; A. Bryson, *From courtesy to civility: changing codes of conduct in early modern England*, Oxford 1998; and L. Gent and N. Llewellyn (eds), *Renaissance bodies: the human figure in English culture, c. 1540–1660*, London 1990. See also A. Davies, *The Quakers in English society, 1655–1725*, Oxford 2000, 43–63. The work of the anthropologist Mary Douglas is important for understanding the political meaning of the physical body: *Natural symbols: explorations in cosmology*, London 1973, and *Purity and danger: an analysis of the concepts of pollution and taboo*, London 1979. I am grateful to Rebecca Newport for allowing me to consult her unpublished work on this subject.

[40] Gouge, *Domesticall duties*, 277; Dod and Cleaver, *Godlie forme of householde government*, 218; Gataker, *A good wife's God's gift*, 21, and *Marriage duties*, 11–14; M. R., *The mother's counsel; or, live within compasse: being the last will and testament to her dearest daughter*, London 1630, 6; Whately, *Bride-bush*, 38–9; Allestree, *Ladies calling*, 6, 11–14.

inferiority: the next to carry her selfe as inferior.'[41] In similar vein, Dorothy Leigh wrote in her book of advice about her children's upbringing that women should 'not be ashamed to show their infirmities but to give men the first and chiefe place'.[42] The significance of adherence to rules of bodily comportment was given added weight by the widespread belief that outward bodily gesture reflected inner spiritual character.[43] As William Gouge explained, 'a wives outward reverence towards her husband is a manifestation of her inward due respect for him'.[44] Inappropriate demeanour denoted moral as well as social disorder. Dorothy Leigh warned that 'it is not enough for a woman to be chaste but even so to behave herself that no man may think or deem her unchaste'. 'Carriage' not 'chastity alone', kept a woman's name 'chaste from suspicion'.[45]

Male moralists repeatedly reminded their female audience that they had to learn that modesty should steer 'every part of the outward frame'.[46] Writers then proceeded to define in detail the physical abilities that had to be acquired at home to achieve this form of bodily respect. Control of the countenance was believed to be very important. Submission had to show in the face in 'calm and meek looks', in the eyes 'as doves eies' and in the lips that 'droped as honie comb'. 'Boldness' of countenance signified the sin of pride and self-conceit to which women were especially prone.[47] It is interesting to note in this regard that modesty at male examination meant that in the late seventeenth century a medical practitioner was not permitted to gaze on his female patient's face.[48]

Gouge further recommended that a married woman should show her subordinate 'place' in relation to her husband within the household by lowering her body in his presence. Mindful of the independent spirit of his female audience, he was cautious in his recommendations as to when and where these forms of respect should be offered, emphasising that a wife should not 'bow at every word that she speaketh to her husband'. But on certain occasions, for example when a husband went on a journey, or when he arrived home, if a wife had a 'solemn and great suit to make' or reason to be grateful for an 'extraordinary favour', Gouge advised that she should lower her body to demonstrate respect and submission. He added a final observation that some wives 'as know what beseemeth their place, and are not ashamed to manifest as much', declared their reverence by 'some obeisance' when they sat down or rose up from the table, although his tentative tone suggests that he

---

41 Whately, *Bride-bush*, 36.
42 D. Leigh, *The mother's blessing*, London 1627, 39–41.
43 K. Thomas, 'Introduction', to Bremmer and Roodenurg, *A cultural history of gesture*, 8.
44 Gouge, *Domesticall duties*, 277.
45 Leigh, *Mother's blessing*, 16; M. R., *Mother's counsel*, 6.
46 Allestree, *Ladies calling*, 6; Gouge, *Domesticall duties*, 278; Gataker, *Marriage duties*, 11–14.
47 Allestree, *Ladies calling*, 6; Gouge, *Domesticall duties*, 276.
48 E. Shorter, *A history of women's bodies*, London 1983, 123–38, 141.

was not entirely confident that women would look favourably on his recommendations.[49] More commonly conduct writers stayed on safer ground by
offering the general proposal that a woman's carriage should convey 'mild-
ness' or 'lowlinesse' and 'reverence' of manner as a manifestation of deference.[50] Gesture and demeanour should demonstrate esteem. 'Gayety' of
deportment was 'unbecomeing a wife'.[51] Assertive gestures such as 'standing
with arms akimbo', were deemed inappropriate for ordinary women, fitting
only for males or Amazonian woman rulers.[52] Contemptuous gestures such
as 'pouting and lowring', 'a sullen looke', 'a scornefull cast of the armes', or a
'fretfull flinging out of her husbands presence', were also roundly condemned
as 'thick clouds overspreading the heavens in a summers day'.[53] Women were
warned that passionate gestures betrayed their disorderly nature. For 'to laugh
as women do sometimes, with their hands on both sides and with a lascivious
agitation of their whole body is the height of indecency and immodesty'.[54]

The covering of a wife's head in the presence of her husband was regarded
as an important way of achieving a bodily display of subjection. The Elizabethan homily 'Of the state of matrimony' advised 'Apparel of her Head,
whereby is signified that she is under covert or obedience of her husband',
and William Gouge delivered similar advice, instructing wives that 'cover on
the women's head, as in general it implied subjection, viz, a revrand carriage
and gesture'.[55] That women were discarding these manifestations of marital
status and honesty was widely condemned in several quarters. Most famously,
perhaps, in his *Anatomie of abuses* Stubbes admonished women for 'laiyng
out their haire to the shewe, whiche of force must bee curled, frilled and
crisped, laid out (a world to see) on wreathes and borders, from one eare to an
other ... rather like grim sterne Monsters, than chaste Christian Matrones'.[56]
While his exposition was exceptional in its focus upon pride and sartorial
excess, his anxieties were reiterated regularly in other works.[57] The dying of
hair, the wearing of periwigs and the painting of faces were frequently criti-

[49] Gouge, *Domesticall duties*, 279.
[50] Whately, *Bride-bush*, 38; Gataker, *Marriage duties*, 12.
[51] Mendelson and Crawford, *Women in early modern England*, 131.
[52] Thomas, 'Introduction', 8.
[53] Gouge, *Domesticall duties*, 278; Whately, *Bride-bush*, 38; Gataker, *Marriage duties*, 14.
[54] D. A., *The whole art of converse: containing the necessary instructions for all persons, of
what quality, and condition soever*, London 1683, 37, cited in Capp, 'When gossips meet', 4.
[55] Anon., *Certain sermons or homilies appointed to be read in churches in the time of Queen
Elizabeth*, London 1687, 535; Gouge, *Domesticall duties*, 270, 277; Gowing, *Common bodies*,
55, Mendelson and Crawford, *Women in early modern England*, 131.
[56] P. Stubbes, *The anatomie of abuses: contayning, a discoverie, or briefe summarie of such
notable vices and imperfections, as now reigne in many Christian countreyes of the worlde: but
(especiallie) in a verie famous Ilande called Ailgna: together, with most fearefull examples of
Gods judgementes, executed upon the wicked for the same, as well in Ailgna of late, as in other
places, elsewhere*, London 1583, 33.
[57] A. Walsham, '"A glose of godliness": Philip Stubbes, Elizabethan Grub Street and the
invention of Puritanism', in S. Wabuda and C. Litzenberger (eds), *Belief and practice in
Reformation England: a tribute to Patrick Collinson from his students*, Aldershot 1998, 178,

cised for their corrupting qualities.[58] Thomas Tuke's *Discourse against painting and tincturing of women* warned women of the consequences of meeting their maker with 'these counterfeit flames, or fire-like and yellowish haires' that would be 'punished with the true flames of hell fire'.[59]

Clothing was also believed to be vitally important for female self-presentation of submission. Female apparel aroused very strong feelings indeed. Conduct writers and Puritan preachers shared to the full the notion that chastity should be displayed physically, at home and abroad, by careful regulation of the clothing that covered the female form.[60] They complained about the attachment of men and women to new-fangled fashion, in part because of the social confusion that it created, but also because it served as 'allurements to lust'.[61] However their discussions tended often to drift towards warnings specifically to women partly because of an assumption that the weaker sex was more prone to pride and attachment to extravagant dress, but also because of the close connection between female clothing and immorality in the minds of writers of prescriptive texts. It was widely believed that fashionably dressed women might seduce men into sin.[62] William Averell thundered in his *A mervailous combat of contrarieties* that the 'laying out of their hayres, the painting and washing of their faces, the opening of their breasts, & discovering them to their wastes, their bents of Whale bone to beare out their bummes, their great sleees and bumbased shoulders, squared in to make their wastes small ... and all these outward showes' lured men into lust.[63] More worryingly, extravagant clothing might question a respectable woman's chastity. John Denison warned ominously in 1608, that a woman sumptuously attired 'is a snare and dangerous provocation to leudnesse. Yea, but every one

193. For an excellent analysis of Puritan attitudes to clothing, on which much of this discussion is based, see K. Wright, 'A looking glass for Christian morality? Three perspectives on Puritan clothing culture and identity in England, c. 1560–1620', unpubl. MPhil. diss. Birmingham 2004.

58 P. Lake, *The boxmaker's revenge: 'orthodoxy', 'heterodoxy' and the politics of the parish in early Stuart London*, Stanford 2001, 43.

59 T. Tuke, *A discourse against painting and tincturing of women: wherein the abominable sinnes of murther and poysoning, pride and ambition, adultery and witchcraft, are set foorth and discoured*, London 1616, sigs. B3, C3.

60 N. B. Harte, 'State control of dress and social change in pre-industrial England', in D. C. Coleman and A. H. John (eds), *Trade, government and economy in pre-industrial England: essays presented to F. J. Fisher*, London 1976, 132–65; A. Hunt, *Governance of the consuming passions: a history of sumptuary law*, London 1990; J. Thirsk, *Economic policy and projects: the development of a consumer society in early modern England*, Oxford 1978, 13–15, 44–7; C. Breward, *The culture of fashion*, Manchester 1995; A. J. Jones and P. Stallybrass, *Renaissance clothing and the materials of memory*, Cambridge 2000; A. Ribeiro, *Dress and morality*, Oxford 2003; C. Richardson (ed.), *Clothing culture, 1350–1650*, Aldershot 2004.

61 Harte, 'State control of dress', 143.

62 Gowing, *Domestic dangers*, 2–3, 112.

63 Cited in Wright, 'A looking glass for Christian morality?', 26.

that is thus attired, doth not intend to intrap any thereby. Well, admit there be no such intent, yet may there easily be such an effect'.[64]

There was a widely held assumption that a woman's dress should reflect the social rank of her husband. Thomas Fuller noted that 'our good wife sets up a sail according to the keel of her husband's estate'.[65] But it was repeatedly recommended that modesty should prevail in female clothing and nothing that smacked of vanity or the satisfaction of the peculiarly female human sin of pride should be permitted. Markham's advice to the housewife was that she avoid 'variety of new and fantastic fashions' and dress plainly in garments 'comely and strong … without toyish garnishes, or the gloss of light colours'.[66] Womanly weakness in this regard meant that, according to conduct writers, it was best that their husbands directed their dress. John Manningham recorded in his diary in October 1602: 'At Paules Dr. Dove made a sermon against the excessive pride and vanitie of women in apparraile, &c., which vice he said was in their husbandes power to correct.'[67]

Moralists were equally anxious about the corrosive consequences of female speech and so conduct writers devoted a good deal of attention to control of the female mouth within the home. Women were advised that they could not claim too much personal space through over-mighty speech. Wives were instructed on how to address their husbands respectfully and warned that 'such tokens of familiarity as are not withal tokens of subjection and reverence are unbeseeming a wife'.[68] Authors were also keen to emphasise that as a mark of deference and respect women should avoid interrupting their husbands and maintain a 'sobriety, mildnesse, courtesie and modestie of conversation'. Above all they were to refrain from unnecessary speech. It was widely agreed that silence in women was generally the best option, given the close connection between female speech and sin.[69]

The same prescriptive pattern was repeated in sermons such as 'Of matrimony', preached from local parish pulpits across the country, and in shorter versions of lengthy tomes, such as *The virtuous wife*, published in 1667, sold for a few pence and clearly designed for an audience of modest means. It was a message that was applied with equal intensity to unmarried maidens. A series of conduct books began to be produced at the start of the sixteenth century

---

64 Ibid. See also M. R., *Mothers counsel*, 27; Dod and Cleaver, *Godlie forme of householde government*, 243; Allestree, *Ladies calling*, 167; and *A very fruitfull and pleasant booke, called the instruction of a Christian woman, made first in latin, by the right famous cleark M. Lewes Vives, and translated out of Latin into Englishe, by Richard Hyde*, London 1585, 69–88.
65 T. Fuller, *The holy state and the profane state* (Cambridge 1624), ed. M. Walten, New York 1938, 2.
66 G. Markham, *Cheap and good husbandry*, London 1653, 3–4.
67 *The diary of John Manningham of the Middle Temple, 1602–1603*, ed. R. P. Sorlien, Hanover, NH 1976, 114.
68 Gouge, *Domesticall duties*, 283.
69 Ibid. 277; Whately, *Bride-bush*, 38; Allestree, *Ladies calling*, 8–10; Dod and Cleaver, *Godlie forme of householde government*, 233.

aimed directly at women. Most of these works were divided into sections devoted respectively to maidens, wives and widows. Each stage of life was dealt with slightly differently, reflecting the different responsibilities of the single, married and widowed state. But at the core of this didactic litera-ture was an emphasis upon the acquisition of bodily habits of self-discipline during the formative phases of youth. Young maidens were urged to cultivate qualities of self-discipline that would be reflected in their outward carriage, clothing and comportment. They were to demonstrate modesty, chastity and submission through industry and avoidance of 'all ranke company and unfit-tinge libertie, which are the overthrow of too many of their sexe'. Thus in the enormously popular guide for women written by Juan Luis De Vives in 1523, *De institutione femininae christianae*, reprinted in English many times, he wrote that maids should refrain from 'unsuitable walking and wandring out from the house'.[70] In much the same vein, Becon, in his *Catechisme*, warned maidens to avoid, 'vain spectacles, pastimes, playes, interludes', which fostered frivolity and threatened their chastity.[71] Richard Allestree offered similar counsel to young women after the Restoration. Maidens, like youth in general, were, he advised his readers, 'flexible, and easily warps into crookedness'. Idle gossiping, bad company, irreverent carriage and 'mischievous liberty' should be assidu-ously avoided to preserve their precarious virginity.[72] Moralists repeatedly emphasised that married women had a Christian duty to train their daughters into adherence to these habits through the example that they set. Failure to do so was regarded as serious moral negligence.

These precepts, peddled from the pulpit and prescriptive texts, were heavily underscored in seventeenth-century street stories, satire, poems and jokes. The contemporary motif of gender role reversion, 'the world turned upside down' was a commonplace of popular plays and songs. Ballads like 'The woman to the plow and the man to the hen-roost' offered cautionary tales that showed the need for women to stay at home by describing the chaos that ensued when a wife left the ordering of her house to her husband and meddled in management of outdoor affairs.[73] Street stories also stressed the importance of confinement of the female body for the securing of patriarchal authority. A corpus of ballads depicted the corrosive consequences of female liberty for domestic stability. The seventeenth-century English broadsheet *Tittle tattle; or the several branches of gossipping* warned of women meeting in spaces outside the house to exchange news and gossip. Fighting and unru-

---

[70] *The instruction of a Christian woman*, 9, 13, 79–89.
[71] T. Becon, 'The catechisme', in *The worckes of Thomas Becon which he hath hitherto made and published, with diverse other newe bookes added to the same, heretofore never set forth in print, divided into the tomes or parts and amended this present [sic] of our Lord 1564; perused and allowed, according to thorder appointed in the Quenes maiesties injunctions*, London 1564, fo. cccccxxxvi.
[72] Allestree, *Ladies calling*, 167, 172–3; M. R., *Mothers counsel*, 8; H. Wolley, *The compleat servant-maid*, London 1685, sig. A4.
[73] *The Roxburghe ballads*, ed. W. Chappell and J. Ebsworth, London 1866–99, vii. 185.

liness were the result, together with the dangerous dissemination of lewd stories of love. The tale ends with an admonition advising women to 'go Knit and Sew and Brew and bake and leave off this Tittle Tattle'.[74] In similar vein a series of verses by Samuel Rowlands, entitled variously *Tis merrie when gossips meet* and *A whole crew of kind gossips*, told light-hearted tales of the antics of women who frequented public spaces that were meant to amuse but there is no doubting the sober reflection on the consequences of female freedom that these texts contain. Gadding women who drank in taverns and alehouses were denounced as idle, extravagant and perfidious wives.[75] The moral failings of women who went on excursions to playhouses, bowling alleys and taverns were another favourite theme. *The cuckold's complaint* dwelt at length on the miseries of a husband whose unfaithful wife wasted away his money and loitered with her lover in the tavern. A different tale told of a group of women who met at a tavern on market day, and stayed late into the night drinking 'sherrie' talking all the while of treachery and luxury. Another depicted seamen's wives drinking brandy in the alehouse late at night and seducing other women's husbands.[76] Stories also told of subversive wives who arranged sexual assignations under cover of supposed social gatherings.[77] Violence was more overtly recommended as a punishment for wifely disobedience in these popular texts. The recommended solution for the subjugation of an independent scolding wife was more often than not a severely savage beating.[78]

The links between gender, time and space were also important in these stories. A growing literature imagined night streets as sites of sexual immorality, symbolically opposed to the orderliness of domestic life. Ballads such as 'News from the tower-hill' depicted the risks to maidenly modesty posed by 'walking abroad' too late.[79] Thomas Dekker's pamphlet *Lanthorne and candlelight* (1608) included an anecdote about a woman, accosted by a constable, and interrogated 'Where have you bin so late? ... Are you married? ... What's your husband? ... Where lie you?'[80] Social space in these texts thus carried sharp social connotations, which defined who could and should have access to public spaces in sharply gendered terms. As a consequence female respectability was defined spatially. Women were repeatedly warned of the moral dangers they faced as they moved out into spaces away from the protections

74 Anon., *Tittle-tattle: or, the several branches of gossipping*, London 1603. See also R. West, *The court of conscience, or Dick Whippers sessions* (1607), sig. F, cited in Capp, 'When gossips meet', 52.
75 *The complete works of Samuel Rowlands*, ed. S. J. Herrtage, Glasgow 1880; W. P., *The gossips greeting; or, a new discovery of such female meetings*, London 1620.
76 *The Pepys ballads*, ed. W. G. Day, Cambridge 1987, i. 436; iv. 184–5.
77 Rowlands, *Crew of kind gossips*, 27–8.
78 *Pepys ballads*, iv. 132.
79 Ibid. i. 266–7.
80 T. Dekker, *Lanthorne and candle-light*, London 1608.

of the domestic sphere. The gadding woman was widely associated with whoredom in the satirical imagination.[81]

The problem was that these discursive constructions of a seemingly simple patriarchal spatial system were shot through with complexities, ambiguities, inconsistencies and outright contradictions. Difficulties arose in the first instance when moralists tried to define in detail what staying at home actually meant. The repeated recommendation within prescriptive texts that women should remain within the home was frequently followed by a list of reasons why they should go outside it. Dod and Cleaver, for example, regularly restated the axiom that a chaste and modest woman 'must also love her house', but then proceeded to provide a detailed discussion of the many reasons why women would be required to 'go abroad'.[82] The oft-repeated obligation of 'good neighbourhood' was very important in this respect. Its maxims meant many things but amongst them was the expectation that women be hospitable to neighbours and strangers who came to the house and that they would 'visit such as stand in need' outside it, complicating constructions of the virtuous wife as solitary and enclosed.[83] Another layer of intricacy was added by the reluctant acknowledgement by many moralists that, despite its dangers, women should be permitted some recreation beyond the house. Allestree emphasised to his female readers that it was always better to 'be a prisoner to ones home, then a stranger' but admitted that he did not write 'to Nuns', and had no purpose 'to confine them to a cloister'. He accepted that 'Mutual visits may often be necessary, and so (in some degree may be several harmless and healthful recreations)'.[84] Even the pious Puritan preacher William Gouge admitted that while 'tavernes, ale-houses, play-houses, and such places' were not suitable spaces for husbands to take their wives they were 'businesses as beseemeth maidservants'.[85] In similar vein the celebrated recommendation by Daniel Rogers that women should remain riveted to the house was accompanied by the acknowledgement that 'there is a general liberty to be permitted to a woman's liberties, companies, merriments, toys and trinkets, which the gravity of an husband should shame itself into peering into'.[86] Robert Abbott echoed these sentiments, using the Virgin Mary and her friendship with Elizabeth as a biblical precedent to support the view

[81] L. Gowing, 'The freedom of the streets: women and social space, 1560–1640', in P. Griffiths and M. S. R. Jenner (eds), *Londinopolis: essays in the cultural and social history of early modern London*, Manchester 2000, 140; P. Griffiths, 'The structure of prostitution in Elizabethan London', *C&C* viii (1993), 39–56, and, 'The meanings of night-walking in early modern England', *Seventeenth Century* xiii (1998), 212–38.

[82] Dod and Cleaver, *Godlie forme of householde government*, 228.

[83] Ibid.; Gouge, *Domesticall duties*, 262; Allestree, *Ladies calling*, 61–2, 79.

[84] Allestree, *Ladies calling*, 167. There may be an anti-Catholic dimension to this. Writers may have been anxious to avoid association with Catholic claustration. Thanks to Alex Walsham for this suggestion.

[85] Gouge, *Domesticall duties*, 376.

[86] Rogers, *Matrimoniall honour*, 251.

that women should be permitted to go to 'friendly meetings, for visiting one another'. Scriptural stories like these complicated prescriptive emphasis upon the destructive potential of female liberty, making the distinction between 'the virtue of visiting and the vice of gadding' very hard indeed to define.[87]

The second complication to the recommendation that women should stay within the home arose when writers of conduct manuals set out the finer points of the duties of husbands and wives. There was an enduring tension in these discussions between coexisting but conflicting models of marriage as both a partnership and a hierarchical relationship. Conduct writers aimed to resolve these inconsistencies with their elaboration of the definition of complementary but separate duties related to the different and unequal qualities and characteristics of each sex. Dod and Cleaver offered the most detailed exposition of the system, which was reproduced at the beginning of this book. Its traditions dictated that a husband should have absolute control of his wife and that the duties of spouses should be divided by giving to the man the external activities and to the woman the responsibility 'to give order for all things within the house'.[88] Inconsistencies arose within this spatial and social system however because of the domestic managerial responsibility it assigned to women. Within their detailed discussions of the internal spatial arrangements of households, male moralists gave the mistress considerable responsibility and autonomy with regard to the ordering of the family home. It was her sole duty, according to Dod and Cleaver, 'to see to those things that belong unto the kitchen, and to huswiferie'. Gouge gave her 'power and liberty to do in the household affaires what she thought good' and Daniel Rogers condemned men who meddled in domestic affairs.[89] Sir Thomas Smith, the Elizabethan lawyer and diplomat, noted in his De republica anglorum in the late 1570s that, while by law English women were completely subject to their husbands, in practice 'they have for the most part all the charge of the house and household ... which is indeed the natural occupation, exercise, office, and part of a wife'.[90] In their own domestic spaces women were to rule with minimum supervision, interference and restriction, somewhat at odds with the model of the household as a space of female submission.

Further inconsistencies were added as writers were forced to acknowledge the need for a degree of overlap in the duties of husbands and wives.[91] It was accepted that the preservation of the prosperity of a household required that women and men work in partnership and that wives had a joint if unequal role in the accumulation as well as preservation of material goods. Gouge,

---

[87] Citations from Capp, 'When gossips meet', 28.
[88] Dod and Cleaver, Godlie forme of householde government, 167–8.
[89] Ibid.; Gouge, Domesticall duties, 288; Rogers, Matrimoniall honour, 198.
[90] T. Smith, De republica anglorum: a discourse on the commonwealth of England, ed. L. Alston, Cambridge 1906, 126–7.
[91] On overlap in the productive roles of men and women see J. Bailey, Unquiet lives: marriage and marriage breakdown in England, 1660–1800, Cambridge 2003; Shepard, Meanings of manhood, 195–205; and Capp, 'When gossips meet', 28–9.

for example, stated that a wife ought to be 'an helpe in providinge such a sufficiency of the goods of this world, as are needful for that estate wherein god hathe set them'.[92] Dod and Cleaver agreed that the wife, 'according to her abilitie and power, must helpe her husband to get [goods]. The care and burthen to maintain the familie is common to both.'[93] In similar vein Thomas Gataker assigned to women the duty of 'constant and painefull endeavour of doing something, as abilitie, leisure and opportunitie shall give leave, towards the supporting and upholding, or the raising and advancing of their state, and further enlarging of their meanes'. He went on to suggest that if a wife produced goods that were surplus to the requirements of her household then she should 'sell and make merchandise of; and that no discredit or discommendation at all to her neither'.[94]

Recognition that women might make a contribution to 'matters of profit' meant that conduct writers, somewhat contradictorily, had to allow women several activities outside the house. Authors on farming and husbandry, for example, assigned women the responsibility for selling surplus produce from their yard and garden at the market and the purchase of items the household could not produce for itself. John Fitzherbert accepted these activities as part of the housewife's role, and he insisted on the husband and wife's mutual accountability when it came to marketing transactions. A wife, after her day at the market, was 'to make a true reckoning and account to her husband what she hath receiveth and what she hath paid'. The man was to do the same to his wife.[95] A married woman was also expected to support her husband in all tasks and to act as his deputy when he was away.[96] Gervase Markham asserted that 'in time of nede' it would be appropriate for a wife to go out into the fields to 'helpe her husbande to fyll the mucke wayne or donge carte, dryve the plough, to lode hey, corne & such other'.[97] Many texts urged women to follow the virtuous example of Bathsheba, the mythological biblical housewife of Proverbs xxxi, and her celebrated abilities in trade, manufacture and agriculture. Industry and adaptability were all-important in these representations, and as a consequence, whether moralists liked it or not, their precepts permitted a wide spectrum of female spatial practices provided activities could be justified as part of work or domestic duties. Everything depended on context.[98]

The third and related reason why inconsistencies emerged within these

---

92 Gouge, *Domesticall duties*, 253.
93 Dod and Cleaver, *Godlie forme of householde government*, 183.
94 Gataker, *Marriage duties*, 20–1.
95 Cited in Amussen, *Ordered society*, 68.
96 Dod and Cleaver, *Godlie forme of householde government*, 86, 183; Gouge, *Domesticall duties*, 288.
97 Cited in A. Clark, *Working life of women in the seventeenth century*, London 1919, 149.
98 Dod and Cleaver, *Godlie forme of householde government*, 60, 86. On the role of 'deputy husband' see L. Ulrich, *Goodwives: image and reality in the lives of women in northern New England, 1650–1750*, New York 1980, ch. ii.

discursive constructions was that gender was only one in a complex system of hierarchies that ordered the family home. There was a widely held conception amongst male moralists and political thinkers that the proper government of the household and by extension the whole commonwealth depended upon the maintenance of a series of social hierarchies – gender, age, marital and social status. Power relationships within prescriptive texts were understood and explained as a kind of grid in which an individual who held a dominant role in certain circumstances could be subject in another.[99] As William Gouge explained:

> we must distinguish the severall places wherein men are: for even they who are superiours to some are inferiours to others: as he that said, I have under me and am under authoritie. The master hath servants under him, may be under the authoritie of a Magistrate. ...The wife, though a mother of children, is under her husband.[100]

Magistrates ruled over male householders. Husbands ruled over wives; masters and mistresses ruled over servants and fathers and mothers over children. The patriarchal system was complicated by these principles in that they placed young and poor men in contradictory positions to older, married and/ or wealthy women. The position was often one of subjection and dependence.[101]

These intricacies created inconsistencies in the gendered ways in which space was construed. They raised questions about how to understand the organisation of domestic space as a template for gender order because the home was not represented simply as a school of female subordination; it was also constructed as an arena of female government. Texts repeatedly emphasised the principle that husbands and wives were joint, if unequal, governors of the house. It was believed to be both divinely ordained and natural that wives should wield authority and control over the organisation and use of their houses and the individuals who lived under their roof. Thus Dod and Cleaver explained that the first and most important division within the structure of government of the household was between the 'Governours' and 'Those that must be ruled'. The governors, whose authority was divinely ordained, included 'the father and mother, master and mistresse'.[102] Gouge also affirmed that 'the wife is by God's providence appointed a joint governor with the husband of the Family', 'the husband and his wife are the chiefest

99 Braddick and Walter, *Grids of power*, 11; Shepard, *Meanings of manhood*, 2–3, 34–5.
100 Gouge, *Domesticall duties*, 5.
101 Shepard, *Meanings of manhood*, 2–3, 34–5. See, for example, Katherine Hodgkin, 'Thomas Wythorne and the problem of mastery', *HWJ* xxix (1990), 20–41; A. Wood, *The politics of social conflict: the Peake country, 1520–1770*, Cambridge 1999, 24–5.
102 Dod and Cleaver, *Godlie forme of householde government*, 16.

in the familie, all under them single persons: they governors of all the rest of the house'.[103]

Furthermore, while writers consistently emphasised the potential unruliness of gender, they also dwelt at length upon the destructive potential of youth. Concern thus focused on the one hand on the organisation and use of domestic space to control women, yet on the other on the 'bridling' of disorderly youth.[104] Not only wives and daughters but sons and male servants had to be kept in line and mistresses and mothers as well as fathers and masters had the duty of discipline and education of the young. Whately described the wife's authority 'to diligently looke into the behaviour of all under the roofe, that no disordered nor sinfull practice may find quiet entrance or abode there'.[105] Gouge asserted that 'mistresses are as ordinary as masters. The duties which are enjoyned to be performed to masters may answerably be performed to mistresses ... and also by maidservants, and also by men-servants that are under mistresses'.[106] Children were repeatedly advised that sons and daughters owed duties of obedience and deference to mothers and to fathers. The mother was below the father in the household hierarchy 'by reason of her sex', but Scripture showed that children 'beare equal respect to both their naturall parents'.[107] In similar vein, servants of both sexes were admonished to respect the authority of the mistress as well as the master. What is also distinctive in these discussions is the assumption that the discipline of servants and children by household governors would involve the regular exercise of authoritarian violence. This was in sharp contrast to advice to husbands that counselled restraint with respect to the use of violence in the correction of their wives.[108] Distinctions in corporal punishment of maidservants and man-servants were recommended in so far as several writers expressed the view that it was fitting for the master to correct men-servants and the mistress to correct maidservants. But impropriety did not equate with lesser authority. Treatises on domestic government repeatedly restated the principle that obedience, reverence and respect were due in equal measure to 'masters, mistresses and dames'.[109]

Servants and children were admonished to 'frame their gestures to a reverent and dutiful behaviour' to parents, 'masters, mistresses and dames'.[110] Bending of the body before their betters was important as a display of deference. Obeysance 'as becometh the age and sex' had to be offered to both household governors in the form of giving 'place', 'uncovering the head,

---

103 Gouge, *Domesticall duties*, 3.
104 Shepard, *Meanings of manhood*, 23–38; P. Griffiths, *Youth and authority: formative experiences in England, 1560–1640*, Oxford 1996.
105 Whately, *Bride-bush*, 17.
106 Gouge, *Domesticall duties*, 161.
107 Ibid. 484.
108 Ibid. 419; Whately, *Bride-bush*, 100.
109 Dod and Cleaver, *Godlie forme of householde government*, 380.
110 Ibid.

35

bending the knee, bowing the body, standing up with the like'. Children were reminded that 'Joseph and Solomon, bowed, the one to his father, the other to his mother', to show equal respect and deference to both parents.[111]

An increasingly popular literature that offered advice to young men emphasised that they had to learn to understand their inferior 'place' in relation to their superiors.[112] What is implied, if not explicit, is that their subordination in relation to the mistress as well as the master had to be constantly and assiduously physically and spatially enacted.[113] Young men were reminded by Abraham Jackson in his advice book *The pious prentice, or the prentices piety* of the need to maintain a 'disdainful cast of the eye' to convey submission to their betters.[114] Richard Mayo's *Present for servants* urged readers to show 'respectful honour that your place requireth' and to avoid 'fawcy carriage' in the presence of their superiors.[115] Great emphasis was placed upon the need for young men to uncover their heads by removing or 'doffing their cap' before superiors of both sexes. William Phiston refers to these matters in some detail in his advice book for children *The schoole of good manners* where he states that, 'in standing thus before thy betters, hold thy hat in thy left hand, with both hands mannerly before thee'.[116] Speech was also important and young people were warned against claiming too much personal space by speaking up to superiors. Phiston advised children and youth 'in speakinge to your superiors ... let these words that thou speakest be uttered with reverence'.[117] Gouge suggested that as a mark of respect children should, 'if they observe their parents to be unwilling to heare them speake any more of such and such a matter, then ought they to lay their hand upon their mouthes. ...This is a token of great respect.'[118] Printed advice to female servants was much more rare but the first manual written by a woman in 1685, Hanna Wolley's *The compleat servant-maid*, placed similar emphasis upon obedience and respect.[119]

Later elaboration of physical and verbal manners determined that in the negotiation of private and public interactions age and rank took precedence over sex. Respect was to be demonstrated to superiors of both sexes by giving 'place'. Persons of higher rank and age were to be given more personal space than inferiors. Rules of civility recommended that the space of a 'span' (nine

---

111 Gouge, *Domesticall duties*, 437.

112 On advice literature for male youth see Shepard, *Meanings of manhood*, 21–46.

113 Gouge, *Domesticall duties*, 402.

114 A. Jackson, *The pious prentice, or the prentices piety*, London 1640, 58.

115 R. Mayo, *Present for servants*, London 1693, 27–9.

116 W. Phiston, *The schoole of good manners*, London 1609, sig. B2; P. Corfield, 'Dress for deference and dissent: hats and the decline of hat honour', *Costume* xxiii (1989), 64–79.

117 Phiston, *The schoole of good manners*, sig. B2.

118 Gouge, *Domesticall duties*, 433–4.

119 Wolley, *The compleat servant-maid*, sig. A4.

inches) should be maintained between gentleman and young.[120] Inferiors had to keep to the left of superiors (men and women) and walk one step behind. To enter into a lady's bedchamber was forbidden unless invited to do so and to sit upon her bed was only ever to be undertaken with great caution and by invitation.[121]

Conduct writers prescribed a series of spatial strategies that were intended to mark out and enforce the superior age and 'place' of the wife and mother in relation to other subordinates. According to William Gouge the mistress's superior 'place' should be reflected in the quality and quantity of her clothing and the food that she ate at table:

> Both in the measure and manner of providing, there must be a difference put betwixt a wife, and servants or children. These may have their portions of meat, apparrell, and like necessaries, proportioned out and stinted unto them, which is unmeet to be done to a wife. Neither is it needfull that so plentifull a provision be made for them as for her.[122]

The greater inferiority of the age and rank of servants and children in relation to the mistress also demanded an extra margin of courtesy towards fathers and masters. The 'obeysance of children and servants ought to be more submissive and more frequent' than that of wives.[123]

Advice writers worked consistently to erase these inconsistencies, and to reinscribe the binaries upon which the patriarchal edifice was based. Yet the contradictory features of their discussions consistently undermined the integrity of these categories. This is not to imply that the impact of the patriarchal spatial model was not powerful. Its structural effects were obvious at every turn. Yet exploration of the flawed and uneven ways in which space and gender order was represented in these texts is illuminating in several respects. It allows us to see that while the organisation, control and use of space was regarded as vitally important for the marking out and maintaining of gender order in early modern culture, space was a ground of gender construction whose meaning could shift, that the purchase of patriarchy could change and, perhaps more important, so could the position and power of women in different settings. The ideological assumption that there were two basic groups of social actors, men and women, and that all women were subject to all men was flawed. All women were not inevitably oppressed or confined, nor were men always assertive, active and independent. As will be seen in the remaining chapters of this book, the patriarchal ideal that placed the

---

[120] Bryson, *Courtesy to civility*, 98, citing *Youth's behaviour: or decencie in conversation amongst men*, trans. Francis Hawkins, London 1661; Gowing, *Common bodies*, 52–81.
[121] A. De Courtin, *The rules of civility; or, certain ways of deportment observed amongst all persons of quality upon several occasions*, London 1685, 44, 58, 18–23, 61–5, 121; Roodenburg, 'The hand of friendship', 166.
[122] Gouge, *Domesticall duties*, 402.
[123] Ibid. 279.

primary emphasis upon women's relationship of subordination to men and the need for their confinement within the household undoubtedly informed the language that gave shape to spatial experience but the way that men and women lived, imagined and constructed space could not be and was not organised exclusively in these terms.

2

Domestic Space

'the house of everyman is to him as his Castle, and fortress, as well for his defence against injuries and violence, as for his repose'.[1] Edward Coke

The significance of the early modern household, for the marking out and maintaining of gender order, makes it the obvious starting point for an investigation into how men and women experienced, imagined and gave meaning to space in everyday life. Despite the importance of the subject for seventeenth-century moral commentators, modern historians have written little directly about the internal social organisation of houses belonging to people below the level of the elite. Studies have been principally preoccupied with the material aspects of the early modern home. Modern scholarship has given us a thorough understanding of the physical structure and visual features of early modern houses. We know that town housing was generally arranged in rows in narrow streets. Houses were made of wood, with stone or brick foundations; they had narrow frontages that faced the street; they frequently stretched far back and had several storeys that housed more than one family. Village houses were generally single storey although some had an upper level at one end. More prosperous homes had a front doorway that opened onto a main hall where the family lived and ate. There was a kitchen to one side and a parlour that doubled as a bedroom on the other. A back door led to a garden and to other specialised service spaces used as butteries, cheese houses, or for storage of animals and farm equipment.[2] An upper floor or loft was used for additional storage or as bedrooms for apprentices or servants. Chim-

---

[1] Sir Edward Coke, *An exact abridgement in English of the eleven books of reports of the learned Sir Edward Coke, knight, late lord chiefe justice of England, and the councell of estate to his majesty, King James*, London 1651, 221.
[2] For rural housing see W. G. Hoskins, 'The rebuilding of rural England, 1560–1640', *P&P* iv (1953), 44–59; M.W. Barley, 'Rural building in England', in J. Thirsk (ed.), *The agrarian history of England and Wales*, IV: *1500–1640*, Cambridge 1985, 590–685; and Johnson, *An archaeology of capitalism*. Studies which emphasise regional variation in rates of rebuilding include R. Machin, 'The great rebuilding: a reassessment', *P&P* lxxvii (1977), 33–56; M. Johnson, *Housing culture: traditional architecture in an English landscape*, London 1993; and M. Overton, J. Whittle, D. Dean and A. Hann, *Production and consumption in English households, 1600–1750*, Oxford 2004. For urban housing see U. Priestley, P. Corfield and H. Sutermeister, 'Rooms and room use in Norwich housing, 1580–1730', *Post-Medieval Archaeology* xvi (1982), 93–123; P. Guillery, *The small house in eighteenth-century London*, London 2004; W. C. Baer, 'Housing the poor and mechanick class in seventeenth-century London', *London Journal* xxv (2000), 13–39; Brown, 'Continuity and change in the urban house', 558–90; and S. M. Jack, *Towns in Tudor and Stuart Britain*, Basingstoke 1996.

neys, glazed windows and wainscoting reflected improvements in comfort and design.

However, with the exception of recent work by Jennifer Melville, the history of early modern middling-sort domestic space has not benefited from the anthropological approaches that have been so fruitfully adopted to explore the social meaning of domestic spaces belonging to different social groups in other periods and places. These have highlighted the intricate links between space and the formation of gender identities and relations.[3] These links have been addressed implicitly in work on early modern marriage, the family, women and gender that has focused upon the long-standing debate among historians about the significance of the separate spheres analogy for the reality of life for men and women in the pre-modern past. Most historians have simply concluded that rhetoric bore little relation to domestic reality. The household was not organised towards a rigorous spatial segregation of the sexes. Keith Wrightson has long argued that early modern marriage was an economic partnership, characterised by interdependence and companion-ship. Recent studies of marriage and masculinity, by Joanne Bailey and Alex Shepard, have highlighted the importance of domestic life for both men and women and the ways in which household work strategies blurred boundaries between male and female spheres of activity. Ralph Houlbrooke and Robert Shoemaker have emphasised that, while there was a sexual division of labour within the early modern household, there was also considerable overlap in terms of the tasks and spaces in which activities were performed. Men and women, married and unmarried, old and young, mingled together inside and outside the house, in productive and domestic tasks.[4]

Yet beyond this rejection of the applicability of the separate spheres model for the early modern period, there is still much to learn about the relationship between gender and the domestic interior. In the relatively confined condi-tions of middling-sort houses, it would not be likely that spaces could be iden-tified that were strictly segregated according to gender, or any other social factor, as can be found in studies of the elite. But we have seen that non-segregated spaces can express and enforce social differences between indi-viduals and groups by the different ways that space is used and the manner in which it is controlled. In the light of these findings we need to know a great deal more about how gender influenced the spatial organisation of the

---

[3] Melville, 'The use and organisation of domestic space'. For studies of the influence of gender upon the organisation of elite domestic spaces see, for example, Friedman, *House and household*, and Wall, 'Gendering rooms'. For western Europe see R. Sarti, *Europe at home: family and material culture, 1500–1800*, London 2002; for socio-anthropological studies of domestic spaces see Massey, *Space, place and gender*; Moore, *Space, text and gender*; Reiter, 'Men and women in the south of France', 21–49; Roubin, 'Male space and female space', 252–82; and Spain, *Gendered spaces*.

[4] Wrightson, *English society*; Bailey, *Unquiet lives*; Shepard, *Meanings of manhood*; R. Houlbrooke, *The English family, 1450–1700*, London 1984; Shoemaker, *Gender in English society*; Smail, *The origins of middle-class culture*; Hunt, *The middling sort*.

integration of the activities of various members of the household during day-to-day life.

Exploration of these issues has the potential to offer considerable insights into early modern gender relations, since the house was the most immediate context that determined how and when men and women met and mingled in the pre-modern past. It was also the most important environment within which crucial distinctions between the relative roles and status of different categories of men and women were organised and defined, on the basis of age, marital and social status as well as gender. An understanding of the variety of ways in which different types of men and women experienced and used domestic space should expose how gender intersected with the other hierarchies that ordered the domestic world, in ways that complicate the polarised picture of relations between men and women presented by prescriptive literature and, subsequently, by historians who have relied upon it.

Control

To understand properly the possibilities as well as the limits of gendered powers of control over access to the house and use of its spaces, a number of factors need initially to be considered. First amongst these is the different legal position of men and women with respect to the properties in which they lived. Laws pertaining to property ownership were highly gendered in early modern society. Proverbial wisdom and common law declared an Englishman's home to be his castle.[5] Formal and legal authority rested entirely in the husband's hands.[6] Common law assigned different legal status to single and married women. A single or widowed woman was termed a *feme sole* who theoretically had the same legal rights as a man to own property and to take legal action to defend those rights in court. A married woman was termed a *feme covert*. Her husband upon marriage subsumed her legal identity and thereafter she had no legally enforceable rights of ownership of the property in which she lived.[7]

---

[5] F. Heal, *Hospitality in early modern England*, Oxford 1990, 7; Melville, 'The use and organisation of domestic space', 125.

[6] Approximately 20% of household heads were female. For early modern single women see J. Boulton, *Neighbourhood and society: a London suburb in the seventeenth century*, Cambridge 1987, 128–9; B. J. Todd, 'The re-marrying widow: a stereotype reconsidered', in M. Prior (ed.), *Women in English society, 1500–1800*, London 1985, 54–92; P. Sharpe, 'Literally spinsters: a new interpretation of local economy and demography in Colyton in the seventeenth and eighteenth centuries', EcHR xliv (1991), 46–65; R. Wall, 'Women alone in English society', in *Annales de demographie historique*, London 1981, 303–17; Mendelson and Crawford, *Women in early modern England*, 165–184; J. M. Bennett and A. Froide (eds), *Single women in the European past, 1250–1800*, Philadelphia 1999; and L. Botelho and P. Thane (eds), *Women and ageing in British society since 1500*, Harlow 2001.

[7] Sommerville, *Sex and subjection*, 97–105.

Equity and ecclesiastical law moderated and protected the interests of some married women against these common law disadvantages to the extent that many women were able to make settlements that protected personal property that they had brought to the marriage.[8] But a married women's legal position with respect to the property in which she lived was never equal to that of her husband. The house in which she lived was literally his.

There is no doubt that the basic assumption governing the organisation of domestic space, underpinning attitudes and backed by law, was that absolute authority was invested in male household heads. Yet it is important to understand that women were not entirely subordinated by the early modern domestic system. Contemporary conceptions of household government also included the power of the mistress. A simple model of absolute male control was further complicated by moral and political stress on the importance of the ordered household for social and political stability, which blurred boundaries between public and private power. The borders of early modern houses had considerable social, legal, metaphysical and gendered significance, and legal regulations limited official intervention into household affairs.[9] But belief in the patriarchal family as the bedrock of social order meant that the internal affairs of households were considered to be a matter of legitimate 'public' interest and interventions by neighbours were relatively routine. It was perfectly permissible for neighbours to spy through windows or cracks in walls to secure proof of sexual misdoings. If circumstances were considered serious or blatant enough, then there was a range of circumstances in which the secular and ecclesiastical courts were permitted to enter privately owned domestic spaces, without the consent of the owner. Suspicion of illegal activities taking place in a private dwelling might prompt official intervention. The constable was also permitted to make forcible entry if he had cause to suspect that the crime of adultery or fornication was being committed inside the house. Justices of the Peace could issue warrants to constables empowering them to enter houses and arrest 'all nightwalkers', especially those keeping 'suspicious company' at night time. Parish officers could intervene in domestic relations in extreme cases of marital cruelty or disharmony on the grounds that the peace of the neighbourhood was being disrupted.[10]

Some historians, notably Matthew Johnson, have argued that the architectural improvements that were made to many homes during the seventeenth

---

[8] A. L. Erickson, *Women and property in early modern England*, London 1993; T. Stretton, *Women waging law in Elizabethan England*, Cambridge 1998.

[9] Heal, *Hospitality in early modern England*, 7; Melville, 'The use and organisation of domestic space', 125. For the metaphysical significance of thresholds for early modern people see S. Wilson, *The magical universe: everyday ritual and magic in pre-modern Europe*, London 2000, 4–10.

[10] For discussions of the complex distinctions between public and private forms of regulation of the early modern household see Collinson, 'The Protestant family', 60–2; Amussen, *An ordered society*, 34–66; and Melville, 'The use and organisation of domestic space', 123–4.

century led to significant changes in the ways that they were controlled and relations between the people who lived in them. On the basis of prescriptive evidence from house plans and inventories, he argues that new concepts of privacy developed during this period, middling-sort families retreated behind glass windows into more comfortable homes, household life was lived less publicly and neighbourly and parochial interventions diminished. He also suggests that domestic spaces became increasingly segregated with respect to gender and status. Women and servants were ousted from the 'front', 'public' living spaces of the hall and parlour and relegated, marginalised and 'privatised' to the 'back' spaces of the kitchen and service areas around the yard, as specialised service areas within middling-sort homes increased.[11]

The findings of this study are somewhat different, emphasising that different sets of sources produce very different pictures. Incidental details in the depositions that provide a point of contact with routine spatial practice suggest that men, women, servants and children of both sexes appeared regularly in all the rooms and service areas of the house throughout the period. These conclusions are corroborated in Rachel Garrard's study of seventeenth-century probate inventories from just over the county border in Suffolk and Mark Overton's work on Kent and Cornwall. They have concluded that most rooms continued to be multifunctional spaces, especially in smaller homes, throughout the period.[12] The hall had a front door opening on to the street. Service rooms at the back of the house were not closed 'private' spaces, but had 'back' doors opening on to the yard. These were often the first entry point for visiting servants or tradesmen. In these circumstances, strict segregation of working and living space according to gender or status was impractical and unworkable. It is noteworthy that deponents did not describe their houses as private. The term was applied to spaces within and beyond the house in two main contexts. 'Private' sometimes equated with 'secret', implying the numbers of people present (or absent) from a space.[13] It was also used to distinguish between socially select and socially inclusive spaces. Taverns, for example, were sometimes divided into 'private' and 'public' rooms. The distinction was not made between rooms used by the family and those used by paying customers, but between socially select spaces paid for by customers for their exclusive use, and socially inclusive spaces open to all. In 1683 at the Chequer Inn at Hatfield Broadoak, for example, William Little and Martha Crook 'took a room and continued for aboute three hours in a publicke roome and then went abroade together for about two houres and then returned agayne and asked for a private room'.[14] There is no evidence to suggest that usage of the term equated with the domestic or the feminine.

---

[11] Johnson, An archaeology of capitalism, 174–7.

[12] Garrard, 'English probate inventories', 67; Overton, Whittle, Dean and Hann, Production and consumption, 121–36.

[13] For examples of this usage see Scott c. Whitehead (1619), LMA, DL/C/225, fo. 218v; ERO (Ch.), Q/SBa 2/61.

[14] Crooke c. Little (1683), LMA, DL/C/240, fo. 410v.

A male public world and a female private and domestic sphere were certainly not the meaning implied.

Unsurprisingly, the organisation of domestic space in rural and in urban middling households in early modern Essex underpinned patterns of integration, rather than separation, of the sexes during everyday life. Melville and Lorna Weatherill have drawn similar conclusions from their studies of middling-sort domestic spaces in other places. Melville has concluded that in Restoration London, 'popular domestic spaces may be characterised as unsegregated', while Lorna Weatherill has suggested that within the house, 'no "space" was regarded as specifically female. Rooms and the goods in them were used by men and women alike.'[15] None the less, the power geometries that were drawn out and defined within these modest and mixed social spaces were still highly significant. Spaces could be gendered, even when they were shared, by the different ways in which they were perceived, individuals making 'mental maps' to tell them which spaces were safe or secure to enter. These distinctions depended to a significant extent upon the degree of autonomy an individual possessed within a space and the power that they could exercise over how a space was used.[16] We find that prerogatives of control were determined not simply by gender, but by a complex interrelation of age, status and sex.

Powers of control over access to the house and use of its rooms rested firmly with both governors of the household. Moreover, the managerial role of the mistress meant that she was often in day-to-day charge. Prescriptive discourses that granted to mothers and mistresses positions of power to exercise control over their domestic spaces, unequal but comparable to masters and husbands, did inform practice. Their power was manifested in a number of ways.

Married women controlled access to their houses by outsiders. They intervened to repel or to expel public officials from their homes, especially if they posed a threat to the integrity and economic interests of the family. For example, in 1645 Edmund Palmer of Barking informed the court of quarter sessions that 'hee being then constable & going to demand of Thomas Edwards of Barking Fisherman some money due upon a rate' was confronted by Margaret, Edwards's wife, who abused him and forced him on his way.[17] Women refused entry to constables, or sheriff's officers, who appeared at the house to forcibly distrain livestock.[18] They also denied access to state

---

[15] Melville, 'The use and organisation of domestic space', 173; L. Weatherill, 'A possession of one's own: women and consumer behaviour in England, 1660–1740', *Journal of British Studies* xxv (1986), 154.

[16] P. Thompson, 'Women in the fishing: the roots of power between the sexes', *Comparative Studies in Society and History* xxvii (1985), 21.

[17] ERO (Ch.), Q/SBa 2/55. See also F. G. Emmison, *Elizabethan life: disorder*, Chelmsford 1971, 179.

[18] F. G. Emmison, *Elizabethan life: home, work and land*, Chelmsford 1991, 236.

officials who arrived to arrest their husbands.[19] One especially aggressive Essex matron, Margaret Gransfield of Rettendon, assaulted parish officials and tore the clothes from their backs when they came to her house to force her husband to pay his taxes. In the end the army had to be brought in to exact payment.[20]

Women wielded sufficient social authority to be able to expel customers who entered the house for commercial purposes. Many alehouses were run from domestic spaces and although the husband had to hold the legal licence, married women often acted as *de facto* managers of these businesses.[21] Their position required a difficult balance between maintaining order and making the most profit by accommodating guests of varying degrees of respectability. But landladies intervened regularly to prevent an individual leaving the house if he/she had not paid the bill, or to eject someone who was behaving badly. Their authority to do so was generally accepted. For example, in 1613 Joan Thomwright deposed that one evening while she was working in the alehouse belonging to Edward Allfeild of Hatfield Peverell, 'some wrangling' developed between Allfield and one John Curtis over a matter of businesss. Allfield's wife Jane intervened and 'willed him to depart the house'.[22]

Married women claimed the right to defend household boundaries.[23] Runaway hens, pigs or unruly children who trespassed into a neighbour's territory detonated many defamation disputes. For example, in 1725 Sarah Sayer and Martha Plantin were involved in a violent verbal altercation, 'by reason of her ye said Sarah's fowles eating up and destroying of ye currants and gooseberries' growing in Martha Plantin's garden.[24] Quarrels about these incursions were frequently conducted between women as they stood in their own doorways, hurling insults at each other across the street. Their spatial strategy was deliberate, designed to demonstrate, physically and symbolically, their dominance over their domestic territory.[25]

---

[19] For the prominence of married women in rescues see G. Walker, 'Expanding the boundaries of female honour', *Transactions of the Royal Historical Society* 6th ser. vi (1996), 235–45.

[20] ERO (Ch.), Q/SBa 2/60; Emmison, *Disorder*, 174.

[21] When a widow was the licensee, as was often the case, patterns of authority were reasonably straightforward, since a widow possessed legal rights of control over property equal to that of a man.

[22] Allfeild c. Curtis (1613), LMA, DL/C/221, fo. 1378v. For further examples of married women expelling men from alehouses see ERO (Col.), D/B5 Sb2/9, fo.181v; ERO (Ch.), Q/SBa 2/78; Frost c. Copsheafe (1610), LMA, DL/C/219, fo. 251–v.

[23] On women, witchcraft and the policing of household boundaries see D. Purkiss, 'The house, the body, the child', in her *The witch in history: early modern and twentieth-century representations*, London 1996, 91–118.

[24] Plantin c. Sayer (1725), ERO (Ch.), D/AXD 2, fo. 80v; Snowden c. Walker (1650), D/AXD 2, fo. 8v; Goodwin c. Elliott (1710), D/AXD 2, fos 56v–57; Cox. c. Poos (1722), D/AXD 2, fos 70v–75; Grenerise c. Pinge (1610), LMA, DL/C/219, fos 174v–180, 227v–228; Pinge c. Grenerise (1610), DL/C/219, fos 290v, 301v–306, 345v, 354v–357, 440v.

[25] Gowing, *Domestic dangers*, 98.

Married women exercised practical control over access to the house and use of its rooms, through their possession of the keys. Both household heads had a monopoly of control of the keys.[26] But, because of their domestic managerial role, married women very often kept charge of the keys during the day.[27] Social historians have long been out of sympathy with an evocation of the early modern past as a kind of idyllic golden age. The risks of robbery were very real and by the middle of the seventeenth century locks were routinely fitted to doors to houses and outbuildings in the countryside as well as in the town.[28] The depositions provide a plethora of examples of married women locking the doors to their houses if they were to be left unattended, and it seems that women often kept possession of the key. For example, in 1634 Margery Ellinett, wife of Thomas Ellinett of Dedham, informed the court of quarter sessions that 'on 14th May last about nine of the clock she went out of her house, [and] locked her dore'. When she returned home, she found that her landlady had broken in. In 1636 a Colchester wool comber complained that his house had been burgled, even though his wife had 'locked her doore … haveing occasion to go out'.[29]

In seventeenth-century England it was also common practice to keep rooms locked when they were not in use, probably to prevent sticky-fingered servants, neighbours or customers from purloining the valuable goods inside. Masters and mistresses locked individual rooms, but again because of the practical obligations of household management the mistress often kept charge of the keys. For example, Susan Galloway explained to the magistrate that her dame's chamber was 'locked and there could goe nobody into the same'.[30] According to her servants, Isobel Collin locked the door to the bedchamber when she and her husband went inside. It was also alleged that she locked the door to the 'old parlour' and the 'cheese house', to prevent her servants from spying on her adulterous liaisons with her lover Robert Carter.[31]

Landladies held keys to rooms that they rented out to paying guests and required that their lodgers lock themselves into their rooms after dark.[32] The mistress also kept keys to the coffers and chests in which valuable items of

---

[26] On keys see Melville, 'The use and organisation of domestic space', 176–82.

[27] Sixteenth-century morality tales represented housewifely authority and responsibility as well as chastity in painted portraits of the prudent housewife with her key. According to Thomas Tusser it was the mistress's task to lock up her house at night: M. Warner, *From the beast to the blonde: on fairy tales and their tellers*, London 1994, 34.

[28] For inventory evidence of locks and keys possessed by Essex householders see Emmison, *Home, work and land*, 9.

[29] ERO (Col.), D/B5 Sb2/7, fo. 226v. See also ERO (Ch.), Q/SR 425/104; D/AEA 41, fo. 231v.

[30] ERO (Ch.), Q/SBa 2/12.

[31] 'Records of an English village: Earls Colne, 1400–1750', ed. A. Macfarlane and others, Cambridge 1980–1 [microfiche], nos 700084, 700330, 703155, ERO (Ch.), D/ABD 1, not foliated; D/ABD 2, not foliated.

[32] ERO (Ch.), Q/SBa 2/28; Q/SBa 2/19.

food, linen, clothing and money were kept.[33] William Sethe, 'bonesetter' of Hatfield Peverell, made the mistake of entrusting £9 into the hands of Marie Spacie, his landlord's light-fingered wife. He told the Essex bench that she 'locked the same upp' in a 'hutche' in her house', and later stole it.[34] Many other references to women handling money provide indirect additional evidence of their control of the keys to the cupboards in which money was kept. Wives paid household bills, dealt with rent and bought and sold a variety of goods at home. For example, the wife of a Writtle yeoman paid the sum of £55, the half yearly rent, to her landlady.[35] One Church's wife was tricked into paying Enoch Garrett £5 for a 'black gelding', that he said her husband had bought. Another woman, of Feering, paid him £3 for a 'mylche beaste' that he told her he had sold to her husband.[36]

Householders might entrust care of the keys to their servants for a short time if, for instance, they were required to lock up the house at night. Masters and mistresses also left servants in temporary charge of the keys to the house, its rooms and its cupboards if they went away. But depositions relating to theft clearly display the disparities in status and power between servants and both household governors in these contexts. Insecure and defensive servants emphasised that their master or mistress delegated responsibility for care of the keys to them. Married women made no such justifications: possession of the keys was recognised and accepted as part of their greater privilege and power.[37]

The ability of the mistress, as well as the master, to control access to the house and use of its rooms, contrasts sharply with the position of other subordinates who lived under the same roof. The low status of servants within the household hierarchy was reflected and reinforced, spatially, in a number of ways. Servants had extremely limited power to exercise control over any space within the house. They did not expel outsiders, unless delegated to do so by their superiors.[38] Although servants, like almost everybody else in early modern England, kept keys to their own chests in which they stored precious personal possessions, there is only one reference to a servant who held the key to the room in which her chest was stored.[39] In 1678 Elizabeth Poole, servant

---

[33] ERO (Col.), D/B5 Sb2/7, fo.205v.

[34] ERO (Ch.), Q/SBa 2/43.

[35] ERO (Ch.), Q/SR 422/89. For further examples of women's business dealings at home see Macfarlane and others, 'Records of an English village', nos 701109, 701318, ERO (Ch.), D/ABD 2, not foliated; Smith c. Harrison (1702), LMA, DL/C/247, fo. 282v; and *The diary of Ralph Josselin, 1616–1683*, ed. A. Macfarlane, Oxford 1976, 208, 241, 266, 267, 269. On married women's business activities see Shepard, *Meanings of manhood*, 195–205, and Bailey, *Unquiet lives*, 85–108.

[36] ERO (Ch.), Q/SR 104/9, 9a.

[37] ERO (Col.), D/B5 Sb2/2, not foliated; D/B5 Sb2/3, not foliated; D/B5 Sb2/9, fo. 90v.

[38] For examples of masters and mistresses instructing subordinates to secure the house or to expel or repel outsiders from their houses see ERO (Col.), D/B5 Sb2/3, fo. 8v; D/B5 Sb2/2, fo. 5v; D/B5 Sb2/9, fo. 90v; ERO (Ch.), Q/SBa 2/19.

[39] ERO (Ch.), Q/SR 416/44; Q/SR 425/104; Q/SR 428/143; 'William Holcroft his booke':

to Sarient Conyers, told the Essex Bench that she kept several silver spoons belonging to her master 'in a roome which shee alone had ye key of'.[40] In other households, even in the few that had sufficient space to provide serv-ants with specific rooms, there are no references to suggest that these rooms were locked from the outside.

Without their own keys, servants could not develop the sense of personal space and privacy that their employers began to enjoy in the late seventeenth century in the new 'refuges of intimacy' such as bedchambers, great chambers, closets and studies that began to appear in larger households by this date and which could be equipped with locks and keys.[41] By contrast, family members could constantly and casually pass through the rooms in which servants slept and employers entered whenever they wished. For example, one morning in March 1621 Isobel Collin 'suspecting [her servant] ... Marg[are]t to be lousy did one day go into her chamber and ... searching her bed did find the same full of lice'.[42]

More serious than these violations of personal privacy, lack of spatial control left young women extremely accessible to masters who could sexually assault them. Servants sometimes took temporary control of space and locked themselves into a room, if the key had been left inside the door. On one occa-sion Leonard Whiting's maidservant locked herself in the milkhouse when her master tried to sexually assault her while his wife was away.[43] But in most instances servants had few opportunities to resist the advances of masters who were able to exploit their absolute power of access to, and control over, all rooms within the house to access and abuse their servants' bodies. Young women like Dorothy Baker, whose master Mr Kemp 'would locke her up at night to have his pleasure of hir', were left vulnerable to the violence that habitually characterised their experience of domestic life.[44]

The low status of servants (and children), reflected and reinforced by their lack of spatial autonomy, meant that they often experienced their own domestic spaces as arenas of direct power. Subordinates were closely super-

---

local office-holding in late Stuart Essex, ed. J. A. Sharpe, Chelmsford 1986, 57; ERO (Ch.), Q/SBa 2/22; Q/SBa 2/72; Q/SBa 2/23.

[40] 'Holcroft his booke', 67.

[41] On the significance of these spaces for the creation of a sense of personal privacy see O. Ranum, 'The refuges of intimacy', in Chartier, A history of private life, 207–63, and Sarti, Europe at home, 131. The wife of the rector of Fryerning retreated to her closet to pray alone: A. Walker, The holy life of Mrs Elizabeth Walker, London 1690, 33. For the growing importance of the great chamber as an intimate space for separateness for middling and better sort householders in the late seventeenth century see Overton and others, Production and consumption in English households, 133–4.

[42] Macfarlane and others, 'Records of an English village', no. 700698, ERO (Ch.), D/ABD2, not foliated.

[43] F. G. Emmison, Elizabethan life: morals and the church courts, Chelmsford 1973, 45.

[44] ERO (Col.), D/B5 Sb2/6, fo. 72v. For further examples of the isolation and sexual assault of female servants by their masters see D/B5 Sb2/6, fo. 129v.; D/B5 Sb2/6, fo. 129v.; ERO (Ch.), Q/SR 188/77; ERO (Col.), D/B5 Sb2/6, fo. 129v.

vised and often exploited. Their manners and gestures were minutely measured to ensure that deference and obedience were performed. Contemporary
accounts suggest that in higher status households, kneeling before parents
was practised. Elizabeth, countess of Falkland, continued to kneel before her
mother when speaking to her, even into adulthood, despite rising above her
in social rank and though she was always considered to be an 'ill-kneeler and
worse riser'.[45] At middling social levels, a respectful demeanour was required
by servants (and children) as well. In 1664 Samuel Pepys noted in his diary
that he feared his new servant Susan would be 'over-high for us, she having
last been a chambermaid and holds up her head'.[46] Thomas Yeldham was
admonished for standing 'very close to his master facing him boldly with his
hat on his head'.[47] Another insubordinate servant, Christopher Woods, was
rebuked for 'playinge with his fingers by way of derision'.[48]

Unlike their superiors, servants could not come and go, into and out of the
house, as they pleased. Their movements were carefully monitored. Mistresses
and masters sent them on errands, ordered them to stay indoors, dictated
when they should eat or where they should sleep. Susan Chaplin, servant to
Mr Smithies, minister of Milende, Colchester, told the court that she went
out for a few hours on Christmas Day 1701, but was careful to emphasise
that her 'mistress gave her leave to go'.[49] Thomas Yeldham was disciplined
by 'a blowe on the eare' from his master for lingering too long on an errand
and neglecting his work.[50] Mistress Westwood of Kelvedon allegedly beat her
servant Elizabeth Williams quite brutally because she 'behaved herself very
ill, and lay out of her master's house one or two nights without her Master *or
Mistresses* leave'.[51]

Children too could be highly supervised. In the early spring of 1606,
for example, Anne Bailey's father was so anxious about the attentions of
his daughter's suitor that he 'kept her at home from coming to market to
Romford'.[52] In another case, in the spring of 1652, Matthew Palmer locked
his daughter into her bedroom and left his wife to stand guard over her during
the day to stop her meeting Matthew Percevall.[53] It also seems that mothers
were not to be trifled with. In 1605 twelve-year-old Thomas Haskins told the
borough court of Colchester that he dared not go out into the fields with his

---

[45] M. Hewitt and I. Pinchbeck, *Children in English society*, I: *From Tudor times to the eighteenth century*, London 1969, 18.
[46] *The diary of Samuel Pepys*, ed. R. C. Latham and W. Matthews, London 1970, iv. 113.
[47] ERO (Ch.), Q/SR 81/47.
[48] ERO (Ch.), Q/SBa 2/42; Q/SBa 2/30.
[49] Smithies c. Harrison (1701), LMA, DL/C/247, fo. 426v.
[50] ERO (Ch.), Q/SR 81/47.
[51] Staines c. Westwood (1684), LMA, DL/C/240, fo. 147v (my emphasis); ERO (Col.),
D/B5 Sb2/7, fo. 205v.
[52] Harrison c. Bailey (1606), ERO (Ch.), D/AED 5, fos 108r–110.
[53] ERO (Ch.), Q/SBa 2/78; Q/SR 353/148; Q/SR 353/115–17.

friend John Rudland, 'for if his mother cam home and founde him abroade she woulde beat him'.[54]

The important difference between the spatial experience of servants and children, which reflected and reinforced the distinct and low status of the hired servant, was the servant's vulnerability to eviction. Because servants had no title to property and their customary contracts were difficult to enforce, they were extremely vulnerable to eviction.[55] Household heads frequently violated verbal agreements upon which servants' contracts of employment were often based, and simply turned them 'out of doors'. Mistresses did not expel adult male servants, but there were several cases in the records of mistresses throwing their female servants out. Sometimes eviction was a form of punishment for dishonesty or inefficiency. For example Elizabeth Brand confessed to the court of quarter sessions that she was 'turned out of doores' by her mistress goodwife Parker of Barking after stealing some of her clothes.[56] Mary Lord explained that in 1586 she had been 'servant to one Mrs. Gyttins, who put her away, from whence she went to one Mrs. Archer, with whom she made covenant for a year, but Mrs. Archer, misliking her service after she had been there a fortnight, released her of her covenant'.[57]

Servants of both sexes were vulnerable to eviction in these circumstances, but gender did have its part to play in all of this, because of the additional risk for young women of expulsion due to extra-marital pregnancy.[58] According to law, pregnant servants were not to be turned away, but in many cases they were, especially if the bastard was their master's child. A poignant example is the case of Susan Lay, who had sexual relationships with her master and his son. When she became pregnant, her mistress shipped her off to London, presumably to avoid the prying eyes of neighbours.[59] Sarah Eyon, who was 'put out of service' when she became pregnant in 1601, and Priscilla Carter, who suffered a similar fate when it was discovered that she was with child while in service in 1638, are two of numerous other examples of young girls who were made homeless when it was discovered that they were pregnant.[60]

It would be wrong, of course, to imply that servants were entirely passive or always confined. Day-to-day household life created a vast array of circum-

---

54 ERO (Col.), D/B5 Sb2/6, fo. 139v.

55 Anne Kussmaul has found that although contracts implicitly bound the servant to reside with the master for one year, and bound the master to maintain the servant for the year and to pay the wages agreed upon, whether or not there was work and whether or not the servant remained fit, household heads frequently breached the terms of these oral contracts and expelled their servants: *Servants in husbandry in early modern England*, Cambridge 1981, 32.

56 ERO (Ch.), Q/SBa 2/2.

57 ERO (Ch.), Q/SR 98/78.

58 For the eviction of male servants see ERO (Ch.), Q/SBa 2/42; Q/SBa 2/44.

59 ERO (Ch.), Q/SBa 2/74. For more details of this case see L. Gowing, 'The haunting of Susan Lay: servants and mistresses in seventeenth-century England', G&H xiv (2002), 183–201.

60 ERO (Ch.), Q/SBa 2/34; Emmison, *Morals*, 11.

stances that enabled young people to negotiate a good deal of social freedom. Some servants were also prepared to contest the social and spatial boundaries set by their employers.[61] Occasionally they went out without permission. William Cope confessed that 'he departed out of his master's house in the night season without his master's knowledge, knowing that his master would mislike of it, if he should know it'.[62] Robert Coo was sent to the Bridewell for 'having on two nights run out to dances, ... the first times he was out all night and the last time till midnight, for he would not come home until the dancing was over, though Sir John sent for him. The last time he carried away the key of the hall door to get in again.'[63] Night time, in particular, allowed servants more freedom. They sometimes admitted friends into the house without permission, or conducted sexual liaisons with their lovers, after their employers had gone to bed.[64]

Control by household heads was never absolute. The day-to-day demands of domestic management compelled masters and mistresses to make several spatial arrangements that compromised their control over their domestic spaces. Complicated work routines meant that men and women were coming and going all the time during the working day and frequently had to delegate charge of the house to hired servants, who were often unable or unwilling to prevent access by intruders. In one case a landlord coaxed the key of the front door from his tenant's servant, took over the house and had the locks changed.[65]

Few locks had duplicate keys and the practical mechanics of keeping house meant that, if both the mistress and the master went out, they had to leave the keys to doors and cupboards in 'safe' spaces such as 'mortis holes' or on top of 'mantletraces' inside the house, so that members of the household could come and go as necessary. Predictably, burglars found hidden keys quite easily, and simply unlocked the door to steal the goods inside.[66] Servants also had intimate knowledge of all these arrangements and those of a less dependable disposition were not slow to exploit opportunities for petty pilfering.[67] Feckless servants could prove even more of a threat to competent management and control than dishonest ones. In one case an arrangement of convenience for servants, apprentices and non-resident workers, whereby a Colchester cloth manufacturer left the key to his workshop on a hook in his hall, culminated in catastrophe. Late one evening in March 1637 an inept apprentice,

61 Griffiths, *Youth and authority*, 297.
62 ERO (Ch.), Q/SR 55/4.
63 *The notebook of Robert Doughty, 1662–65*, ed. J. Rosenheim (Norfolk Record Society, 1989–91), 47.
64 Griffiths, *Youth and authority*, 205–13; ERO (Col.), D/B5 Sb2/3 (not foliated); ERO (Ch.), Q/SR 124/61, 62.
65 ERO (Ch.), Q/SR 403/84, 85. See also ERO (Col.), D/B5 Sb2/9, fo. 90v; D/B5 S/b 2/9, fo. 42v.
66 ERO (Col.), D/B5 Sb2/7, fo. 318v.
67 ERO (Ch.), Q/SR 394/91, 92; Q/SBa 2/25; ERO (Col.), D/B5 Sb2/9, fo. 90v.

John Liveinge, took the key without permission and returned to the shop to finish his work. When he had done, he locked up and put the key back on to the hook in the hall, but left oil on the lighted stove, which caught fire and burned down his master's workshop.[68]

The violence of servants could undermine the ability of household governors to maintain control over their domestic spaces.[69] The authority of married women was especially vulnerable in these contexts because of their lesser physical strength and their gender. Gestures of disrespect and/or violence inflicted by men-servants on mistresses were probably expressions of resentment by male subordinates against a complex system of gendered domestic spatial control that rendered them relatively powerless.[70] For example, when Thomas Yeldham was challenged by his mistress, Rachel Skynner of Braintree, for his 'lewdness', whilst at work in her shop, he 'gave her such a thrust against the shop chest that in her conscience he was the very and only occasion of the death of her child and put her in great peril of death'.[71] The astrologer Simon Foreman relates in his autobiography that, during his apprenticeship in Salisbury, he got on well with his master, but had a difficult relationship with his mistress, who favoured her maidservants and often beat him. When he became older and stronger, at the age of seventeen, he challenged her and seized the stick as she was about to strike him one day, but he knew that such insubordination could not be tolerated and that he must leave. The Lancashire apprentice Roger Lowe was relieved to leave his master's house, to take up residence in his shop, despite its discomfort, because of his mistress's 'pestilential nature'.[72]

The image of the house presented by contemporary legal and social commentators, as a space of security and boundedness for household heads, was contradicted in many contexts by the reality of spatial arrangements. In addition to their dependence on often unreliable servants, the flimsiness of the fabric of houses facilitated a number of affronts to the security that house-holders might feel entitled to expect within the walls of their homes. Words could be dangerous intrusions that breached established boundaries, through thresholds such as windows and doors.[73] Neighbours could mind one anoth-

---

[68] ERO (Col.), D/B5 Sb2/7, fos 231v, 232v.

[69] ERO (Ch.), Q/SBa 2/42. See also Q/SBa 2/30.

[70] For an interesting case study that explores the complexities of relations between mistresses and female servants see Gowing, 'The haunting of Susan Lay', 183–201.

[71] ERO (Ch.), Q/SR 81/47.

[72] *The autobiography and personal diary of Dr Simon Foreman, the celebrated astrologer, from A.D. 1552 to A.D. 1602*, ed. J. O. Halliwell, London 1895, 276–81; *The diary of Roger Lowe of Ashton-in-Makefield, Lancashire, 1663–74*, ed. W. Sachse, London 1938, 119. For an excellent analysis of the complex relationships between mistresses and man-servants see Hodgkin, 'Thomas Wythorne and the problem of mastery', 20–41. See also Capp, 'When gossips meet', ch. iv.

[73] Snowden c. Walker (1650), ERO (Ch.), D/AXD 2, fo. 8v; Stoale c. Rawkins (1606), D/AED 5, fo. 94v. For discussion of the material and moral threat posed by defamation see

er's intimate business by spying through holes and cracks or listening through thin walls.[74] The fragile fabric of houses also facilitated entry by any half-determined housebreaker. A Norfolk labourer, on the road at West Bergholt, gained entry into a house in 1631 simply by breaking through a wall, even though he was frightened off by the mistress of the house and only stole a pair of gloves.[75]

The multifunctional character of the early modern household severely weakened structures of control. Shops, workshops, lodging houses and alehouses were often run from home, which meant that the access of outsiders had to be relatively unrestricted. Boundaries between commercial space and living space were fairly unstable, and despite efforts to safeguard possessions, paying guests often stole sheets or clothes from rooms or chests in the alehouses where they lodged. Opportunist petty thieves also crept in through back doors to dwelling houses to steal food or goods, while householders were occupied in the shop in the front.[76]

More seriously, fluid social and spatial boundaries continually exposed family members to the risk of violence inflicted by neighbours and strangers who visited. The Colchester records furnish a distressing number of examples of cases of sexual assault of young children; several abusers were customers or tradesmen who gained access to the house on the pretext of business of some kind.[77] Women were also vulnerable to violence at home, challenging or, at least, undermining contemporary rhetoric that represented the domestic environment as safe for women.[78] Alehouses that were run out of domestic spaces carried particular risks. The toxic mix of drunkenness and male custom of varying degrees of respectability meant that women were often targets of drink-induced violence. Male hosts occasionally met with physical opposition, but the weaker physical strength of women made them more vulnerable.[79] In Colchester in the summer of 1650, for example, Phoebe Grire worked as

---

J. A. Sharpe, *Defamation and sexual slander in early modern England: the church courts at York* (Borthwick Papers lviii, 1980); Ingram, *Church courts, sex and marriage*, 292–319; Gowing, *Domestic dangers*; Foyster, *Manhood in early modern England*, 148–64; and Shepard, *Meanings of manhood*, 152–85.

[74] ERO (Ch.), Q/SBA 2/30. See also D/AED 4, fos 171r–172, 174r–175; D/AED 5, fos 199r–201.

[75] ERO (Col.), D/B5 Sb2/7, fo.30v.

[76] ERO (Col.), D/B5 Sb2/9, fo.152v; ERO (Ch.), Q/SBa 2/42; Q/SBa 2/45; Q/SBa 2/70.

[77] ERO (Col.), D/B 5 Sb2/8, fo. 101v. On the sexual abuse of young children see M. Ingram, 'Child sexual abuse in early modern England', in Braddick and Walter, *Negotiating power*, 63–84.

[78] ERO (Ch.), Q/SBa 2/19.

[79] A study of women's stories of rape has found that out of 70 accounts of women who made complaints of rape to the Northern Circuit Assize magistrates between 1647 and 1798, 14 women described having been sexually assaulted in their own homes. Only 17 out of the 162 men accused of sexual assault were described as 'strangers' by the female complainants: J. Gammon, 'Ravishment and ruin: the construction of stories of sexual violence in England, c. 1640–1820', unpubl. PhD diss. Essex 2000, 91–155.

a servant in an alehouse in West Bergholt, owned by George Holton and managed by his wife Hannah. One July morning six men assaulted Phoebe when she refused to serve them beer. Her mistress faired little better. When the men returned in the afternoon and demanded more drink, Hannah also refused to serve them, whereupon they locked her up in a room next door, helped themselves to beer and stole two pounds of cheese.[80]

Male neighbours could also be threatening.[81] There were several cases of assault of married women, committed by male visitors who entered the house on the pretext of neighbourly sociability. For example, Edward Davenante sexually assaulted Etheldreda Eliston of Sible Hedingham while she was 'alone in her said house'.[82] Faith Virgin told the Essex bench that John Sewell 'did manye tymes assalte her and allure her to committee filthynes' by use of force within her own house.[83]

Outbuildings were especially hazardous, since they were isolated and separated from the main house. These spaces were used regularly by women during the course of their daily work and were popular sites for assignations between maidservants and their suitors. Hence the frequent linguistic association between barns and illicit sex.[84] But barns, butteries and cheese houses could also be dangerous places for women at work alone, as Elizabeth Talbot of Colchester found to her cost one Sunday afternoon in 1623, when Nicholas Kemball assaulted her when she was alone in her buttery.[85]

In sum, the permeability of domestic spatial boundaries and the complex demands of multifunctional household management meant that access to the living spaces over which householders presided was difficult to control. In matters of domestic government, wives and mistresses as well as masters were able to control access to the house and use of its spaces in ways that the servants and children they supervised could not. But while status was highly significant, it was not wholly determining. Control was always fragile, unstable and hard to maintain.

So far the discussion has focused on the different positions of governors and subordinates. The relative powers of husbands and wives within patterns of domestic spatial control need now to be addressed. The position of the wife was always contradictory, since according to law and ideology she was a partner, manager and dependant, powerful in relation to her subordinates, but owing subjection and obedience to her husband. As supreme household governor, the husband had legal power to exercise control over his wife's spatial autonomy in several ways. He could wield power over her body through physical punishment. He could expel her from her house if

---

80 ERO (Col.), D/B5 Sb2/9, fo.45v; ERO (Ch.), Q/SR 527/6, 7.
81 ERO (Col.), D/B5 Sb2/7, fo. 26v; D/B5 Sb2/1, fo. 68v.
82 ERO (Ch.), Q/SBa 2/55.
83 ERO (Ch.), Q/SR 93/43. See also Q/SBa 2/80; Q/SR 527/13.
84 Homan c.Yonge (1647), ERO (Ch.), D/AXD2, fo. 8v; Q/SBa 2/28.
85 ERO (Col.), D/B5 Sb2/7, fo. 75v; ERO (Ch.), Q/SBa 2/20.

she committed, or was suspected to have committed, adultery. By the eighteenth century English law also established a limited right to chastise a wife by confinement, if a husband believed his wife kept 'bad company' or was being extravagant. Women did not possess comparable legal powers to limit their husband's autonomy or to put away unfaithful husbands, although they could seek a separation if extreme cruelty could be proved.[86]

The greater prerogatives of the husband and master are reflected in the records in several contexts. There were, for instance, very few examples that show women controlling the movements of their husbands within and beyond the house. Exceptional occurrences occasionally come to light such as the case of Robert Abbott, a neighbour of Ralph Josselin, the vicar of Earls Colne, who confessed to the clergyman that 'his wife kept him bound in bed to force him to sell his lands'.[87] Specific occasions, in particular childbirth, also undermined an underlying pattern of gendered space. According to custom, the childbed chamber was an exclusively female arena. Some historians argue that this tradition, momentarily at least, overturned the positions and power of the sexes with regard to control of domestic space. Yet cases of cruelty show that, even on these most intimate female occasions, women did not possess sufficient power to enforce a man's exclusion if he chose to enter the childbed chamber by force.[88]

The many more references to men who controlled access to the house by their wives demonstrate the different and unequal position of men and women with regard to rights of possession of their domestic spaces. This superior male prerogative can be seen most clearly in cases of marital conflict. Some men justified violence against their wives because they were not allowed access to their domestic spaces.[89] Accounts of abuse also repeatedly refer to husbands who forcibly expelled women from their homes. The violent domestic tyrant and notorious philanderer, Robert Jordan, tallow chandler of Barking, threw his wife Sarah out of the house, after the birth of their first child.[90] Another violent and unfaithful husband, John Hayward, moved his mistress into his house and forced his wife Dorothy out in 1644.[91] Confinement was also cited in some cases as a form of cruelty.[92] According to witnesses, goodwife

[86] M. E. Doggett, *Marriage, wife-beating and the law in Victorian England*, Columbia 1993, 15–27; E. Foyster, 'At the limits of liberty: married women and confinement in eighteenth-century England', *C&C* xvii (2002), 39–62.

[87] *Josselin diary*, 406. See also ERO (Ch.), D/ACD 2, fo. 69.

[88] A. Wilson, 'The ceremony of childbirth and its interpretation', in V. Fildes (ed.), *Women as mothers in pre-industrial England*, London 1990, 68–107; Gowing, Common bodies, 166.

[89] Gowing, *Domestic dangers*, 210.

[90] Jordan c. Jordan (1713), LMA, DL/C/254, fo. 140v; Rule c. Rule (1675), DL/C/237, fo. 334v.

[91] ERO (Ch.), Q/SBa 2/56.

[92] Foyster, 'At the limits of liberty', 39–62.

Holborrowe was kept 'with stealth', by her husband, who placed 'a halter about her neck'.[93] Men occasionally expressed their superior power symbolically in these conflicts, ripping off their wives' headgear to display their power to deny women's claims to modesty or domestic authority. For example Henry Grigges tore off his wife's 'carcheffe from her headd and did pull her by the heire of her hedd' and then beat her with his fist 'about her head' in his own house.[94]

Wives were not simply objects of control in these cases. Depositions generally describe battles between spouses, as women tried to defend their right to remain in their own houses. Susan Bridge, wife of Thomas Bridge, husbandman, informed the Essex justices that:

> going to the house of Sir Henry Mildmay to tell him how her husband had abused her and finding him not at home returned home and finding her sister Fortune Dellaway put out of the said house whom she left there and the dore being locked by her husband she saith she tooke a boarde and opened the said dore by hitting it off from the hinges and desired her sister to go into the howse which she did.

However, when Thomas returned home later that day, he threw Fortune out of the house and gave his wife several blows 'with a brickbatt'. In the end few women had the physical strength to stand up to the brutality of their husbands.[95] The Essex records confirm the findings of Melville and Hunt, in their studies of the records of the London courts, that men might choose to leave their houses but they were never forcibly ejected.[96] As Hunt has argued, 'it was only men who threw women and children out of the house and not the reverse; the home was literally his'.[97] The advantages possessed by male heads of households, in terms of their physical strength, their property rights and their legal entitlement to control and to discipline the movements of their wives, meant that men held the balance of power in conflicts over control. A mistress's dominance of domestic space, in terms of managerial responsibility or usage, could not equate with legal or political control of it, when marital relations broke down.

Given the likely under-reporting of cases of cruelty, experiences of this kind cannot be ignored, producing as they did untold physical and psychological misery for married women. However, even in a culture that accepted physical punishment and acknowledged limited male rights to control the

---

[93] Emmison, *Morals*, 163. See also Sumner c. Sumner (1697), LMA, DL/C/245, fo. 398v.
[94] See also M. Ingram 'Sexual manners: the other face of civility in early modern England', in P. Burke, B. Harrison and P. Slack (eds), *Civil histories: essays presented to Sir Keith Thomas*, Oxford 2000, 99.
[95] ERO (Ch.), Q/SBa 2/1.
[96] ERO (Ch.), Q/SBa 2/56; Jordan c. Jordan (1713), LMA, DL/C/254, fo. 140v.
[97] M. Hunt, 'Wife beating, domesticity and women's independence in eighteenth-century London', *G&H* iv (1992), 19.

movements of their wives, cases that came to court were probably exceptional and extreme expressions of the exercise of male power and control. Studies of marital violence warn against models of explanation simply as severe manifestations of the patriarchal prerogative embedded in the domestic and social order. Martin Ingram and Joanne Bailey have pointed out that witnesses often attributed male abusive behaviour to pathology rather than to patriarchy.[98] The difficult question to answer is the relation that these extreme forms of male control bore to acceptable assertions of male authority.

The behaviour of abusive men is perhaps best understood as an exaggeration, rather than an aberration of dominant modes of masculine behaviour. Court narratives suggest that abusive husbands derived a degree of justification for their actions from legal and ideological constructions of patriarchal systems of spatial control. Non-abusive husbands evicted their wives upon suspicion of adultery. William Collin turned his wife Isobel out of doors after her alleged extra-marital affair.[99] William Wheeler of South Weald expelled his wife because she 'used such company that he liked not of, and he often warned her to forbear and she would not'.[100] Daniel Pryor 'upon discontent' forced his wife out of her house.[101] Testimonies about suspected adultery refer repeatedly to unfaithful women, who disregarded husbandly powers of social and spatial constraint. Isobel Collin was accused of entertaining male guests in her house, against her husband's wishes.[102] John Playle complained to the Essex Bench in 1574 that his wife, 'forgetting the duty and obedience of a wife unto her husband' entertained Robert Foxe and William Turner 'unlawfully', against his wishes and while he was asleep in bed, adding that, as a consequence, he stood 'in great fear as of his life as of his goods'.[103] There are also occasional references to jealous husbands who imposed social and spatial boundaries on their wives. Mr Holborough, a watchmaker of Colchester, was wary of the amorous attentions of Mr Smythies, minister of Milende, and allegedly forbade the minister from visiting his wife at home.[104]

Legal and prescriptive spatial theory had some bearing on legal and cultural spatial practice. Yet it is also clear from cases of complaint that women, and those who listened to them at court, understood that there were limits to the exercise of male prerogatives of control. Conscience set boundaries to wifely obedience.[105] In 1577, for example, Olive, wife of William Browne, a Finchingfield husbandman, complained to the court of quarter sessions that

98   Ibid. 23; Ingram, *Church courts, sex and marriage*, 183; Bailey, *Unquiet lives*, 30–61.
99   Macfarlane and others, 'Records of an English village', nos 700042–2063, ERO (Ch.), D/ABD 1, not foliated; D/ABD 2, not foliated
100 Emmison, *Morals*, 163.
101 ERO (Col.), D/B5 Sb2/9, fo.108v.
102 Macfarlane and others, 'Records of an English village', nos 702602, 700378, ERO (Ch.), D/ABD, 1, not foliated; D/ABD 2, not foliated.
103 ERO (Ch.), Q/SR 49/4 1.
104 Harrison c. Smythies (1701), LMA, DL/C/247, fo. 289v. On jealousy see Foyster, *Manhood in early modern England*, 136–8.
105 Sommerville, *Sex and subjection*, 87–9.

'whereas heretofore her husband was wont to go to Sermons and to suffer her to go, through the persuasions of George Binkes and William Binkes [Roman Catholics] by certain books which they have read unto him, he will neither go himself nor yet suffer her to go, to her great grief'.[106] Women also complained about spatial and social constraints when they took cruel husbands to court. Loss of possession of the keys, for example, was presented as indication of abuse. When Mary Jones sued for separation from her husband Charles in 1614, she presented the court with evidence of economic as well as physical hardship. Witnesses reported that her husband had refused to allow her any maintenance and that he 'did many tymes take from her her keyes'.[107] Added to this evidence are complaints from women who objected to restrictions imposed by their husbands upon their social and spatial autonomy. In 1590, for example, Margaret Percy sought a separation from her husband Christopher. In her deposition she complained that he 'used very hardd cruell and unkynde words to [her], threatening that he would have her into the country not for any love that he bore her ... but only to hamper her and lock her into a chamber'.[108] In the eighteenth century Henry Fielding's fictional Mrs Western told her brother that 'English women were not to be locked up like the Spanish and Italian wives' since they had as much right to liberty as English men.[109]

Some husbands praised the quality of meekness in their wives, suggesting a 'natural' adherence to bodily codes of submission so stressed in conduct books.[110] But there was always the problem of personality in the determination of the degree of deference that a husband could expect. There is little evidence that men punished their wives for gestures of disrespect.[111] Given the seriousness with which insolence was taken in this society and the

106 ERO (Ch.), Q/SR 64/44. See also Q/SBa 2/58.
107 Gowing, *Domestic dangers*, 210. See also Bailey, *Unquiet lives*, 79–83; S. Amussen, '"Being stirred to much unquietness"': violence and domestic violence in early modern England', *Journal of Women's History* vi (1994), 80.
108 Gowing, *Domestic dangers*, 224. Even though confinement was and still is a depressingly persistent tactic employed by abusive husbands, and women complained about this behaviour to the courts throughout this period and beyond, it is important to stress that, as Joanne Bailey has highlighted in her recent study of marital violence, until the second half of the eighteenth century wives who sought a separation from the church courts had to emphasise that their lives were at risk. It was not until the second half of the eighteenth century that legal definitions of cruelty expanded to include confinement and courts gave more credence to less physically violent acts of abuse. Elizabeth Foyster has found that despite growing convictions that men needed to be subjected to more control in order to prevent violence, changing notions of femininity left gentlewomen more vulnerable to accusations of madness and confinement in a madhouse: Bailey, *Unquiet lives*, 124; Foyster, 'At the limits of liberty', 39–62.
109 Fletcher, *Gender, sex and subordination*, 4.
110 *Two East Anglian diaries, 1641–1729: Isaac Archer and William Coe*, ed. M. Storey (Suffolk Records Society xxxvi, 1994), 117.
111 Wrightson, *English society*, 97; Capp, '*When gossips meet*', 72–84.

frequency with which other subordinates were reprimanded for repudiation of these social and spatial rules, this absence is perhaps significant.

It would be wrong to be lured by legal and moral prescription into believing that early modern domestic relations were always a life or death struggle for control, in which men battled daily to subdue and to confine women. Contemporary commentators noted the freedoms that England afforded to its women. English culture contrasted with the continent, in that it condemned men who coerced and confined their wives.[112] Diary evidence offers glimpses of the ways that husbands and wives, for the most part, constructed a domestic world based upon compromise and negotiation. William Stout, for example, told how his mild-mannered brother Josias opted for outward quiet rather than trying to assert control over the movements of his young and strong-minded wife, allowing her to 'treat her friends at pleasure ... more than would have been allowed by most of husbands'.[113] Adam Eyre gave way to pressure from his wife to stay at home, recording ruefully in his diary on July 1647 that he was confined to quarters, 'by reason my wife was not willing to let mee goe to bowles to Bolstertone'. On another occasion, when he stayed out too late at the alehouse, she locked him out and he was forced to break open the gates.[114] An alternative strategy to confrontation, as numbers of rooms increased in more wealthy homes, was to retreat into a closet or study if relations became especially tense.[115] The non-conformist minister Oliver Heywood recalled in the summer of 1672, for example, that 'being in my house, upon some slight occasion, my wife gave out some peevish discontented words, I durst not speak for fear of grieving her but withdrew myself into my study'.[116]

Most importantly, focus on the physical locations where power was constructed and maintained exposes ways in which the everyday imperatives of organisation of middling-sort domestic spaces mitigated, moderated and even rendered irrelevant patriarchal prerogatives of control. The relatively open and multi-functional character of domestic space, with its constant flow of neighbours, customers and paying guests, meant that absolute social and spatial control was impossible to achieve. In addition, as chapter 3 will show, the organisation and division of the spatial and sexual division of labour, especially in rural households, meant that the husband was out of the house for most of the working day. In these circumstances he could not be involved

[112] Smith, De anglorum, 126–7.

[113] The autobiography of William Stout of Lancaster, 1665–1752, ed. J. D. Marshall (Chetham Society, 3rd ser. xiv, 1967), 159.

[114] A. Eyre, 'A dyurnall or catalogue of all my actions', in Yorkshire diaries and autobiographies in the seventeenth and eighteenth centuries, ed. C. Jackson (Surtees Society lxx, 1877), 51, 65, 66.

[115] According to some historians the study was used mainly but not exclusively by men: Ranum, 'The refuges of intimacy', 228; Sarti, Europe at home, 131.

[116] The Rev. Oliver Heywood BA, 1630–1702: his autobiography, diaries, anecdote and event books, illustrating the general and family history of Yorkshire and Lancashire in three volumes with illustrations ed. J. H. Turner, Brighouse–Bingley 1881–5, i. 112. See also Walker, Holy life, 33.

in everyday decisions about who came into and out of the house. Finally, and most important, the considerable managerial and material agency of middling-sort married women within the early modern household economy afforded them, indeed demanded, that they had the freedom to leave and to enter the house as necessity not patriarchy dictated.

Eating

The meal table was an important arena for marking out the boundaries of belonging to the early modern household. It was, as Jack Goody has commented, 'the domestic household writ large'.[117] A husband was expected to make adequate provision for his wife and children.[118] Board and lodgings also formed part of the wages paid to servants and apprentices.[119] Eating together was so important to the definition of early modern marriage that a man and wife seen at a meal table alone could arouse suspicion of adultery.[120] Similarly, the break up of a marriage manifested itself in the separation of spouses *a mensa et thoro* – from bed and board. Eating also had an undoubted importance in early modern society for the marking out of social difference. An investigation into who cooked the meal, where a person ate and what they ate is highly illuminating for the understanding of the way in which the use and organisation of space marked out distinctions between men and women, masters and servants, old and young.[121]

It is clear from the records that women were predominantly responsible for preparing meals. The gendered character of cooking is vividly, if unintentionally, demonstrated by one William Ffuller, late of Alford who, in 1634, confessed to the theft of his master's hens. He explained that he took them to one 'Mumfords howse at which the said Mumford promised him a feast *when his wife cam home*'.[122] Of course poorer households were to a large degree

---

117 J. Goody, *Cooking, cuisine and class: a study in comparative sociology*, Cambridge 1982, 204.

118 Wrightson, *English society*, 90, 108.

119 Kussmaul, *Servants in husbandry*, 40.

120 Gowing, *Domestic dangers*, 71; Poulter c. Valentine (1615), LMA, DL/C/223, fo. 214v; Office c. Cophead and Cophead (1628), DL/C/231, fo. 63v; Macfarlane and others, 'Records of an English village', nos 702602, 700378, ERO (Ch.), D/ABD1, not foliated; D/ABD 2, not foliated.

121 Studies of the historical, social and cultural significance of food include S. Mennell, *All manner of foods: eating and taste in England and France from the Middle Ages to the present*, Oxford 1985; Goody, *Cooking, cuisine and class*; Heal, *Hospitality in early modern England*; D. Sabean, *Power in the blood: popular culture and village discourse in early modern Germany*, Cambridge 1984; and C. I. Hammer, 'A hearty meal? The prison diets of Cranmer and Latimer', *Sixteenth Century Journal* iii (1999), 653–80; Sarti, *Europe at home*.

122 ERO (Ch.), Q/SBa 2/19 (my emphasis); D/ACA 37, fo. 134v; Grove c. Spencer and Spencer (1618), LMA, DL/C/225, fo. 175v.

dependent on outside cooking. Plebeian women worked for wages most of the day, did not enjoy the benefits of an oven or even a secure supply of grain, and so could not and did not always prepare family meals themselves. In the cloth towns of north and central Essex early modern 'fast food' was available, cooked and sold by women and men, and many labouring women in the countryside bought bread and beer from local alehouses instead of doing their own cooking.[123] In 1600 the parish of Finchingfield petitioned to be allowed to license another victualling house; the town's one victualler could no longer supply the more than eighty households that had to buy their food. Over the next few years similar petitions came from Langham, Great Oakley, Halstead and High Easter.[124]

Wealth probably determined that some women delegated day-to-day cooking and baking to female servants. Inventory evidence suggests that as levels of wealth increased amongst the middling and better sort in late seventeenth-century south-east England, more genteel lifestyles were adopted; cooking became more complex, larger numbers of servants were employed and the wife took on a predominantly supervisory role.[125] Age also blurred distinctions between male and female work. For example young male servants were allocated peripheral preparatory tasks such as lighting the oven for baking or the fetching of water. Husbands also helped on occasion. For example when the newly married Revd Ralph Josselin and his wife arrived at Earls Colne and had to entertain their farm servants to a hay harvest supper in June 1646, the young clergyman noted in his diary, that 'I neyled my oven and made cakes in it for our workemen'. However we should not be mislead by his efforts. He finished his note with the remark that 'this was the first I ever made for such an use in my life'.[126] Judging from his diary entries it was also the last. It can be confidently concluded from a variety of evidence that cooking was a predominantly female activity at middling and lower social levels in early modern England.

The depositions confirm conclusions, drawn from inventory evidence, that food preparation in rural households continued to be performed in the hall during the first half of the seventeenth century, but activities were transferred to kitchens as domestic spaces became enlarged and specialised kitchens became more common.[127] However kitchens were not simply female spaces.

---

[123] C. Johnson, 'A proto-industrial community study: Coggeshall in Essex c. 1500–1750', unpubl. PhD diss. Essex 1990, 46–8; ERO (Ch.), Q/SBa 2/58. See also ch. 4 below.
[124] ERO (Ch.), Q/SR 151/99; 155/31. By the eighteenth century, the poor probably purchased almost all their food: Mendelson and Crawford, Women in early modern England, 269.
[125] Overton, Whittle, Dean and Hann, Production and consumption in English households, 80; T. Meldrum, Domestic service and gender, 1660–1750, London 2000, 40.
[126] Josselin diary, 62.
[127] Weatherill, Consumer behaviour, 150; Melville, 'The use and organisation of domestic space', 214; Johnson, An archaeology of capitalism, 174–7; Emmison, Home, work and land, 25–9; Overton, Whittle, Dean and Hann, Production and consumption in English households, 130–1.

The six cases of murder by poison that came before the Essex courts allow us to glimpse the social character of the spaces where food was prepared. Three of the six persons accused were male – two were husbands and one was a male servant, all of whom had open access to food and drink and to the spaces in which hot drinks and meals were made.[128] Gendered experience of these spaces may have been different in the vast majority of ordinary homes, insofar as women probably spent a great deal of time standing inside the hearth watching over the meal, while men sat outside the hearth beside the fire, waiting to be served. But these spaces were not separated or segregated in any straightforward or binary sort of way. The organisation of space for cooking did not stress female separation because it was not performed in an exclusively female space.[129]

Different meals were taken in different spaces at different times of the day. Breakfast probably consisted of bread, beer and butter if it was available and was taken sometime between 6 o'clock and 8 o'clock in the morning.[130] In smaller homes, in the earlier period, everyone ate breakfast in the multifunctional hall.[131] As numbers of rooms increased in more wealthy homes, servants ate breakfast separately in the kitchen.[132] Supper was also an informal and simple meal, taken between 5 o'clock and 9 o'clock in the evening, eaten with family and friends, or alone, almost anywhere in the house – in the hall, the parlour, the kitchen or upstairs in a bedchamber.[133] By the late seventeenth century, in larger households, great chambers were popular for taking small meals.[134] Depositions also contain numerous references to married couples and single men and women taking their supper at the local tavern even if the experience could be insalubrious. When Ralph Josselin travelled north with the Parliamentary forces in 1645 he put up at a 'pretty course lodging' and supped on a 'harde egge and tough cheese'; a few days later he

---

[128] ERO (Ch.), Q/SBa 2/ 85; Q/SR 390/32; ERO (Col.), D/B5 Sb2/4, not foliated; D/B5 Sb2/7, fos 255v–258; Sharpe, *Crime in England*, 131. For an illuminating study of early modern literary representations of husband murder by poison see F. Dolan, *Dangerous familiars: representations of domestic crime in England, 1550–1700*, New York 1994.

[129] A study of probate inventories from the north-west and southern regions of Restoration England has shown that the contents of kitchens included items of 'comfort and colour' varying from books to weaponry, birdcages, time-pieces, looking glasses and prints: S. Pennell, 'The material culture of food in early modern England c. 1650–1750', unpubl. DPhil. diss. Oxford 1997, 236–8.

[130] H. Hall, *Society in the Elizabethan age*, London 1902; *Foreman autobiography*, 271; T. Hitchcock, 'Sociability and misogyny in the life of John Cannon, 1648–1743', in T. Hitchcock and M. Cohen (eds), *English masculinities, 1660–1800*, London 1999, 36.

[131] Davis c. Greengrasse (1610), LMA, DL/C/219, fos 373v–374.

[132] *Foreman autobiography*, 271, Overton, Whittle, Dean and Hann, *Production and consumption in English households*, 130.

[133] Crowe c. Ffoster (1586), ERO (Ch.), D/AED 3, fos 1v–2; Boulton c. Eaton (1583), D/AED 2, fos 83v, 112v; Walker, *Holy life*, 15; ERO (Col.), D/B5 Sb2/2, not foliated. See also ch. 4 below.

[134] Overton, Whittle, Dean and Hann, *Production and consumption in English households*, 133–4.

stayed at another 'poore house' and was given 'pitifulle black bread' and 'a white loaf crust'.[135]

The main cooked meal was midday dinner. At busy times of the year, in particular during harvest, wives took their husbands' meal out into the fields, but most of the time working men returned home at midday to eat their 'dinner'.[136] The spatial ordering of the dinner table explicitly articulated distinctions between the different degrees of status and power possessed by individual members of the household. A complex interrelation of gender, age and place determined where a person sat to eat their dinner. In the earlier period, in more affluent homes, servants and apprentices of both sexes ate separately at a lower table.[137] Parents and children ate together at the 'upper' table, often joined by an employee who was considered to be of the same social standing.[138] For example, the status-conscious Elizabethan tutor, Thomas Wythorne, stipulated to his employer that he should be 'used as a friend and not a servant. Upon this, they not only allowed me to sit at their table but also at their own mess, so long as there were not any to occupy the place ... that was a great deal my better.'[139] Samuel Pepys, on the other hand, symbolically defined his sister Paulina's status downwards in the domestic hierarchy when he agreed to let her come and live with him and his wife in November 1660. He decided that she would take her place 'not as a sister but as a servant', and declared, 'I do not let her sit at table with me.'[140] A marital case that came before the bishop of London's consistory court in 1574 vividly illustrates the powerful symbolism of these spatial distinctions for the marking out of fine gradations within the hierarchy of place. In the view of those who prosecuted Elizabeth Denham for adultery, she scandalously disrupted domestic order, when she moved her lover, Isaac Binge, an apprentice with her husband, printer Henry Denham, from the lower table to the upper table to sit beside her to eat.[141]

Inventory evidence suggests that the development of houses during the seventeenth and early eighteenth century accentuated processes of spatial and social separation. The number of rooms increased, tables reduced in size and increased in number. Servants ate in the kitchen or in the hall, while

---

135 *Josselin diary*, 28.
136 ERO (Ch.), Q/SBa 2/73; Q/SBa 2/7; Boucer c. Irnard (1710), LMA, DL/C/252, fo. 26v.
137 Overton, Whittle, Dean and Hann, *Production and consumption in English households*, 130.
138 Melville, 'The use and organisation of domestic space', 216; P. Earle, *A city full of people: men and women of London, 1650–1750*, London 1989, 240–1; Meldrum, *Domestic service*, 146.
139 *Autobiography of Thomas Wythorne*, ed. J. Osborn, Oxford 1961, 94.
140 *Pepys diary*, i. 288; ii. 232.
141 Cited in Gowing, *Domestic dangers*, 190. For the prevalence of the practice of servants sitting at separate tables see Melville, 'The use and organisation of domestic space', 221–3, and Earle, *City full of people*, 240–1, 243.

the master and his family ate in the parlour.[142] In households of more modest means, with fewer rooms and less furniture, servants and apprentices probably continued to eat at the same table as the master and mistress. But power differentials within the household hierarchy were still defined and displayed symbolically by systems of seating. The overlapping influences of gender and status are apparent in these contexts. The master sat at the head of the table, often in the only single chair. The distinct position of the wife, as partner, was also marked out by her superior place at the other end of the table, where she sat in a chair, above servants and children of both sexes.[143]

Legal and literary discussions recognised how the spatial order at the dinner table reinforced a domestic order that granted to married women positions of domestic authority distinct from other dependants. In 1721 a case came before the prerogative court of Canterbury over a will of a bookseller Henry Rhodes. Evidence given in support of Jane Lillington, whose status as wife or servant was at issue, emphasised that she 'sat at the upper end of the table and carved as mistress of the family'.[144] In a disputed marriage case in 1610, it was noted by neighbours that when Richard Warren sat at supper with friends in his house and proposed marriage to Margaret Perry, he moved her to the top of the table, to display spatially and symbolically her new position as his wife and mistress of his household.[145] A deponent, supporting the case against the abusive husband of one Mistress Chambers in 1698, noted her symbolic humiliation at the hands of her husband one evening when he placed his daughter in his wife's place at table.[146] Contemporary travellers noted of English wives that, in contrast to practice on the continent, they were given the uppermost place at table. A book published in England in 1724 claimed that in Germany wives were 'not allowed at the upper end of the table'.[147] The wives of London citizens, on the other hand, were 'in all banquets and feasts … shown the greatest honour; they are placed at the upper end of the table, where they are first served'.[148]

Subordinate members of the household of both sexes were expected to sit lower down the table, on less comfortable forms, stools and benches, or if chairs were in short supply, children probably had to stand. An extract from a

---

[142] Overton, Whittle, Dean and Hann, *Production and consumption in English households*, 94, 119, 130–4.
[143] A pilot count of seating furniture made from 160 probate inventories from just over the county border in eastern Suffolk in 1584 found an average ratio of 1 chair to every 4.3 other seat places. Over time chairs became more common and also more comfortable but seating continued to reflect rank. Inventory lists invariably distinguished between 'great', 'little', 'small' or 'ordinary' chairs: Garrard, 'English probate inventories', 59. For chairs see F.W. Steer, *Farm cottages and inventories of mid-Essex, 1635–1750*, Chelmsford 1950, 13; Johnson, *Archaeology of capitalism*, 175.
[144] Meldrum, *Domestic service*, 163.
[145] Perry alias More c. Warren (1610), LMA, DL/C/219, fos 83v–84.
[146] Chambers c. Chambers (1698), LMA, DL/C/246, fo. 94v.
[147] Sarti, *Europe at home*, 155.
[148] Fletcher, *Gender, sex and subordination*, 3–4.

chap-book of the period highlights the disadvantages of age with regard to the allocation of place at table. In 1685 an unknown commentator on courting couples wrote: 'above all let them [young maids and men] be respectful to their parents and when they come to the Table, seat themselves last in a place suitable for their degree, not contending therein, nor seeming dissatisfied, though they sit below their inferiors'.[149]

The depositions provide few clues about the order and manner in which members of the household took their meals. Roger Lowe's amusing account of his first meal at the servant's table of a local cleric, implies an absence of even the rudiments of ceremony at the lower table:

> Every servant [had] a bowlful of podige [pottage] anon a great trencher like a pott lid I and all the others had, with a great quantity of podige. The dishes else were but small and few. I put bread into my podige thinking to have a spoon, but none came. While I was thus in expectation of that I could not obtaine, every man having a horn spoon in their pocketts, having done their podige fell to the other dishes. Thought I, these hungry Amallkites that I am gotten amongst will devour all if I do not set upon a resolution. ... Thought I what must I do with all these, wished in my heart many times that those hungry Rogues had them [dishes of food] in their guts, but that would not do, for still they were there before me, and I durst not set them away, though it was manners so to have done.

Lowe decided to eat his potttage as quickly as possible, but burnt his tongue, preventing him from finishing his meal. He left his food, 'with a hungry belly but a lamenting heart, and ere since I have been cautious how to supp pottige'.[150] Yet Lowe's obvious horror at what he experienced suggests that meal times in middling households may often have followed more orderly rules.

A case of poisoning in one late seventeenth-century London household provides some insight into the pecking order of eating in middling-sort family homes. It involved the attempted murder of his master Thomas Dymock by Edward Frances, his 'blackmore servant' (probably a slave), over a nine-month period in 1692, in an attempt to gain his liberty. On one occasion Frances managed to put rat poison into some water gruel in preparation on the kitchen fire. Thomas Dymock's wife Rebekah told the court that she tried to tempt her husband into eating some supper after he had fallen ill from drinking ale poisoned by Frances a few days before. After her husband refused the gruel Rebekah decided to eat a portion herself and ordered her maid to bring some to her. The maid, Joanne Lichfield, duly brought the gruel to her mistress and then asked her 'if shee may eate the rest of the water grewell'. Rebekah agreed. However it is interesting to note that before Joanne actually sat down to eat the food she felt obliged first to ask her master's daughter and

---

[149] Cited in Pennell, 'The material culture of food', 228.
[150] *Lowe diary*, 39–40.

then Frances if they would eat it. Only when they both refused did Joanne feel able to take 'the water grewell' and eat it herself. From this small vignette we can tentatively suggest that the master would be offered food first, followed by the mistress, the children of the nuclear family, the male servant and then the female servant. Gender, age and place interrelated in complex ways to determine who ate when.[151]

In this instance the master was waited upon by his wife, who was then served by her maidservant. In more wealthy homes it may well have been the case that serving was considered demeaning and left to servants. In 1715, when Elizabeth Vickers's status as wife or domestic servant was in question following the death of Edward Atwood, Elizabeth Coote testified that she often observed Vickers 'dress his victuals, wash the dishes, wait on him at table … and to behave herself in all respects as a common servant in doing all the mean and servile work of Atwood's household'.[152] But accounts in the depositions suggest that in many ordinary households married women served the meal, assisted by their female servants. For example, when William Stapleton called at the house of William Woods, a husbandman of Dedham, to ask goodwife Woods to accompany him to a neighbour's house to discuss the sale of some household goods, she explained that she 'was not at liberty to go along to Ellivett's howse', because she was busy serving her husband's 'folks [who] were at breakfast'.[153]

It was assumed in early modern culture that social factors also influenced what people ate and how much. According to prescriptive literature the key determinants were status, age and 'place'. Conduct writers advised that the subordinate position of servants and children in relation to both household governors should be reflected and reinforced by their lesser quantity and quality of food. In practice it seems that male and female servants sometimes consumed the same food as their employers.[154] Robert Loder, for example, a Berkshire yeoman farmer, in trying to prove to himself that keeping servants was too costly, adopted the assumption that each member of the household, including his five servants, ate equal shares of the food purchased and consumed similar quantities of candles and firewood.[155]

On the other hand, evidence from a wide variety of sources shows how differences within the household hierarchy could be marked out and enforced by the allocation of different qualities and quantities of food according to rank. Complaints of starvation of male and female apprentices and servants that reached the Essex bench during the period provide evidence of the most

[151] Cited in Melville, 'Use and organisation of space', 221.

[152] Meldrum, Domestic service, 146 n. 53.

[153] ERO (Col.), D/B5 S/b2/7, fo. 253v.

[154] Peter Earle found that servants of both sexes in London households of middle and upper rank ate well but those in artisan homes were likely to be less well fed and lived in conditions which 'were often very unpleasant': City full of people, 125–6.

[155] Cited in Kussmaul, Servants in husbandry, 40.

extreme end of the spectrum of this form of differential dietary control.[156] But even in more orderly and especially in larger households, consumption could be status-related. In 1656 Edward Barlow noticed that in the household of his prospective employer apprentices were seated at the same table as their master and mistress and their children, but at the lower end. They were given pudding without suet and plums and meat of poorer quality.[157] Thomas Wythorne, on the other hand, stipulated that he should be distinguished from more humble domestic servants by sharing the dishes served to his employers.[158] Simon Foreman's autobiography provides insights into the disadvantages of age when it came to the allocation of food. He claimed that 'being little and small of stature and young of yers, everyone did triumph over him', especially the kitchen maid Mary Roberts. It was not until he beat her 'black and blue one day' that she treated him more respectfully, giving him 'many a pound of butter' for his breakfast 'which before that she wold never doe'.[159]

Patterns of consumption also expose complex interrelations of gender and class. Prescriptive rules required that husbands should provide their wives with a quantity and quality of food that reflected their husband's rank and their superior 'place' within the household hierarchy. Cases of marital abuse, while offering a stark reminder that prescription did not always inform practice, do reflect an expectation that these rules should be adhered to.[160] When, in January 1644, Dorothy Hayward pleaded to the court for protection from her violent husband, she told the Essex bench that he had allowed her 'neither fitting clothes nor victualls, threateninge to make her glad of a crust of bread'.[161] Margaret Percy, suing her husband for cruelty and adultery in 1590, recounted harrowing tales to the court of the economic hardships and humiliations he had inflicted on her, leaving her 'in very bare estate for provision and forbidding the butcher to let her have any meat'.[162] In another London case an abused wife complained that her husband forced her to eat 'bread and chese', complaining, 'can't you eat that as well as the children?' She replied, 'No ... I want a bit of meat.'[163]

Kitchen accounts from the Bacon estate in the late sixteenth century, on the other hand, show that larger amounts of meat and drink were provided for male than for female workers. Mendelson and Crawford have also suggested that in poorer households wives may have deliberately given themselves smaller portions of food, so that their husbands, whose wages were higher,

---

156 ERO (Ch.), Q/SR 348/44. See also Griffiths, *Youth and authority*, 322.
157 Cited in Houlbrooke, *The English family*, 176.
158 *Wythorne autobiography*, 94.
159 *Foreman autobiography*, 273.
160 Sommerville, *Sex and subjection*, 35.
161 ERO (Ch.), Q/SBa 2/56. See also D/AEA 3, fo. 23.
162 Cited in Gowing, *Domestic dangers*, 224.
163 Cited in Earle, *A city full of people*, 245.

could continue working.[164] Popular culture implies that husbands generally expected and received the best and most food. An inversion of the accepted gender order during the family meal was a favourite device deployed by ballad writers to depict loss of male control: the married man's complaint that 'Of every several dish of meat, she'll surely be first taster, And I am glad to pick the bones, *she is so much my master*' implies that the normal expectation was that husbands had preferential access to the household meal and the wife ate what was left over.[165]

Sleeping

Sleeping, like eating, provided a clear context for the expression of inequalities of status and power within the household. Legal accounts confirm that the mistress and the master slept in the best and most comfortable bed, although the disparities in the status and power of husbands and wives were exposed in cases of marital conflict when women were most often displaced. In 1693 Mary Danvers told a group of friends that when her (pretended) husband came home drunk and fell out with her, 'she went and sate up in the Garret all night' where the servants lay.[166] Similarly in 1647 Judith Smith complained to the court of quarter sessions that 'on Monday night last the said Robert Smith her husband came home about 8 or 9 of the clock at night (she being in bed) haveing (as she conceiveth drunk too much) and did beate her aboute the head and pinched her in divers places of her body and kicked her in so much that she was forced to go out of her bed lest he should have done some further misrule to her and she still goes in fear of her life'.[167]

The unfortunate consequences of the fight between the rector of Alphamstone and his wife, as reported to the court of quarter sessions in 1572, offers a vivid insight into the enforcement of gender hierarchy in the allocation of space for sleep. It appears that the household only had three beds. After an argument the rector remained in the best bed and his wife was forced to take the second, displacing their son, Symond Callye, who joined their maidservant Joan Rayner in the third bed. Joan was forced to sleep with Symond from two weeks before Christmas to Candlemas, and, 'not having the feare of God before her eyes, being overcome with the entyceing and alurement of the same younge man, consenting to his wicked demand, is now become with child by the same Symond'.[168]

---

164 Mendelson and Crawford, *Women in early modern England*, 263.
165 *Roxburghe ballads*, ii. 576.
166 Danvers c. Danvers (1693), LMA, DL /C/ 244, fo. 93v.
167 ERO (Ch.), Q/SBA 2/65; Q/SBa 2/56.
168 ERO (Ch.), Q/SR 79/5.

The example of Symond and Joan provides further evidence of the lack of ability of individuals of lower status to exercise control over the spaces that they used for sleep. Details from the depositions suggest that very often a combination of age, rank and gender determined the bed on which a person slept. The subordinate status of servants, apprentices and to a lesser extent children of both sexes in the hierarchies of 'place' and age was signified powerfully by the order and quality of beds assigned to them. They were typically allocated the third, fourth or fifth 'best' or 'worst' 'flock' or 'boorded bedd steddles'. Alternatively, they might be expected to sleep on 'trundle' or 'truckle beds', low beds on wheels that could be stored under larger beds during the day.[169]

The rooms in which members of the household slept reinforced conventional conceptions of authority and order. The master and mistress took precedence of place in the parlour, considered to be the 'best room' in the house.[170] Later, as spheres of life began to separate out in more affluent homes, the 'chief bed' was removed upstairs into the 'parlour', 'fore' or 'great' chamber on the first floor.[171] The lower status of servants, apprentices and children was indicated by the variety of less comfortable, less exclusive circumstances in which they were expected to sleep. They were less likely to be allocated a space specifically for sleeping. In the earlier period they frequently slept on trundle beds in the hall, a room used for a variety of different purposes during the day including cooking, working and eating. Elizabeth Retteridge, apprentice with Thomas Fyersham, linen draper of Colchester, for example, slept in the hall of her master's house. Similarly, in 1578, Anne Glover, widow of Colchester, reported that her servant, Anne Fforde, lay 'in the halle in a trundle bed'.[172] Apprentices sometimes slept on a trundle bed in their master's shop so that they could serve customers late into the evening.[173] Several Essex wills of the period refer to the 'soller where my servants lie', suggesting that servants sometimes slept in the unheated 'solars' or attics of the house, presumably amongst the sacks of grain or raw materials often stored there.[174] Evidence from the courts also confirms that servants frequently slept in boarded beds in the chambers over service rooms, which were sometimes separated from the main dwelling house. For example in 1620 Thomas Jones, servant to William and Isabel Collin of Halstead, told church court officials that he usually slept

[169] Emmison, *Home, work and land,* 30; Steer, *Farm cottages and inventories,* 17.

[170] ERO (Ch.), D/AED 8, fo. 71v. Nuncupative will of Alice Bowles alias Mosse (1630); Harrison c. Bayley (1607), D/AED 5, fo. 115v.

[171] Garrard, 'English probate inventories', 57; Emmison, *Home, work and land,* 3–4, 12–16; Weatherill, *Consumer behaviour,* 159–60; Johnson, *Archaeology of capitalism,* 169; Steer, *Farm cottages and inventories,* 4, 12–16; Overton, Whittle, Dean and Hann, *Production and consumption in English households,* 133.

[172] ERO (Col.), D/B5 Sb2/3, fo. 120v; D/B5 Sb2/6, fo. 41v.

[173] *Lowe diary,* 6.

[174] In medieval and Restoration London, servants frequently slept in the attic: B. Hanawalt, *Growing up in medieval London: the experience of childhood in history,* Oxford 1993, 180–1.

in a chamber over the cheesehouse. He alleged that the room had cracks in the floorboards that were wide enough for him to spy on his mistress while she made love to Robert Carter in the outhouse below.[175] That bedrooms hardly existed for servants in many homes is further indicated by the confession made by Susan Newman to the borough court in Colchester in December 1654. She accidentally set fire to her master's barn when she was startled by a cat and knocked over a candle, while she was 'about the makeing her masters servants bed in the same barne'.[176]

Servants' sleeping arrangements also tended to be more temporary. They were expected to move wherever and whenever their superiors commanded them.[177] In July 1650, for example, a servant of one Mr Amatt of Hutton was ordered to sleep in the barn to keep watch over the vagrants lodging over-night.[178] Earlier, in 1628, Katherine Butcher of Belchamp St Paul informed the court of quarter sessions that her servant, Susan Galloway, 'did lye with her two or three nights by reason her husband had required her she should keep with her until he returned in the same chamber'.[179]

The sleeping quarters of servants were often more crowded than the bedchambers of their superiors. It was common practice, for example, for servants to share a bed with the children of the household. In 1592 Mary Clarke, maidservant to Rebecca Purcas of Thaxted, informed the court of quarter sessions that she shared a bed with 'one child of thirteen years of age'.[180] Such crowding had tragic consequences for the daughter of Isaac Archer, minister of Chippenham, in Cambridgeshire. In December 1682 he recorded details of her death in his diary, explaining that 'She had a tender hearted nurse, but we feare 'twas overlaid, ... there being 4 in the bed'.[181]

The subordinate status of servants of both sexes was further signified by the order and manner in which they retired to sleep. There was an expectation that servants should wait up until their employers came home at night, to warm their beds and light them to their chamber. Mary Day, who worked as a servant for Joseph Rule, a yeoman of Upminster, reported that her master refused to pay for candles, 'that she might see to warm her [her mistress Mary Day] to bed'.[182] William Winter, apprentice to John Sumner of Barking, explained that one Sunday about 11 o' clock at night, his master came home

---

175 Macfarlane and others, 'Records of an English village', no. 700084, ERO (Ch.), D/ABD1, not foliated.
176 ERO (Col.), D/B5 Sb2/9, fo. 95v.
177 Melville also noted what she describes as the 'shiftability' of servants' sleeping arrangements: 'The use and organisation of domestic space', 227.
178 ERO (Ch.), Q/SBa 2/74.
179 ERO (Ch.), Q/SBa 2/12.
180 ERO (Ch.), Q/SR 124/59, 60. See also Q/SBa 2/21.
181 Two East Anglian diaries, 166.
182 Rule c. Rule (1675), LMA, DL/C/237, fo. 391v.

late and 'went upstairs immediately and this deponent waited upon him up to his Chamber doore and att the doore gave him a candle and he the said John then went into the chamber and immediately blew out the candle and this dep[onen]t then went his way in order to goe to bedd'.[183] Sara Wentrose confessed to the ecclesiastical court in 1635 that her mistress expressed her displeasure when she found Sara 'in her master's chamber one night to carry up his slippers'.[184] Elizabeth Pepys expected help with undressing and Samuel became disgruntled if his boy did not help him to bed.[185]

Occasionally details emerge about the sleeping arrangements of elderly or sick relatives that expose their liminal status within the household. It seems that old age or dependence granted few privileges to individuals when it came to the allocation of space for sleep. Indeed it seems to have consigned men and women to a position similar to children and servants.[186] We find for example that George Hayward's elderly father slept in a chamber with a female servant and the children, while he and his wife slept in a separate room upstairs.[187] Another unfortunate example is the ailing sister-in-law of Robert Fleate, a glover of Colchester, who shared a bed with his three children, while he and his wife slept in comfort in the room next door.[188]

The depositions also provide occasional glimpses of the dangers, particularly for women and children, of the insecure and overcrowded sleeping spaces provided for inmates in the lodging houses erected in industrial towns like Colchester during the period. John Baron, his wife and two children were one of many cloth-working families who lived out of one room and slept in a single bed in Colchester. One afternoon a male neighbour sexually abused his daughter while he and his wife were out of the lodging house during harvest time.[189] In another Colchester case in 1668, Mary Prigg was sexually assaulted by a fellow lodger, who had easy access to her sleeping space. She explained to the borough court officials that 'her lodging being a hall room was a thoroughfayre from the streetdore into the rest of the said house'.[190]

Many individuals in better-off households slept in overcrowded conditions. For the most part gender had less of an influence on these arrangements than age, status and place, although some distinctions can be discerned between the experiences of male and female servants. There were no references in the depositions to male servants sleeping with their employers and only

[183] Sumner c. Sumner (1697), LMA, DL/C/245, fo. 398v.
[184] ERO (Ch.), D/ACA 51, fo. 68v; Q/SBa 2/32.
[185] *Pepys diary*, vii. 200.
[186] On adults sleeping in their own beds by the end of the seventeenth century see Weatherill, *Consumer behaviour*, 160.
[187] ERO (Ch.), Q/SBa 2/56.
[188] ERO (Col.), D/B5 Sb2/2, not foliated. Unfortunately evidence from the depositions does no allow us to see at what age children were given separate beds or whether, for instance at the onset of puberty, they were given beds and rooms of their own.
[189] ERO (Col.), D/B5 Sb2/9, fo. 256.
[190] Ibid. fo. 168.

one example of a 'boy', probably a male apprentice, sleeping in his master's bedchamber, but maidservants were frequently expected to sleep in the same chamber as their masters and mistresses.[191] Sharing a room meant that copulation could be a fairly public affair. In 1608 Elizabeth Lucas, who worked as a servant for Richard Gilder, a butcher of Colchester, confessed to the borough court that an apprentice 'with whom she did dwell did begett her with childe and that he had the carnal use and knowledge of her bodie at Easter last on her bedd wher she did lye att her masters beddfote when her master and dame were abedd in the night tyme'.[192]

Lawrence Stone has argued that these arrangements were common at middling social levels at least until the end of the eighteenth century when increasing stress began to be laid on personal privacy and servants began to be lodged in separate chambers.[193] However, evidence from the depositions suggests that change began to occur much earlier in middling-sort households in early modern Essex. Alterations in arrangements may have been made in part to protect personal reputation. From around 1580 the Church began to condemn the communal sleeping of mixed sexes, and regular presentments began to be made to the archdeaconry courts for sexual offences, which focused on the unsuitability of such arrangements. In 1600, for example, some searching questions were put to one Edwards of Manningtree as to 'whether he hath sent his wife commonly by the tide to Harwich market in the night season, his maid lying at his bed's feet in the chamber'.[194]

The extent of church influence on household sleeping arrangements is difficult to assess. Comfort, convenience and the status associated with the ownership of several expensive beds probably also contributed to change. But there is considerable evidence to indicate that from the early part of the seventeenth century servants of both sexes were provided with sleeping accommodation separate from their superiors whenever possible or practical, and when rooms were shared single-sex sleeping accommodation seems to have been provided.[195] In 1685 Mary Everett, apprentice to Samuel Shedd of the parish of St Giles, Colchester, confessed to the borough court that 'on Monday 8th of February last she did sitt up late att worke that night with her master and after they had done work her master bid her goe and lye down on the boyes bed in the chamber'.[196] Edward Spooner and Richard Brewer shared a chamber in an outhouse while they worked as servants for one Widow Porter in 1633, while the maidservant slept in the dwelling house.[197]

---

191 ERO (Ch.), Q/SBa 2/56.
192 ERO (Col.), D/B5 Sb2/6, fo. 190v.
193 L. Stone, *The family, sex and marriage in England, 1500–1800*, London 1977, 254–5.
194 Emmison, *Morals*, 15; ERO (Ch.), D/AEA 15, fo. 125v.
195 ERO (Col.), D/B5 Sb2/9, fo. 90v.
196 Ibid. fo. 256v.
197 ERO (Ch.), Q/SBa 2/41; Q/SBa 2/12.

By the latter half of the seventeenth century regular references to a 'Mayds Chamber' and a 'Mans Chamber' can be found in yeomens' inventories.[198]

Obviously sleeping arrangements depended to a significant degree on the size of the house, the number of beds and the number of people in it. Shortage of money and space might mean that servants sometimes shared a bed with the master and mistress. In 1650 Thomas Porter informed the court of quarter sessions that when he searched the house of Thomas Guier, a labourer of Widford, he found 'Thomas Guier and Mary his wife and Mary Dagenett [Guier's niece and maidservant] were all in bed together'.[199] In more suspicious circumstances, Ann Ellis of Kelvedon was presented before the archdeacon of Colchester on a charge of incest after her sixteen-year-old son was overheard to say that 'he desyered to fele other children's secret p[ar]t[es] sayinge further that he Lyinge nughtly with his mother and grandmother knewe ther secret p[ar]t[es] to be hearye'.[200]

Change did not therefore develop in a uniform manner. Specialised spaces for sleep were on the increase, but rooms in many houses remained multipurpose and people continued to eat, sleep and even work in the same space for much of the period. Nor were patterns of specialisation and differentiation related entirely to differences in wealth and class. One of the most interesting developments that took place in middling and gentry households in the late seventeenth and eighteenth centuries was the increasing popularity of the great chamber, a room which was probably used for eating, sleeping and entertaining guests.[201]

Yet domestic space remained an arena that resonated with power and symbolism. Hierarchical distinctions between men and women, masters and servants, old and young, continued to be expressed and enforced by the way that space was used for eating and sleeping, and the manner in which it was controlled. Married women were by no means excluded from power within this spatial system. In the extremes of marital breakdown, their inferior position in relation to their husband, with respect to the domestic space in which they lived, was starkly expressed. Yet in most other contexts patriarchal authority was less obvious and there is little evidence of heavy-handed husbandly control. Indeed, while the authority of the mistress did not carry the legal, institutional and social weight of her husband, the difference between her position and that of the servants and children whom she supervised was stark. Responsibility for daily management of domestic space did bring with it a good deal of autonomy and *de facto* powers of control.

It would be wrong, however, to interpret such spatial patterns as static. Spatial organisation was fluid and highly variable according to a number of

---

198 Steer, *Farm cottages and inventories*, 123, 128, 135, 148; Overton, Whittle, Dean and Hann, *Production and consumption in English households*, 81.
199 ERO (Ch.), Q/SBa 2/73.
200 ERO (Ch.), D/ACA 34, fo. 52v.
201 Overton, Whittle, Dean and Hann, *Production and consumption in English households*, 133–4.

factors including the personality of individuals, time of day, size and wealth of the household, the local economy and occupation. It also varied according to context. Several studies have argued that work created contexts of cooperation and mutual dependence in which social and spatial relations were not wholly or even partially expressed in hierarchical ways. We will now go on to explore these ideas through an investigation into how social and gender relationships were expressed and ordered through the organisation of space for labour.

3

The Spatial Division of Labour

'Paul willeth that women be house-keepers, or keepers at home, as we call
them hous-wives'.[1]

Conventional assumptions about a spatial and sexual division of labour that
was linked to supposedly 'natural' differences between the sexes, and which
determined that women were made to run the home and men were suited
to work outside it, were central to early modern ideological theories about
gender.[2] The organisation of the sexual and spatial division of labour has also
been fundamental to the scholarly analysis and explanation of the construction of gender identities and relations across time and place. Discussions in
gender history have been conditioned, to a large extent, by the pioneering
research of Alice Clark, and her arguments about the impact on female status
of changes in the spatial organisation of work brought about by the onset of
capitalism. According to Clark, the pre-industrial economy, in which production often went on in the household, offered women opportunities for wide-
ranging participation in trade and agricultural work. The spatial organisation
of the household economy had positive social consequences for women
because husbands and wives frequently worked together, in a manner that
encouraged an association of male and female interests. Female participation in economic activity and status steadily decreased, it is argued, with the
advent of capitalism, the resulting end of domestic production and the separation of work from home.[3]

More recently several scholars have challenged Clark's notion of a 'golden
age' of harmonious partnership in domestic production, and criticised her
theories of progressive decline. They argue that the sexual division of labour,
and consequently gender relations, were characterised more by continuity of
economic subordination than change and decline over the long term. Women's
work in the medieval and early modern period was low status, badly paid or
unpaid, frequently shifting and perceived as marginal, although essential to

---

1   Gataker, *Marriage duties*, 20.
2   Sommerville, *Sex and subjection*, 12–16.
3   The classic account is Clark, *Working life of women*. For studies that follow Clark's argument quite closely see I. Pinchbeck, *Women workers and the industrial revolution*, London
1930; B. Hill, *Women, work and sexual politics*, Oxford 1989; K. D. M. Snell, *Annals of the
labouring poor: social change and agrarian England, 1660–1900*, Cambridge 1985. M. Roberts,
'Sickles and scythes', *HWJ* vii (1979), 3–28; and D. Valenze, 'The art of women and the
business of men: women's work and the dairy industry, c.1740–1840', *P&P* cxxx (1991),
142–69.

the economies of households and communities.[4] Female occupations were commonly quite separate from male and often performed in separate places. Peter Earle has argued that Augustan London, for example, 'was a world of parallel spheres', and predominantly gender-specific working environments.[5] Equally, in her study of women's employment in the rural proto-industrial village of Colyton in Devon in the late seventeenth century, Patricia Sharpe found that bone lace-making provided women with work quite separate from male employment patterns.[6] Local studies of gendered agricultural work in a number of regions throughout England in the seventeenth century have concluded that women's farm work was 'complementary to men's but not the same'.[7]

The creative consequence of such intense debate about the impact of socio-economic change on female economic activity and status has been a critical re-examination of theoretical, evaluative and practical approaches to the organisation of the sexual division of labour in the pre-modern past.[8] Conventional assumptions about a 'natural' division of space and of labour between male production and female consumption have been undermined by the immense amount of writing and research that has recovered the 'public' productive working lives of women.[9] Historians have also begun to look critically at the notion that men were excluded from unpaid domestic labour inside the house.[10] The idea of marriage as an economic partnership remains

[4]   Vickery, 'Golden age to separate spheres?'; J. M. Bennett, 'History that stands still: women's work in the European past', Feminist Studies xiv (1988), 269–83.
[5]   Earle, A city full of people, 122, and 'The female labour market in London in the late seventeenth and early eighteenth centuries', EcHR xlii (1989), 328–53.
[6]   Sharpe, 'Literally spinsters', 46–65, quotation at p. 55.
[7]   A. Hassell-Smith, 'Labourers in late sixteenth-century England: a case study from north Norfolk', C&C iv (1989), 11–52, 376–94; P. Sharpe, Adapting to capitalism: working women in the English economy, 1700–1850, London 1996, 74.
[8]   For pioneering studies of the sexual division of labour see Hill, Women, work and sexual politics, and A. Lawrence, Women in England, 1500–1760: a social history, London 1994, 109–15. For the most recent critical appraisals see Shepard, Meanings of manhood, 195–205; Bailey, Unquiet lives, 61–84; and Capp, 'When gossips meet', 42–55.
[9]   For further studies of women and work see L. A. Tilly and J. A. Scott, Women, work and family, New York 1978; M. Roberts, 'Words they are women and deeds they are men: images of work and gender in early modern England', in L. Charles, and L. Duffin (eds), Women and work in pre-industrial England, London 1985, 122–80; M. Roberts, 'Women and work in sixteenth century towns', in P. J. Corfield and D. Keene (eds), Work in towns, 850–1850, Leicester 1990, 86–102; W. Thwaites, 'Women in the market place: Oxfordshire, c.1690–1800', Midland History ix (1984), 23–42; D. Willen, 'Women in the public sphere in early modern England', Sixteenth Century Journal xix (1988), 559–75; M. Prior, 'Women and the urban economy: Oxford, 1500–1800', in Prior, Women in English society, 93–117; S. Wright, '"Churmaids, huswyfes and hucksters": the employment of women in Tudor and Stuart Salisbury', in Charles and Duffin, Women and work, 100–21; I. K. Ben-Amos, 'Women apprentices in the trades and crafts of early modern Bristol', C&C vi (1991), 227–63; and J. M. Bennett, Ale, beer and brewsters in England: women's work in a changing world, Oxford 1996.
[10]   H. Medick, 'The proto-industrial family economy: the structural function of house-

central to our understanding of the early modern economy.[11] But it is now recognised that the roles and responsibilities of men and women were rarely rigidly structured, varying across time and place and according to context.

In general, however, the domestic division of labour has not been subjected to investigation at the detailed local level. The comment made almost thirty years ago by Miranda Chaytor that 'we still know very little about sexual divisions within the households of the majority of the rural population, about the different activities and concerns of women and men, old and young', still essentially remains valid today.[12] In particular, given the acknowledged significance of the links between space, work and the dynamics of power between the sexes, we need to know a good deal more about the location of male and female work, and the degree to which the sexes were integrated or separated during the working day. This chapter attempts to add to our knowledge through a case study of the way that men and women used and organised space for work in Essex during the 'long seventeenth century'. The advantage of the analysis is that it moves away from traditional reliance on quantification of female workers to be found in wills, account books and tax listings, records in which women's work often went unrecorded and so its significance is missed. It looks instead at details of day-to-day behaviour included in incidental detail in the depositions that give insights into what women actually did, rather than what they were meant to do, and, more important for this study, where they did it. This chapter looks first at the organisation of unpaid domestic labour; it then examines spatial patterns of work in agricultural and non-agricultural households. The division between these two occupational groups was admittedly blurred in early modern England. Many men and women engaged in both activities but at different times of the year. Here I will concentrate on where each type of work was done and on the patterns of association or separation between the sexes generated by different types of occupation.

Unsurprisingly, evidence from the depositions confirms that women did most of the domestic chores in middling-sort households in early modern England, although the fact that not all housework was done inside the house emphasises the limited relevance of a male public, female private and

hold and family during the transition from peasant society to industrial capitalism', *Social History* iii (1976), 291–315; Hill, *Women, work and sexual politics*, 39; C. Davidson, *A woman's work is never done: a history of housework in the British Isles, 1650–1950*, London 1982, 185–7; Clark, *Working life of women.*

11 For discussion of the idea of marriage as an economic partnership see Wrightson, *English society*, 93–4; Houlbrooke, *The English family*, 106–10; Clark, *Working life of women*; Tilly and Scott, *Women, work and family*; and Hufton, *The prospect before her*, 134–72, and 'Women in the family economy in eighteenth-century France', *French Historical Studies* ix (1975), 1–22. For studies that emphasise the inequality of power relations within the marital partnership see Mendelson and Crawford, *Women in early modern England*, 256–301; Prior, 'Women and the urban economy'; and Hunt, *The middling sort*, 129–31.

12 M. Chaytor, 'Household and kinship: Ryton in the late sixteenth and early seventeenth centuries', *HWJ* x (1980), 30.

domestic dichotomy for the understanding of the spatial division of labour in this period. We have seen that women cooked the meals. While the division of responsibility for consumption was not as clear-cut, since men did buy food, evidence from the records suggests that women purchased most of the provisions for family meals.[13] Shopping could take different forms in different places and wealth, geography and occupation determined that some women spent more time out of the house shopping than others. Middling-sort rural women spent a good deal of time at home working on the production of food for their families, cultivating the kitchen garden, making bread, beer and clothes. Nevertheless, very few households were self-sufficient by the seventeenth century, and it is clear that countrywomen also shopped for some food and consumer goods. 'Private' trading between individuals, outside of official control, was rapidly increasing in the region during this period, and it is not surprising to find women making private purchases of grain or flour from the mill or meat from neighbouring farmers who sold produce door to door; books, ribbons, tobacco and cloth were purchased at home from itinerant traders who travelled around country districts; other necessities were bought on weekly visits to the nearest market.[14] Poorer women in rural villages, who were occupied full-time in working for wages, bought most of their food, mainly bread and beer, from local victualling houses; itinerant sellers of foodstuffs also visited villages that lay at some distance from a local town, so that working women did not have to lose valuable time walking long distances to market to buy their food.[15] By the end of the seventeenth century rural shopkeepers had become more numerous and their stock was sometimes quite extensive.[16] Poorer women in towns purchased ready-cooked food from cook shops, as we have seen; but they also had to spend time trading for basic foodstuffs. Female consumers of all social types are highly visible in the records, haggling over exchanges with farmers and merchants or their wives at shops and market stalls. More affluent urban women probably spent the most time out and about on the street shopping, because they almost always cooked for

---

[13] Examples of men purchasing food for the household include ERO (Ch.), Q/SBa 2/30; Q/SBa 2/74; Mircocke c. Plummer (1635), D/AED 8, fo. 95v; Greene c. Burrows (1632), LMA, DL/C/232, fo. 82v; Large c. Browne (1630), DL/C/231, fo. 654v. See also Eyre, *Dyurnall*, 32, 34, 36, 49, 55.

[14] On the expansion of private marketing see A. Everitt, 'The marketing of agricultural produce', in J. Thirsk (ed.), *The agrarian history of England and Wales, IV: 1500–1640*, Cambridge 1967, 552–62. For examples of women making private purchases of grain and meat see Warwick c. Marshall (1742), ERO (Ch.), D/AXD 2, fo. 144v; Macfarlane and others, 'Records of an English village', nos 701109, 701138, D/ABD 2, not foliated; Q/SR, 332/106; Q/SBa 2/11; and Rule c. Rule (1675), LMA, DL/C/237, fo. 334v. On petty chapmen see M. Spufford, *The great reclothing of rural England: petty chapmen and their wares in the seventeenth century*, London 1984, 4, 21.

[15] ERO (Ch.), Q/SBa 2/58; Q/SBa 2/70; Q/SR 157/30; Q/SR 151/99; Q/SR 155/31; Q/SBa 2/30.

[16] A. F. J. Brown, *Prosperity and poverty: rural Essex, 1700–1815*, Chelmsford 1996, 37.

themselves and their families, and relied less on domestic production than their counterparts in the country.[17]

Women also did the washing, although it does appear that because washing was perceived as a more menial activity than cooking, and because it was such a time-consuming task, the mistress of the house delegated the work to professional laundresses or to female servants whenever possible.[18] The frequency of washing depended to an extent on the availability of time and spare clothes; those who did not possess more than one set of clothing would not be able to go without them to wash them when it was cold. Even in more affluent households washing was probably not performed every week, because it was such an arduous and time-consuming task. Samuel Pepys quite often recorded washing days in his diary, because they were so inconvenient for him, as his wife and maid did not have time to cook and he was obliged to dine on cold meat.[19] Nevertheless, because of the increasing association between clean underwear and respectability in this period, most people changed the 'linen' that they wore under their outer garments reasonably regularly, and it is quite clear from the frequent references to washing in the sources, that the laundering of clothes was an important part of housework, even in more modest middling-sort homes.[20]

Where washing was done depended upon the availability of water. Even when women within the home performed washing, it was not necessarily done in the house. Many homes did not have a pump or well, and in the country-side this meant carrying washing sometimes relatively long distances to the nearest stream or river. In the town, women did not have to carry laundry quite so far, but it still meant that the work was performed outside the house, in a conduit or common well. In sixteenth-century Chelmsford regular orders were made to stop women washing their linen and garments in the conduit in the high street where it surfaced, due to the polluting effect of their work on the local water supply. Three street wells in the town were misused in a similar way.[21] By the seventeenth century water supplies to private houses had improved, and sources more often describe women, particularly maidservants,

17 Hunt, 'Wife-beating', 12.
18 For the delegation of washing to professional laundresses see Davidson, *A woman's work is never done*. For examples of the employment of washerwomen see Oliver c. Stephens (1586), ERO (Ch.), D/AED 3, fo. 3v; Q/SBa 2/30; D/AXD 2 (1672), fo. 199v, nuncupative will of Sarah Henchman; ERO (Col.), D/B5 Sb2/7, fo. 175v. For a discussion of washing as a menial task see Weatherill, *Consumer behaviour*, 149–50. For the prominence of washing in the working life of female servants see Meldrum, *Domestic service*, 146–8.
19 *Pepys diary*, 1, 19, 111.
20 For the association between clean underwear and civility in early modern society see J. Revel, 'The uses of civility', in Chartier, *A history of private life*, 189–90, and K. Thomas, 'Cleanliness and godliness in early modern England', in A. Fletcher, and P. Roberts (eds), *Religion, culture and society in early modern Britain: essays in honour of Patrick Collinson*, Cambridge 1994, 56–83.
21 H. Grieves, *The sleepers and the shadows: Chelmsford: a town, its people and its past*, I: *The medieval and Tudor story*, Chelmsford 1988, 86; Emmison, *Home, work and land*, 318.

washing at home, either in the kitchen or outside in the yard. None the less, because the job was so hard and tiring, work was still shared and so at least it remained a sociable activity.[22]

Standards of cleanliness were obviously different from today, but the numerous references to women or their female servants sweeping or 'dressing' the house confirms that general cleaning was an important part of early modern women's domestic routine.[23] There was also an assumption that the day-to-day responsibility of caring for children, at least when they were very young, was a female concern. Numerous references can be found in the records to small children playing beside their mothers whilst they worked in the house. Few refer to them accompanying their fathers.[24] Working women sometimes paid other women to nurse their babies, and defamation cases describe arguments that erupted within networks of female neighbours who nursed children while mothers lay sick.[25] The physical proximity of houses in close-knit communities meant that casual surveillance of one another's children was also possible while they played together out in the street. Of course, this more extensive system of childcare was less feasible for women who lived in scattered rural communities or on isolated farms. For women like Elizabeth Broughton of Chishill, who was presented to the ecclesiastical court 'for seldom coming to church', the support of other women was not as available. Her explanation to the Essex archdeacon, 'that by reason of the sickness of her child she cold not repayer to the church', hints at the isolation of some countrywomen at home with small children. It is significant that the court accepted her explanation; she was simply admonished for her neglect and sent on her way.[26] It is also worth noting that fathers never used childcare as a justification for absence, presumably because they assumed court officials would not regard it as a plausible excuse.

This is not to suggest that men were never involved with childcare at all. Seventeenth-century households were busy places and in such a setting all sorts of people could be left in charge of children if necessity or emergency dictated. Court records reveal, for example, that an oatmeal man of Stanstead washed the wool bedding on which his children lay sick, when they

[22] Overton, Whittle, Dean and Hann, *Production and consumption in English households*, 131; Emmison, *Home, work and land*, 98; Valentine c. Poulter (1615), LMA, DL/C/223, fo.193v; Campion c. Foster (1592/3), DL/C/214, fos 284v–285; ERO (Ch.), D/AXD 2 (1672), fo. 199v, nuncupative will of Sarah Henchman; Oliver c. Stephens (1586), D/AED, 3, fo. 3v.

[23] Early modern attitudes to cleanliness at home are explored in Thomas, 'Cleanliness and godliness', 56–83. For examples of women sweeping or 'dressing' the house see ERO (Ch.), Q/SBa 2/45; Q/SBa 2/30.

[24] ERO (Ch.), Q/SBa 2/12; Mott c. Mitchell (1638), D/ACD 5, fo. 127v; Morris c. Bustard (1630), D/AED 8, fo. 62v; ERO (Col.), D/B5 Sb2/ 9, fo. 229v.

[25] For examples of female neighbours watching over children see Trewell c. Collins (1631), ERO (Ch.), D/AED 8, fos 79v–80; ERO (Col.), D/B5 Sb2/2, not foliated; D/B5 Sb2/9, fo. 184v.

[26] ERO (Ch.), D/ACA 23, fo 123v.

had smallpox during the autumn of 1636.[27] Male and female servants were also frequently left to look after young children, even though they were not always conscientious carers and in some cases could be downright dangerous. In Colchester in 1582 John Water, servant to Lambert Grigson, allegedly murdered Elizabeth, his master's daughter, by poison, while she was left in his charge.[28]

Gender boundaries could be blurred by age in several other contexts. Young male servants were involved in tasks connected to cooking and cleaning, taking grain to be ground at the local mill,[29] or collecting water and wood to light the oven.[30] Older married men also helped with these types of everyday jobs and on rare occasions even took on most of the household tasks.[31] But a degree of flexibility does not undermine the conclusion that women did most of the domestic chores.[32]

One historian has estimated that the time taken for women to complete these daily tasks totalled six or seven hours a day, varying of course with wealth, geography and occupation.[33] But because several of these tasks involved work outside the home, and because the nature and location of other male and female occupations were very diverse, the function of running the household had a very varied impact on patterns of integration and separation of men and women during the working day, depending primarily on how the head of the household made his living.

Where men worked in agriculture, the largest male employment sector in early modern Essex, the coexistence of mixed systems of agriculture with the cloth trade in the county meant that husbands and wives worked in separate places for much of the time.[34] Men and women did different types of agricultural work in early modern Essex, as elsewhere in early modern England.[35] On small family farms, if labour was in short supply, women probably helped with ploughing and harrowing, but in general heavy winter fieldwork was left to men. This work kept men out in the fields from September until the end of November, when they retreated to the house out of the cold and wet weather for a few weeks to mend tools and perhaps to perform non-agricultural

27 ERO (Ch.), Q/SBa 2/27.
28 ERO (Col.), D/B5 Sb2/4, not foliated; D/B5 Sb2/5, fo. 118v; D/B5 Sb2/7, fo. 98v.
29 Gutteridge c. Brett (1680), LMA, DL/C/240, fo. 170v; Mircocke c. Plummer (1635), DL/C/232, fo. 82v; Greene c. Burrowes (1632), ERO, D/AED 8, fo. 95v.
30 Faith c. Burt (1600), ERO (Ch.), D/AED 4, fo. 6v; D/ACA 39; Hertford c. Hove (1609), LMA, DL/C/218, fo. 345v; Q/SBa 2/41.
31 Gowing, Common bodies, 173; Josselin diary, 416.
32 Shoemaker, Gender in English society, 117; Medick, 'The proto-industrial family economy', 291–315.
33 Weatherill, Consumer behaviour, 143.
34 Brown, Prosperity and poverty, 7.
35 Sharpe, Adapting to capitalism, 78; Shoemaker, Gender in English society, 152. For studies that argue for a less marked gendered division of labour in agricultural work during the earlier period see Clark, Working life of women, 62; Snell, Annals of the labouring poor, 52; and Roberts, 'Sickles and scythes', 9–10.

activities such as weaving some cloth. Ploughing and harrowing began again in January and February. Finally, in spring, the fields were ploughed and harrowed again.

Women spent most of the winter working in and around the house and yard, cooking, cleaning and caring for children. They also tended animals including poultry, pigs, cattle and sheep that they kept on common land. Between times they carded and spun yarn for the clothiers, as they did for the rest of the year. For much of the winter, therefore, different work in separate places kept contact between husbands and wives to a minimum.[36] Sites of neighbourly disputes reflect the physical separation of men and women during the working day. Details from defamation cases often describe conflicts between men out in the fields in winter in front of all-male groups of neighbours.[37] Disputes between women more commonly occurred at home, in the street in front of the house or in the bakehouse.[38] It is also noticeable in the records that women commonly discovered cases of theft, because they were working in or around the house, or the first to return home to prepare the meal.[39] It was only at midday that farmhouses saw the temporary return of the male population. In cases of theft farmers frequently mentioned that they were out of the house in the morning and were informed of their losses when they came home at midday to have their dinner.[40]

Whatever the cultural origins of these spatial and occupational divisions, they were undoubtedly reinforced by the structure of the regional economy. A home-based female workforce was economically advantageous in Essex, because it allowed women to maximise their income through the opportunities that they had for spinning work. The cloth trade was the most important economic sector in the county after agriculture and operated under the putting-out system. Male clothiers controlled the organisation of the trade, and purchased and distributed wool to women at home who carded it and spun it into yarn. A petition of Suffolk clothiers in 1575, regarding problems over control of the quality of their yarn, explained that 'the custom of our country is to carry our wool out to carding and spinning and put it to divers

---

36 A comprehensive examination of the act books of the archdeaconries of Essex, Colchester, Middlesex and the bishop of London's commissary in Essex and Hertfordshire from 1630 to 1640, whose jurisdictions extended over different regional economies within the county, reveals predominantly male presentments for ploughing, harrowing, carting, hedging or ditching. Married women and female servants were prosecuted in the main for performing 'domestic' tasks, such as baking, brewing or grinding of corn or conventionally female tasks such as gathering or gleaning.

37 Field c. Aylward (1637), ERO (Ch.), D/ACD 5, fo. 127v; Hyde c. Rooke (1630), LMA, DL/C/232, fo. 200v. See also Sutton c. Rochell (1638), ERO (Ch.), D/ABD 8, fo. 51v; Greene c. Browne (1638), D/ABD 8, fo. 58v.

38 Richardson c. Punt (1626), LMA, DL/C/230, fo. 191v; Morris c. Bustard (1631), ERO (Ch.), D/AED 8, fos 62v–66.

39 ERO (Ch.), Q/SR 425/104. See also Q/SR 138/20, 20a.

40 ERO (Ch.), Q/SBa 2/73; Q/SBa 2/7; Boucer c. Irnard (1710), LMA, DL/C/252, fo. 26v.

and sundry spinners, who have in their house divers and sundry children and servants that do card and spin the same wool'.[41] Detailed local research by Arthur Brown has shown that many more women were employed in cloth manufacture than men. At any time around 1700 there were close to 4,000 weavers, wool combers and other male cloth workers in Essex villages and towns, as against 25,000 female spinners.[42] A wide range of social types of women seem to have been involved in this type of enterprise, from the wives and daughters of yeoman to those of wage labourers. The wills of yeoman farmers sometimes refer to a room fitted out in their homes as a 'shoppe', where cottage cloth production was conducted. An interesting warrant of 1622, sent to parish officials in certain villages just over the county border in Suffolk, also complained that 'yeomans and farmer's wives of good ability' were procuring for themselves and their children and servants the greater part of the spinning work from the packhouses, 'whereby the poor are being deprived of it'.[43] For the wives of small farmers and labourers, spinning was not only more pleasant than agricultural work; it was also more remunerative and provided an essential cushion against fluctuations in male employment, helping to pay the bills for rent, food and fuel. In 1636 the wages of women in spinning in Essex were 8d. a day when the normal rate for female agricultural labour was only 6d. It is likely that these practical considerations, more than patriarchal precepts, shaped the choices made by women about work. Since male wages for agricultural work were always higher, the best 'survival strategy' in Essex was for women to remain responsible for childcare and housework and to take on spinning and carding work at home.[44]

It is important also to emphasise that although female occupations were essentially domestic they were rarely solitary and women were not confined within the walls of the house.[45] Spinners often worked outside when the weather was fine, frequently in groups.[46] Celia Fiennes famously described observing the women of East Anglia who 'knit much and spin, some with

---

[41] A. F. J. Brown, *Essex at work, 1700–1815*, Chelmsford 1969, 3; Sharpe, *Adapting to capitalism*, 30; W. Hunt, *The Puritan moment: the coming of revolution in an English county*, London 1983, 19; G. Unwin, 'The history of the cloth industry in Suffolk', in R. H. Tawney (ed.), *Studies in economic history: the collected papers of George Unwin*, London 1927, 271. Domestic industry also offered women opportunities to add to their income through embezzlement. See J. Styles, 'Embezzlement, industry and the law in England, 1500–1800', in M. Berg, P. Hudson and M. Sonnescher (eds), *Manufacture in town and country before the factory*, London 1983, 173–208; ERO (Col.), D/B5 Sb2/9, fo. 240v.

[42] Brown, *Poverty and prosperity*, 12.

[43] TNA: PRO, STAC 8 259/28.

[44] R. E. Pahl, *Divisions of labour*, Oxford 1984; G. Gullickson, *Spinners and weavers of Auffay: rural industry and the sexual division of labour in a French village, 1750–1850*, Cambridge 1986.

[45] For the links between female work and sociability see Capp, 'When gossips meet', 42–55.

[46] Norris c. Butler (1613) ERO (Ch.), D/AED 5, fo. 200v; Matthewes c. Bennet (1627), D/AED 8, fo. 23v; Dod c. Mann (1627), D/AED 8, fo. 19v.

their rock and fusoe as the French does, others at their wheeles out in the streetes and lanes as one passes'.[47] Corroborative evidence of these communal patterns of work can be found in incidental detail in the depositions. We find, for example, that witnesses in an enclosure dispute in Nazeing, brought before Star Chamber in 1623, remarked that the wives of local farmers and craftsmen met on Nazeing common to do their 'knitting'.[48] In winter women enjoyed friends' company working together in one another's houses.[49] Cloth-iers' correspondence sometimes mentioned 'spinning houses' in rural areas, which might offer an approximate English equivalent to the continental 'spinning bee'.[50] Another common practice was to sit in the doorway of the house, to take advantage of the light. From this vantage point women were able to chat with passers-by and observe the goings-on in the neighbour-hood while they worked.[51] Thomas Baskerville, who travelled round England in the 1660s, observed the communal character of female patterns of work, when he noted that the women of Suffolk:

> go spinning up and down the way ... with a rock and a distaff in their hands, so that if a comparison were to be made between the ploughman and the good wives of these parts, their lives were more pleasant, for they can go with their work to good company, and the poor ploughman must do his work alone.[52]

Paradoxically, therefore, a traditional division of labour determined that yeomen farmers and husbandmen spent their time outside the household working in relative isolation, while women worked around the house and out in the street in close contact with their neighbours. Patriarchal precepts were thus entirely overturned in these small rural communities where streets were probably predominantly female spaces for most of the day.

Of course the separation of husbands and wives in areas of mixed agri-culture did not separate all men and women. In settlements of sufficient size to support a wide range of occupations, farmers' wives did not live in an environment devoid of men. Young male servants, male tradesmen and neighbours were a part of their everyday working world. The material condi-tions of life had a critical effect on the way men and women interacted in these contexts. To overcome the problem of lack of space and light inside the house, work spilled out on to the street. Tradesmen and craftsmen worked in open premises in full view of passers-by, under a wooden canopy or pentice, and this meant that men and women came into frequent contact with one another during the course of the working day. Dispute evidence offers glimpses

---

47 *The illustrated journeys of Celia Fiennes*, ed. C. Morris, London 1982, 136.
48 STAC 8/125/16; Pettit c. Mosse (1633), ERO (Ch.), D/ABD 7, fo. 127v.
49 ERO (Ch.), Q/SBa 2/46; Moore c. Clark (1631), LMA, DL/C/232, fo. 194v.
50 Brown, *Essex at work*, 10.
51 Norris c. Butler (1613), ERO (Ch.), D/AED 5, fo. 199v.
52 'Thomas Baskerville's journeys in England, Temp. Car 11', HMC, *The manuscripts of his grace the duke of Portland: preserved at Welbeck Abbey*, ii, London 1893, 266.

of the connections and occasional collisions of the working and social lives of unrelated men and women placed in often uncomfortably close proximity in these crowded conditions. In Moulsham in June 1626, for example, John Hills heard one Goodman Harry defame Elizabeth Turner on her doorstep whilst her husband was 'abroade at work' and he was 'sitting on his shop board' in front of the house next door.[53]

Obviously rural women who lived outside larger nucleated villages, in parts of Essex with the settlement patterns of small hamlets and scattered farms traditionally associated with areas colonised from woodland, lived a more solitary life. However even they were not entirely isolated. It is quite clear that the nature of women's occupations in rural areas ensured that they moved around a great deal.[54] The sexual division of labour within the household, within the cloth trade and within agriculture in Essex encouraged women out on to rural roads on a routine basis. Most middling-sort rural women rode to the local market town to shop at least once a week. They also used the expanding number of country carriers that linked farms and villages to market towns.[55] The prevalence of married women, who travelled to market as traders, is also striking in the records. Age, geography and status determined that some countrywomen had a closer and more regular connection with the market than others. The wives of well-to-do yeomen travelled for purposes of trade, but the wives or widows of more humble farmers or craftsmen did so more often. Women from the dairying district around Epping or the marshlands on the coast had a more significant involvement in the market than their counterparts in corn-growing areas further north around the Rodings. An analysis of the records suggests that the average distance travelled by both sexes to market was no more than ten miles. Women from the dairying districts in the south and east of the county, on the other hand, regularly rode fifteen miles to the city to sell their dairy produce every week during the summer, because of the lucrative profits to be obtained from the London markets. Norden refers to women in parts of Essex and other counties adjacent to London selling their surplus milk, butter, cheese, eggs and fruit in the capitals' markets in the early seventeenth century, and his observations are corroborated by evidence from the depositions.[56] It was the regular habit, for example, of Anne Sibley, wife of William Sibley of Theydon Garnon, Malen Clark, widow of Lambourne

---

[53] Turner c. Harvye (1626), ERO (Ch.), D/ABD 4, fo. 77v; Fenne c. Thompson (1627) D/ABD 4, fo. 77v–r.

[54] On female mobility in London see R. B. Shoemaker, 'Gendered spaces: patterns of mobility and perception of London's geography, 1660–1750', in J. Merritt (ed.), *Imagining early modern London: perceptions and portrayals of the city from Stow to Strype, 1598–1720*, Cambridge 2001, 144–65.

[55] *Josselin diary*, 351. For the expansion of carrier and coach services in the county see K. H. Burley, 'The economic development of Essex in the later seventeenth and early eighteenth centuries', unpubl. PhD diss. London 1957, 98–128.

[56] Cited in Sharpe, *Adapting to capitalism*, 94.

and Jane Casse, wife of Richard Casse, husbandman of Stapleford Tawney, to ride up to London, 'in the somer tyme to sell commodities'.[57]

Women's home-based labour in the cloth trade took them out of the house on a regular basis to collect and to deliver spinning work. Usually clothiers' servants took wool to a village shop or alehouse to be collected by the women spinners, who spun it at home and handed it back as yarn when they obtained their next supply of wool. There are several references in the records to women delivering 'dutche worke' to clothiers' houses, as well as to shops and to inns some distance from their homes. One Saturday in 1600, for example, Rose Honeyball, wife of Daniel Honeyball, a carpenter of Stoke By Nayland, just over the county border in Suffolk, brought 'some spynninge work to Colchester to Erasmus Hedde's house', a distance of some ten miles. The same market day Bridget Barber, wife of John Barber, a husbandman of the neighbouring village of Nayland, 'brought her dutchworke to Colchester at a house'.[58] Whatever the distance or purpose of their journey, because roads were so dangerous in this period, whenever possible women rode or walked together in groups, and so routine journeys were transformed into companionable social occasions. So it was that in 1619 Jane Casse, wife of a husbandman of Stapleford Tawney, 'upon a markett daye rydinge from her owne house to London to sell herr commodities was overtaken by the way by Elizabeth Lake ... and this deponent glad of her companie rode together'.[59] What these examples also indicate are ways in which, because of the nature of their occupations, women were important links between villages and urban centres.

Although spinning was by far the most important female occupation for women in rural Essex, it was not the only one, and the many different activities that they performed impacted upon women's spatial experience in a variety of ways. Many households in this period were multi-occupational and yeoman farmers, as well as more modest husbandmen, carried on other businesses on the side. Depending on the time of year, the head of the household might set his hands to the enterprise. Very frequently, however, and especially when men were out at work in the fields, the wife managed the business. Many of these activities were home-based although they involved a good deal of contact with neighbours outside the household unit. The wife of William Barrett, a husbandman of Lowton, for example, ran a lodging house from home. Elizabeth Dyer, wife of a husbandman of Greenstead, was also a landlady.[60] Elizabeth Copsheafe, another small farmer's wife of Purleigh, was a brewer and victualler.[61]

[57] Rogers c. Lake (1619), LMA, DL/C/226, fo. 26v.
[58] ERO (Col.), D/B5 Sb2/6, fos 9v–10; ERO (Ch.), Q/SR 400/131.
[59] Luke c. Rogers (1619), LMA, DL/C/226, fo. 26v.
[60] ERO (Col.), D/B 5 Sb2/9, fo. 152v.
[61] ERO (Ch.), Q/SBa 2/28; Holinshed c. Yonge (1650), D/AXD 2, fo. 7v; Q/SBa 2/28; Frost c. Copsheafe (1610), LMA, DL/C/219, fos 170v–177.

Other female occupations took them out of the house on a regular basis. It was common practice, for example, for women to sell surplus produce from their gardens or their dairy to other women door-to-door.[62] Historians have also underestimated how much households relied on the exploitation of common rights in the past, and the extent to which women were responsible for this kind of work. There is abundant evidence in the records that labouring women and the wives of small farmers spent a significant proportion of their time outside, working in the fields, gathering food and fuel and caring for pigs, cattle and sheep that they kept on common land.[63] As a rule, wives of well-to-do yeomen probably left labour of this kind to their servants, possibly because this work was not regarded as fitting for women of their rank.[64] However scattered references in a variety of sources suggest that notions of respectability and status boundaries could be flexible and adaptable to economic circumstances. The wife of the vicar Ralph Josselin, for example, did not regard it as beneath her station to manage a flock of sheep.[65]

The spatial division of labour was nevertheless a dynamic process. Fieldwork was seasonal and this meant that degrees of cooperation and integration between spouses altered significantly with changes in the agricultural calendar. Most couples spent time together for a few weeks in the winter when farmers were at home, and husbands and wives were occupied with different tasks in the same place. In the spring women were employed in the fields planting and weeding, sometimes working alongside their husbands.[66] Most important, during haymaking in June, and when harvesting of corn began in July, whole households worked together out in the fields reaping, gathering and binding to bring the grain back into the barns. Incidental detail in the depositions and the many defamation cases that were staged out in the fields in summer demonstrate how harvest work drew husbands and wives, old and young, different social groups, indeed entire neighbourhoods together to work in the fields to help as best they could.[67]

Once harvest was over, a sexual and spatial division of labour came into operation in arable fields again, although for a few weeks arrangements were quite different from the male-oriented spatial patterns that characterised arable fields for the rest of the year. By tradition, when the grain had been

---

62 Marshall c. Waylett (1631), ERO (Ch.), D/AED 8, fos 49v–50.

63 Sharpe, *Adapting to capitalism*, 11–18, 71–94; Mendelson and Crawford, *Women in early modern England*, 256–75; Hufton, 'Women and the family economy' 1–22; J. Humphries, 'Enclosures, common rights and women; the proletarianisation of families in the late eighteenth and early nineteenth centuries', *Journal of Economic History* l (1990), 17–42. For examples of women and maidservants tending livestock in the fields see Goodwin c. Deane (1628), LMA DL/C/231, fo. 129v; ERO (Ch.), Q/SBa 2/17; Q/SBa 2/19; Q/SBa 2/31; Q/SBa 2/58; Q/SBb 100/19; ERO (Col.), D/B5 Sb2/9, fo. 33v.

64 STAC 8/259/28.

65 *Josselin diary*, 455, 577; Eyre, *Dyurnall*, 36, 58, 114.

66 Sharpe, *Adapting to capitalism*, 78–9.

67 STAC 8/152/4; ERO (Ch.), D/ABD4, fo. 61v; Q/SR 187/1; Brand c. Moule (1612), D/ACD 1, fo. 14v.

carted out of the field, men withdrew and women and children took over the fields to glean, clearing the ground of ears of corn left behind after the grain had been gathered in. There is abundant evidence in the records of groups of women gleaning a variety of crops – wheat, barley and oats – out in harvest fields in early autumn, collecting grain that would provide a vital contribution to the household budget, ensuring its survival through the winter.[68] Access to gleaning was not open to all women. Byelaws increasingly confined gleaning rights to women of the parish, and there is evidence that women themselves excluded 'strangers' who tried to glean, as well as those who gleaned prematurely.[69] But while there are references to young boys as well as young girls gleaning with their mothers, it is quite clear that gleaning fields were predominantly female spaces.[70]

Interesting changes can be glimpsed in gendered spatial patterning generated by the growing demands of a London population and specialised agricultural market. Poultry-rearing, fruit and vegetable growing and even the quintessentially female activity of dairying became attractive to men in Essex by the start of the seventeenth century.[71] In 1607 the contemporary commentator William Camden observed that in the marshland and dairying district of Canvey Island, famous for the production of butter and cheeses made from ewes' milk, 'we have seen youths, carrying out a womanly task, milk with small stools fastened to their buttocks, and make ewes' cheeses in cheese sheds which they call there "Witches"'. He also noted that in the Dengie hundred 'men take the women's office in hand and milk ewes, whence those huge thick cheeses are made that are vented and sold not merely into all parts of England but into foreign nations also, for the rustical people, labourers and handicrafts men to fill their bellies and feed upon'.[72] But for the most part gender divisions remained consistently traditional in the region, paradoxically creating complex, varied and dynamic patterns of integration and separation of the work lives of farmers and their wives according to the time of day and the seasons of the year.

The gendering of space for work in households headed by men whose primary source of income was 'manufacturing' was even more varied, depending on the type of trade, the size of the business and, to some extent, according to

---

[68] ERO (Col.), D/B5 Sb2, not foliated; ERO (Ch.), Q/SBa 2/31; Q/SBa 2/58; Q/SBa 2/25; Malt c. Reynolds (1637), D/ABD 8, fo. 2v; Munt c. Sutton (1625), D/ACD 3, fo. 29v; P. King, 'Customary rights and women's earnings: the importance of gleaning to the rural labouring poor', *EcHR* xliv (1991), 461–76; A. Wood, 'The place of custom in plebeian political culture: England, 1550–1800', *Social History* xxi (1997), 56.

[69] King, 'Customary rights', 461–76; Sharpe *Adapting to capitalism*, 80–5.

[70] For a 'boy' gleaning see ERO (Ch.), Q/SBa 2/1.

[71] On dairying see Valenze, 'The art of women'. For examples of women's work in dairying see ERO (Ch.), Q/SBa 2/1; Q/SBA 2/19; D/AEA 15, fo. 23v; Cooke c. Davis (1610/1), LMA, DL/C/219, fos 372v–373, 423r–424; Awsten c. Langley (1609), DL/C/219, fos 3r–4, 9v–10, 45v–46, 52r–53.

[72] Cited in Emmison, *Home, work and land*, 45, 46; ERO (Ch.), Q/SBa 2/25.

the season.[73] The clearest examples found in the records of divergent patterns of daily work, similar to those identified by Earle's study of artisan households in London, were in households involved in the building trade.[74] Bricklayers, thatchers and carpenters obviously worked away from home during daylight hours.[75] The occupations of their wives tended to be more home-based, presumably because they were more compatible with the responsibilities associated with rearing a family.[76] Separate work lives were also common where the business was too small to support the involvement of the wife, although a search for economic survival could have a very varied impact on the location of the work of husband and wife. Where poor journeymen wool-combers and weavers worked in workshops away from home, husbands and wives could be separate for much of the working day. Charles Miller, for example, was a journeyman weaver of Colchester who 'wrought with one Robert Partridge, wever'. Susan Miller, his wife, ran a small-scale pawnbroking business from home.[77] Sometimes both husband and wife could be out of the house during the day. John Gandy of Colchester was a journeyman joiner and his wife kept a stall selling linen. Susan Harrie, who was married to John Harrie, collyer of Halstead, was a 'dresser of hats'.[78] At other times the husband could be based at home while the wife went out to work. Catherine Duffin, for example, wife of Thomas Duffin, a tailor of Chigwell, was employed 'washing in the house of Sarah Henchman'.[79]

Separation in craft-based households could also vary according to the season, especially for precariously paid weavers and their wives, who formed the largest group of artisan households in the county. In summer male weavers left their looms to take advantage of high wages for harvest work to help build up some sort of surplus for the winter. Wives and children could be left to continue work at home.[80] At the end of harvest, spinners would leave the house to their husbands to go out into the fields to glean.[81]

There are some descriptions that imply the existence of single-sex work groups, similar to those described by Earle and Sharpe. Some workshops were probably all-male spaces. For example, a Colchester weaver told the bishop of London's consistory court in 1610 that only he and Edward Buxton were

---

[73] It has been estimated that more than 20% of the adult population of early modern Essex were craftsmen: N. Goose and J. Cooper, *Tudor and Stuart Colchester: an extract from The Victoria history of the county of Essex, IX: The borough of Colchester*, edited by Janet Cooper, Oxford 1994, repr. Chelmsford 1998, 76; Brown, *Poverty and prosperity*, 9–10.

[74] Earle, *City full of people*, 122.

[75] ERO (Ch.), Q/SBa 2/28.

[76] ERO (Col.), D/B5 Sb2/6, fo. 10; Office c. Brown (1704), LMA, DL/C/248, fo. 219v.

[77] ERO (Col.), D/B5 Sb2/8, fos 181v, 191v. Miller mentions returning home around '5 o'clocke'.

[78] ERO (Col.), D/B5 Sb2/7, fo. 306v; ERO (Ch.), Q/SBa 2/30.

[79] ERO (Ch.), D/AXD 2, fo.199v (1672), nuncupative will of Sarah Henchman; Grove c. Spencer and Spencer (1618), LMA, DL/C/225, fo. 176r.

[80] ERO (Col.), D/B 5 Sb2/9, fos 177v–178.

[81] Brown, *Poverty and prosperity*, 64.

in their master's workshop when, 'lookeinge out of the window', they saw Roda Grenerise and William Pinge hurling insults at one another out in the street.[82] We also find references to all-female groups working together in spinning work.[83] There is even some evidence to suggest the possibility that the textile trade may have allowed some unmarried and widowed women to support themselves in single-sex households, as Sharpe found with lace-making in Colyton. In the early eighteenth century Daniel Defoe famously publicised the position of 'poor maidservants who choose rather to spin, while they can gain 9s. per week by their labour than go to Service at 12d. a week to the Farmers Houses as before', a pattern of employment confirmed by poor relief records.[84] Wage rates did not reach such high levels in the seventeenth century, but two cases of embezzlement of yarn by women, brought before the quarter sessions in the 1590s, show that single and widowed women were able to make something of a living in spinning, and could add to their income in less than legal ways. In 1592 Mary Graunt of Earls Colne, single woman, was indicted for theft of 59lbs of wool, worth just over £63, supplied to her by three Dutch clothiers from Colchester. Instead of re-delivering the yarn to them she had sold the wool to three women of Earls Colne, 'converting the same to her own use'. 12lbs of wool was sold to Judith Paine at 5d. the lb. (8d. below the market rate), 30lbs to Cicily Sparrowe at 5d. and 6d. the lb. and 15lbs to Joan Turner at 6d. the lb.[85] In 1595 two widows and one married woman of Earls Colne were charged with a similar offence.[86] Later, in 1653, the constable of St Mary Magdelene parish in Colchester searched the shop of Robert Gooding, looking for 'journeymen and wenches working at their own hand'.[87]

Overall, however, the predominantly gender-specific working environment described by Earle and Sharpe has been difficult to trace from the depositions. There are numerous references in the records to craftsmen and women, married and unmarried, working together in and around the house. This disparity between Earle's evidence for London and Sharpe's for Colyton, may partly be explained by the predominance of poorer women in the sample of witness statements analysed by Earle and in Sharpe's study.[88] Poverty clearly promoted separation of husbands and wives during the working day. The depositions consulted for this study from a wider range of jurisdictions include a broader range of deponents in terms of wealth and social status and focus predominantly upon people of middling ranks.

The greater variety of gendered spatial patterns of work may also be

[82] Pinge c. Grenerise (1610), LMA, DL/C/219, fos 302v–303.
[83] Matthewes c. Benett (1627), ERO (Ch.), D/AED 8, fo. 23v.
[84] Cited in Sharpe, *Adapting to capitalism*, 31.
[85] ERO (Ch.), Q/SR 120/47; Q/SR 153/29, 30. Mary Graunt was prosecuted for bastardy and fornication in 1601.
[86] ERO (Ch.), Q/SR 130/42, 42a.
[87] ERO (Col.), D/B5 Sb2/7, fo. 111v.
[88] Earle, 'The female labour market', 332 n. 15; Sharpe, 'Literally spinsters', 54.

explained by the economic structure of the region. In Essex, unlike Colyton, the cloth industry was an important employer of men as well as women. A rigidly gendered division of labour within the trade was maintained at least in public. Most commonly, women (and children) were involved in the spinning, and some aspects of the finishing of wool. They were occasionally apprenticed to weaving and worked in the trade on an informal basis, when the husband was sick or at work in the fields, but in Essex their involvement in the trade was publicly discouraged, probably because of fears about male unemployment, and weaving remained a predominantly male occupation.[89] However, for most of the period, despite its commercial and capitalist organisation, the industry in Essex remained predominantly domestic. Weavers mostly worked at home and were assisted by their wives, children and servants. This meant that although men and women performed separate tasks they worked side by side. There are many references to weavers, their wives, journeymen and male and female apprentices working together in the house at the same time.[90] In 1725, for example, John Chalkley, weaver of Witham, was in one Hannah Lindsey's chamber with his wife, a journeyman and a boy, when they saw an altercation between Martha Plantin and Sarah Sayer across the street around 2 o'clock in the afternoon'.[91] Overlap of male and female workspace in a domestic context was not, however, confined to the textile industry. There are several references in the depositions to men and women working together in tailoring shops for example.[92] In other types of trade the work of a husband and wife could be different but complementary. John Johnson of Westham, for example, was a clock-maker and his wife 'spinneth threade and maketh lynes for his clocks'.[93]

There is also ample evidence of the importance of the work of married women and female servants in the retail side of the enterprise, which again fostered patterns of integration rather than separation of husbands and wives during the working day. Earle acknowledges that this sort of arrangement was probably common and under-recorded, but does not develop its significance for the gendering of space. Sarah Jordan worked with her husband Robert in his tallow chandler's shop. Margaret and Robert Williamson worked together in a similar sort of enterprise.[94] It is noteworthy that when Jonas Couch,

---

89 Brown, *Essex at work*, 136.
90 ERO (Ch.), Q/SBa 2/14; Fend c. Patient (1613), D/AED 5, fo. 217v; ERO (Col.), D/B5 Sb2/9, fo. 88v; D/B5 Sb2/9, fos 188v, 190v, 191v; Moore c. Clark (1631), LMA, DL/C/233, fo. 190v.
91 Plantin c. Sayer (1725), ERO (Ch.), D/AXD 2, fo. 83v; Moore c. Clarke (1631), LMA DL/C/233, fo. 191v.
92 Allen c. Denham (1615), LMA, DL/C/223, fo. 366v; Wallbanck c. Frewin (1624), DL/C/229, fo. 107v; Dod c. Mann (1627), ERO (Ch.), D/AED 8, fo. 20v; Glascock c. Sargeant (1603), D/AED 4, fo. 106v.
93 Perry c. Warren (1610/1), LMA, DL/C/219, fos 321v–322.
94 Cuff c. Williamson (1702), LMA, DL/C/248, fos 27v–28; ERO (Col.), D/B5 Sb2/ 7, fo. 126v; D/B5 Sb2/5, fo. 2v; Crowe c. Ffoster (1586), ERO (Ch.), D/AED 3, fo. 1v; Warwick c. Marshall (1728), D/AXD 2, fo. 135v.

shoemaker of Colchester, reported the theft of some goods from his house one Saturday in 1589, he told the borough court that he and his wife were in '*their* shop' together.[95]

Jennifer Melville has made the important point that it was also perfectly possible for the work lives and spaces of men and women to overlap even if they had different occupations. At Colchester Mary and Thomas Ansell, for example, worked at home. Thomas was a shoemaker, and Mary ran a lodging house.[96] Hester Stocke and her husband both worked in the house. He was a turner and she 'keepeth a school and teacheth younge children'.[97] It is a mistake to confuse separate tasks with separate spaces.

This point is further emphasised when consideration is given to the layout, structure and multi-functional character of early modern artisan dwellings. Workshops were frequently attached to the house during this period. Rooms were small and walls were thin. Women might be cooking, cleaning or caring for children in the house while men were working in the shop, but the boundaries between these spaces were very blurred. This meant that different household members often undertook different sorts of activities at the same time and in close proximity to one another. As such, they could see or hear exactly what was going on even if they were in a different room.[98] A good example is the defamation suit begun in 1586 when Margery Oliver took her family's laundry to Agnes Bolter's house in Romford, so they could talk while Margery dried and smoothed clothes. As the two women chatted outside in the yard, Elizabeth Stevens, Agnes's neighbour overheard them and thought they were discussing her. She began to shout slanderous comments through the wall at Margery, calling her a 'bridewell bird' and an 'errant whore'. Thomas Bolter, Agnes's tailor husband, who was working in the house, also heard these insults.[99] Such examples show the interesting ways in which the different responsibilities of men and women meant that rooms could have different gendered meanings at set times of the day. However this difference in experience, related to separation of tasks, was not the same as separation of space.

In conclusion we see that historians have perhaps been too eager to dismiss Alice Clark's ideas about close working relations between husband and wife. Some couples worked at different tasks in separate places, but others worked side by side. In practice we see a great diversity in the locations of male and female work and degrees of integration or separation of husbands and wives during the working day. A significant proportion of men were engaged in

95 ERO (Col.), D/B5 Sb2/4, fo. 7 (my emphasis).
96 ERO (Col.), D/B5 Sb2/9, fo. 53v.
97 Cowell c. Day. (1613), LMA, DL/C/221, fo. 1230v; ERO (Ch.), Q/SBa 2/19; ERO (Col.), D/B5 Sb2/9, fo. 200v.
98 Bevis c. Tringe (1607), ERO (Ch.), D/AED 5, fos 120r, 122v; Paris c. Grigson (1737), D/AXD 2, fo. 167r–v.
99 Oliver c. Stephens (1586), ERO (Ch.), D/AED 3, fos 3v–4.

occupations based at home, while women's occupations frequently took them outside it. The spatial division of labour was a highly dynamic process and working arrangements could not be, and were not, organised in a single, predictable pattern. These findings provide further support for the challenge made by scholars to a historiography of gender relations built around bold theories about continuities or changes in spatial and gender relations determined by structural socio-economic transformations. A deeper understanding demands more research into the local contexts in which the gendered division and meaning of work was negotiated. Evidence adds considerable weight to the idea that husbands and wives formed economic partnerships, but it also shows that mutual dependence did not determine the degree to which the workspaces of men and women were separate or the same. Patterns of spousal independence and coexistence were enormously varied, and a number of factors – time, place, occupation and status determined them. It is also clear that the gendered division of labour, whether it emphasised separate or cooperative tasks, was organised, overtly at least, more on flexible and practical than on hierarchical terms. As a consequence, the social effects of the spatial organisation of work were highly dynamic and were the basis for gender relations that were variable, changing and continually negotiated and reconstructed.

Work was very important for women and men, for social contact. Many tasks allowed time for a chat with neighbours in the street, in the house, in the workshop or out in the fields. In early modern England it is very difficult to separate sociability from other day-to-day activities. None the less, recreation was not confined solely to the elite in this period: the next chapter will look at the influence of gender on the use of space for forms of sociability that were sometimes, but not always, determined by tasks that men and women were required to do day-to-day.

4

Social Space

'Here cometh to bee condemned the practice of such wives as are gadders abroad; least acquainted with, or delighting in ought at their owne home … the wise man maketh such gadding abroad the note of a light and lewd housewife or such as though they keepe within, yet sit idle at home: must have their gossips come and sit with them to tell tales and newes, that they may not be idle without company.'[1]

The control of female social space was a central tenet of rhetorical constructions of patriarchal order in early modern England. Male moralists repeatedly recommended that solitude and confinement within the home was a necessary protection for women against temptations to their chastity that they might be unable to resist. Historiographical interest in the evolution of the significance of these classical precepts for the practical social organisation of relations between the sexes, in different times and places, has meant that the gendered organisation of social space has also become a central focus of contemporary research. Work has focused predominantly upon elite patterns of sociability in the eighteenth century. A powerful critique of the public/private divide has recovered the extent of female access to the many new social spaces that emerged in towns and cities at that time, together with the 'public' importance of home-based hospitality and the role of the female host in an age in which politics was dominated by family and faction.[2] With the exception of Bernard Capp's fine study of the significance of female social networks for the negotiation of patriarchy, most studies of sociability in the earlier period have focused upon the importance of hospitality for the maintenance of the honour and political power of male elites and less attention has been given to ordinary people and to gender.[3] There is a tendency in the

[1] Gataker, Marriage duties, 20.
[2] Vickery, The gentleman's daughter; B. Cowan, 'What was masculine about the public sphere? Gender and the coffeehouse milieu in post-Restoration England', HWJ li (2001), 127–57; L. Klein, 'Gender and the public/private distinction in the eighteenth century: some questions about evidence and analytic procedure', Eighteenth Century Studies xxix (1995), 92–109, and 'Gender, conversation and the public sphere in early eighteenth-century England', in J. Still and M. Worton, (eds), Textuality and sexuality: reading theories and practices, Manchester 1993, 100–15; E. Chalus, '"That epidemical madness": women and electoral politics in the late eighteenth century', in H. Barker and E. Chalus (eds), Gender in eighteenth-century England: roles, representations and responsibilities, Harlow 1997, 151–78; A. Foreman, Georgiana, duchess of Devonshire, London 2001.
[3] Capp, 'When gossips meet'. For pioneering studies of sociability amongst the middling sort in early modern Paris, Restoration London and early modern Essex and Cheshire see

literature to dismiss the relevance and importance of the 'separate spheres' model for the organisation of social space in Tudor and Stuart England as inconsistent rhetoric that was separate from the practical reality of a culture organised towards a social mixing of the sexes. This chapter suggests that this is too simple and positive a picture. It proposes that a more fruitful approach that deepens and complicates our understanding of how gender shaped and was shaped by the spatial organisation of sociability in early modern local society moves the focus away from the relevance or lack of it of 'separate spheres' to look at how normative notions of female spatial propriety influenced gendered experience of social *spaces*. The analysis aims to show that while space was not organised towards rigid and static systems of segregation, prescriptive ideas interacted with practice in complex ways to shape practical experience. Inconsistencies within patriarchal rhetoric that admonished women to be 'neighbourly', together with the intricate and sometimes contradictory ways in which gender intersected with other social factors such as age, social and marital status, created social maps that were fluid, flexible and contextually determined. This chapter looks first at use of domestic space for sociability and then at the more 'public' spaces of recreation: drinking houses and open spaces, including the street and the green.

The depositions provide evidence about spatial patterns of sociability of two main sorts. First, comments about individual behaviour, both critical and incidental, offer insights into the underlying attitudes of men and women. Second, it is possible to count examples of social encounters and to identify which type of people were involved in them. There are obvious limitations to the use of this evidence. The figures, taken from three different jurisdictions, dealing with a wide variety of business brought to court by a reasonably broad social range of litigants, provide a relatively representative sample, but cannot be considered to be a precise quantification of different types of social interactions, or the total number of men and women involved. Court narratives were not designed to provide an absolutely exact record of what happened at each encounter and who was there; their purpose was to present events in a way that was thought to be most advantageous to the litigants. Statements varied in accuracy according to jurisdiction and to the type of case. In general, depositions given to the ecclesiastical courts were more detailed than the witness statements recorded by the officials of the secular courts. But even then accounts were often incomplete. Deponents focused primarily on the litigants and frequently gave only vague details of other individuals present, but not directly involved, in the incident described. Thus when Giles Lisrupp gave an account of a heated discussion he had heard in an alehouse in Little Ilford in 1714, he told the court that Joseph Cage called Anne Eve a whore

---

J. Hardwick, *The practice of patriarchy: gender and the politics of household authority in early modern France*, University Park, PA 1998; Melville, 'The use and organisation of domestic space', 231–9; and P. L. Carney, 'Social interactions in early modern England: Cheshire and Essex, 1560–1640', unpubl. PhD diss. Boulder 2002.

'in the presence of this deponent and his fellow witness Henry Reynolds who was sitting with this dep[onen]t] by the fyreside & of *severall others* in & about the kitchen whose names he doth not now remember'.[4] The information is therefore probably a significant underestimate of the numerical presence of both men and women in different social spaces throughout the period, even though it is a reasonably good sample. The second problem, related to the distortions generated by the judicial context, is that the people who appear in certain spaces in the court records are frequently individuals who are coming under official scrutiny as offenders. This of course raises the issue of how far their testimony was shaped by the need to impress the judges. It also requires us to consider how representative these documents actually are, given that several concern themselves with criminal individuals. In fact the variety of this evidence in terms of purpose and type of case, together with the fact that many documents introduce us to litigants and witnesses from a wide social range, means that the degree of distortion varies considerably according to the content of the litigation. In addition, much of the following discussion is based upon evidence of individuals who are mentioned incidentally and upon details included by witnesses more to set the scene than with the intention of influencing authorities in their favour. It should also be remembered that the patterns of behaviour and attitudes described by litigants had to be probable and credible, and so still provide valuable insights into the social experience of people at middling social levels, about which we have very little direct evidence.

Home-based sociability

To begin with home-based sociability, it is quite clear from the records that entertaining at home played an important part in the lives of middling men and women. Despite the admonitions of moralists to women to avoid all but essential social contact at home, the depositions provide evidence of the importance, variety and frequency of female social interaction with outsiders within their domestic spaces. Altogether the gender and marital status of the hosts of 330 voluntary forms of informal home-based sociability amongst members of the middling sort could be identified. Convenient and detailed guest lists for each social encounter do not survive but aspects of the social identity of a total of 806 guests could be traced from the depositions. This information is summarised in table 1.

Two interesting observations can be made from this evidence. First of all it is clear that use of domestic space was closely related to age and marital status. Married men and women were much more likely than single people of either sex to entertain guests in their houses. Out of a total of 806 guests entertained, 351 were received by married women (43.5 per cent), 95 by

4 Eve c. Cage (1714), LMA, DL/C/254, fo. 352v (my italics).

96

Table 1
Gender and marital status of participants in social interactions at home,
c. 1580–1720

Hosts	Guests							
	women (m)	women (um)	women (ums)	widows	men (m)	men (um)	men (ums)	married couples
women (m)	178	23	19	3	32	12	50	17
women (um)	2	2	1	0	3	4	10	1
women (ums)	0	0	0	0	0	0	0	0
widows	66	9	9	1	25	5	8	6
men (m)	18	2	4	2	15	15	31	4
men (um)	0	0	0	0	0	0	0	0
men (ums)	12	4	3	0	3	0	17	0
married couples	12	11	19	4	10	7	25	37

m = married
um = unmarried
ums = unknown marital status

Sources: ERO (Ch.), D/AED 1–8; D/ABD 1–8; D/ACD 1–7; D/AXD 1–3; Q/SBa2; ERO (Col.), D/B5 Sb2/2–9; LMA, DL/C/211–258; GL MS 9189/1–2.

married men (11.7 per cent), 162 by married couples (20 per cent) and 135 by widows (16.7 per cent), but only 24 (2.9 per cent) were received by unmarried women and none at all by unmarried men. 743 (92.1 per cent) of guests were therefore entertained by established householders.

Secondly, evidence demonstrates that home-based hospitality was gendered. We can see from table 1 that married women hosted the majority of interactions either independently or jointly with their husbands. There is also a clear pattern of female predominance in the guests who were entertained. 288 guests were married women (35.7 per cent), 51 were unmarried women (6.3 per cent), 55 were women of unknown marital status (6.8 per cent) and 9 were widows (1.1 per cent). When married couples are taken into account the total number of female guests was 469 whereas the total number of male guests was only 294. This means that in terms of numerical presence in the depositions, women comprised 58.1 per cent of the guests received at home. Home-based hospitality it seems was a female-dominated social space.

It should not be assumed however that female ascendancy within home-based sociability simply reflected and reinforced their subordinate, 'private' and domestic social role. It is clear from the evidence that the early modern middling-sort house was a vitally important stage upon which individuals and households performed acts of hospitality that demonstrated and reinforced their 'public' status and self-worth. Women, as joint domestic governors and autonomous household managers, had an important role in the implementation of this kind of commensality within their own homes. Felicity Heal has shown that for ordinary people as well as elites in this period, generosity or 'good neighbourhood' was a vitally important standard by which both men and women were judged. To be seen to be 'neighbourly' was not only a Christian duty. Performance of hospitality was essential for the maintenance of status, necessary for survival in a society in which a generous and trustworthy reputation was vital for access to the credit networks on which individuals and households depended for economic success.[5] A 'cultural imperative' of reciprocity was built into the conduct of local social relations. Interactions were not merely 'private' expressions of amity; each one had a transactional quality that involved some kind of exchange whether of goods or services, borrowing or lending or, more subtly, the recognition and reception of respect and esteem. Married women were prominent recipients of, as well as participants in, this process of exchange.

Their role is perhaps most apparent in the custom of joint hosting by husbands and wives of lavish dinners to commemorate important family events. Weddings, christenings, churchings and funerals were all marked by celebratory meals at which householders asserted their status as well as entertained their guests. These occasions could therefore be elaborate and expensive.[6] For example, Ralph Josselin spent £6 13s. 4d. 'at least' to celebrate the baptism of his first child in 1642.[7] Among humbler people it appears that it was accepted that guests might share in the cost. As Felicity Heal has commented, it seems that it was the arrangement of the setting, rather than the provision of the food, that was important for preservation of status.[8] A remark included in Thomas Skingley's deposition to the court of the archdeaconry of Essex regarding Anne Bailey's failure to complete a marriage contract is of interest in this regard. His neighbour Richard Harrison told Skingley he wanted to dine at the alehouse but Skingley replied that 'if he soe thought good he sho[u]lde dine with him at one Rameson's howse whose wife was churched that daye'. Skingley added 'yow had as good spend yo[u]r mon[e]y thear as at the alehowse'. Then Harrison and George Newbolt, another acquaintance to Skingley, went with him and his wife to dinner at the Ramesons' house.[9]

Whatever the exact arrangements for this kind of event, it is important to remember that the responsibility for planning it and, where necessary, making the food, fell upon the shoulders of the wife, emphasising her important but distinctive role in making the occasion a success. An interesting vignette included in the diary of the nonconformist minister Oliver Heywood vividly

---

[5] Heal, Hospitality, 388; C. Muldrew, The economy of obligation: the culture of credit and social relations in early modern England, Basingstoke 1998.

[6] Heal, Hospitality, 352–88; D. Cressy, Birth, marriage and death: ritual, religion, and the lifecycle in Tudor and Stuart England, Oxford 1997, 164–88, 201–3, 350–74, 443–9.

[7] Josselin diary, 89.

[8] Heal, Hospitality, 353.

[9] Harrison c. Bayley (1607), ERO (Ch.), D/AED 5, fo. 115v. On the social significance of the churching ceremony to women see Cressy, Birth, marriage and death, 201–3. On self-financing of celebrations see Heal, Hospitality, 366.

highlights these divisions in gendered patterns of responsibility, experience and levels of work. The minister recorded ruefully that on the day after the wedding of his neighbour James Hobsteds in February 1678, he kept a day of prayer at the Hobsteds' house, but once on his knees was 'much distracted and much troubled', by his neighbour's wife and maids 'who passed through the room where we were in the buttery, preparing meat' for the wedding feast.[10]

Interesting gendered spatial distinctions also arose at christening parties. It seems that, if space permitted, the sexes celebrated separately for some of the time. Samuel Pepys recalls that when he and his wife were invited to the baptism of their cousin Benjamin Scott's new son:

> there was a company of pretty women there in the chamber; but we stayed not, but went with the minister into another room and eat and drank. And at last, when most of the women were gone, Sam and I went into my cousin Judith Scott, who was gott off her bed; and so we stayed and talked and were very merry, my she-cousin Stradwick being god-mother; and then I left my wife to go home by coach.[11]

More often the spatial arrangements of celebratory dinners focused around a mixed gathering of spouses. They were an important forum in which to artic- ulate the reputation of the household and demanded the active and collec- tive role of husband and wife as hosts. The regularity with which these events were used as settings to draw communal attention to personal or political grievances suggests their 'public' significance, presumably because individuals were assured a large and listening local audience. It was at a dinner for tenants hosted by Mr Barnard Hyde and his wife of Little Ilford, for example, that Elizabeth Harsnett and her husband heard their minister Mr Rooke defame his hostess Mrs Hyde.[12] Another case records that at a dinner on Christmas Day in 1626, Ann, wife of Thomas Webb of Church End, told a company of neighbours that their Minister Mr Gough, 'could not tell what things not to be spoken of in a pulpit so much so that the master and mistress of the house reprehended her and bade her forbear meddling in church matters'.[13] For middling-sort women as well as men therefore, far from insulating them from the neighbourhood and its affairs, home-based hospitality integrated them into neighbourhood concerns and reinforced local social ties.

The social composition of these occasions reflected their 'public' social character. There were no clear examples in the records of the private chris- tening and churching parties that were apparently becoming popular amongst the propertied classes by the middle of the seventeenth century.[14] It appears

10 *Heywood diary*, 342.
11 *Pepys diary* 11, 216.
12 Hyde c. Rooke (1630), LMA, DL/C/232, fo. 88v.
13 ERO (Ch.), D/AEA 36, fo. 103v.
14 Cressy, *Birth, marriage and death*, 188–94.

from the evidence that these celebratory dinners, together with those that marked feast days and festivals, remained the most socially inclusive forms of hospitality that were staged in early modern middling-sort domestic spaces throughout the period.[15] Individuals of different age, status and gender were included in the celebrations. For example, William Shave and his wife entertained neighbours to a wedding dinner at home in West Ham in 1576 to celebrate the marriage of their servants Edmund and Joan Austen.[16] The Josselins also regularly put on dinners for their 'poore tenants', 'harvest men' and 'some freinds' at Christmas and at harvest time.[17]

There are indications that such open-handed hospitality was under some strain. Accusations of theft made by reasonably well-off householders against humbler guests reflected perhaps a growing mistrust of poorer neighbours.[18] For example, Susan Climster, the wife of a labourer of Waltham Abbey, was accused of stealing a wooden candlestick from her yeoman neighbour, James Bennett, after she had attended his child's christening party in 1636.[19] None the less the wider significance of these occasions for the maintenance of the local social reputation of women and men is indicated by the bitter resentment that was generated by exclusion from the celebrations. Felicity Heal has pointed out that, particularly for women, being left out could cause severe emotional disturbance or even be the occasion for an accusation of witchcraft. When the wife of one Malter was not invited to her neighbour's sheep-shearing dinner in 1570 she allegedly 'bewitched tow of his sheep; for immediately after they were taken with sickness'. Anne Kerke of Broken Wharf, London, was charged with tormenting a child because she was not invited to its christening by a hostile neighbour and when Jane Milburne did not ask Dorothy Strangers to her wedding supper in Newcastle in 1663, she believed that she was afterwards tormented by *maleficium*, inflicted upon her by Dorothy who had disguised herself as a cat.[20] Inclusion or exclusion from family celebration was a vitally important 'public' marker for women and for men of the boundaries of belonging to local communal life.

More intimate forms of hospitality provided for family or neighbours generally had transactional, as well as personal components and women were active participants in these occasions both as hosts and guests. Drinking at home was an important aspect of home-based sociability that was used by both sexes in largely comparable and multi-layered ways.[21] It was sometimes simply part of common hospitality as when two female acquaintances travelled from Dedham to visit the wife of Joseph Tybold, husbandman of Colchester, and

15 Heal, Hospitality, 352–65.
16 ERO (Ch.), D/AED 1, fo. 8v.
17 Josselin diary, 62, 592, 597.
18 Wrightson, English society, 183–221.
19 ERO (Ch.), Q/SBa 2/26.
20 Cited in Heal, Hospitality, 358, 364, 367, 369. See also K. Thomas, Religion and the decline of magic, London 1973, 664.
21 On the social significance of drinking see Weatherill, Consumer behaviour, 157–9.

she offered them some of her 'smale beere', or when the rector of Kelvedon Hatch, Mr Westwood, returned home late one evening from the market and invited his companion, a local blacksmith, into his house to drink.[22] At other times drinking together might be a ritual that signified the sealing of a business deal. Thus Robert Jordan, a tallow chandler, invited his neighbour Anthony Butt 'to drink a pint of wine' once they had completed a business transaction. On several occasions drinking together could symbolise resolution of a conflict. In 1627 Edward Miller and his brother William supped and lodged at Richard Doe's house in Gosfield, at the invitation of his wife Ann. That evening the two men heard a gentleman accuse their hostess of keeping a 'cheating house'. Ann Doe and her guest were apparently reconciled the next day and drank a 'cupp of sacke' together.[23] In similar vein, when Brigit Williams and Hanna Williams of Brentwood fell out over the taking away of a servant, neighbours heard that 'since that falling out they were reconciled and made freindes and have drunke togither friendly'.[24]

Informal meals were also often put on by women and men to discuss business, as when Robert Wright and his wife Helen of Rawreth were invited to dine with Robert Straight and his family to discuss money Straight owed them for beer and which he owed Helen as a bequest from her late husband's father, John Straight.[25] Another good example occurred in January 1573, when Robert Fleate, a glover of Colchester, and his wife Alice entertained his brother-in-law Benjamin Thorpe and his wife Mary to 'supp'. The Thorpes arrived unexpectedly to discuss the renting of some land, and brought with them a 'penny loaf of white bread'.[26] Married women played an active role in the organisation of occasions of this kind, and despite admonitions by moralists to the contrary, appeared to feel free to issue independent invitations to mixed companies of family, friends and neighbours to meals at their houses in a variety of circumstances. In 1707, for example, Elizabeth Miller, a married woman of Barking, met a kinswoman and her reputed husband, John Brown, at the tavern, and 'the next day being Sunday', invited them to dinner.[27]

Clergymen were regular recipients of female commensality. Ralph Josselin was heavily dependent upon the generosity of Lady Honywood, Mrs Harlackendon and Mrs Church for social and spiritual succour and often attended all-female spiritual meetings organised by women in their homes.[28] Nonconformist ministers also looked to married women for support. The boundaries between 'public' and 'private' could become even more blurred in these

---

[22] ERO (Col.), D/B5 Sb2/7, fo. 36v; Jordan c. Jordan (1701), LMA, DL/C/254, fo. 186v; Staines c. Westwood (1684), DL/C/241, fo. 95v.
[23] ERO (Ch.), Q/SBa 2/9.
[24] Redriffe c. Newton (1610), LMA, DL/C/219, fos 273r–274.
[25] ERO (Ch.), D/AED 2, fos 10r–13.
[26] ERO (Col.), D/B5 Sb2/2, not foliated.
[27] Mayle c. Mayle (1707), LMA, DL/C/249, fo. 321v.
[28] Josselin diary, 157, 250, 281, 377, 566.

contexts.[29] Married women motivated and facilitated clandestine worship under cover of hospitality in these households, as was probably the case in January 1631, when the separatist, Mary Purcas, wife of Abraham Purcas of Great Burstead, 'in her husband's absence' entertained 'a strange minister' together with her daughter and son-in-law, to supper and to dinner the next day.[30]

Home-based hospitality of this sort probably held an especially important place in the lives of more wealthy widows. Since, as we will see in the next section, women were more restricted than men from access to drinking houses where men spent a significant proportion of their leisure time, socialising at home must have been very important for strengthening social ties with male neighbours and business contacts. According to witnesses, for example, Mistress Staines, a wealthy widow of Kelvedon Hatch, regularly entertained mixed companies of neighbours to supper at her house to discuss a variety of topics ranging from business to local parish affairs. Even on these relatively intimate occasions, however, women were subject to spatial constraints. It seems that in genteel circles, where more space was available, women withdrew to another room after the meal. When called to court to defend the reputation of Mistress Staines against the insulting accusations of their minister, Mr Henry Glascock and Mr Phillip Wright took care to emphasise that when their widowed neighbour had entertained them to supper one evening in 1683, she was not 'much in their company but spoke to this Respondent to make them welcome and kept company with some Gentlewomen that were in another roome her self'.[31]

Spatial divisions of this sort are naturally not observable amongst humbler folk; lack of room and resources restricted such refinements. But widows amongst a range of social groups used home-based hospitality in similar ways, entertaining mixed companies to dinner and to supper, both on special occasions and less formal ones, for a variety of reasons. A little before Easter in 1584, Margaret Boulton, a widow of West Ham, invited John Ward, husbandman of West Ham, and Agnes his wife, together with Nicholas Boswell and his wife and a bailiff of Ware, to dinner to celebrate a marriage proposal made to her by John Eaton.[32] At Little Laver in 1575 Helen Homeston alias Somner hosted a funeral dinner on the burial day of her husband Reginald, where she showed relatives and neighbours her husband's will.[33]

[29] J. Eales, 'Samuel Clarke and the "lives" of godly women in seventeenth-century England', in W. Sheils and D. Wood (eds), *Women in the Church* (Studies in Church History xxvii, 1990), 365–75. For an excellent case study of the hospitality and patronage proffered to godly preachers in Essex by Lady Katherine Barnardiston of Witham Place see J. Guyford, *Public spirit: dissent in Witham and Essex, 1500–1700*, Witham 1999, 98–103.
[30] ERO (Ch.), D/ABD 6, fo. 207v. A conventicle was held at home in July 1640 by the Colchester Furly family, future Quakers: ERO (Col.), D/B5 Sb2/7, fo. 127v.
[31] Staines c. Westwood (1684), LMA, DL/C/241, fo. 99v.
[32] Boulton c. Eaton (1584), ERO (Ch.), D/AED 2, fo. 107v.
[33] ERO (Ch.), D/AED 1, fo. 165v.

Hospitality to elderly widows also seems to have been important. Widow Wylett of Barking was invited to dinner on a regular basis with Matthew Pearson and his wife, together with married neighbours.[34] When William Brown, also of Barking, was called to court to explain his relationship with his neighbour widow Agnes Franck, he claimed that she had often 'in the waye of honestye and neighbourhoode' visited his house to eat meals with him and his wife.[35] An inheritance dispute records that in 1606 Juliana Thornton, widow of Writtle, went from her house to 'make merrye' with Thomas Parnell in Snoreham, 'as she had done oftentimes before'.[36] Ralph Josselin noted in his diary that in late December 1676 he 'invited a poore widow to dine with mee'.[37] Witnesses and litigants place great emphasis upon ties of friendship in their statements, emphasising that male as well as female neighbours had been 'a good friend' to their widowed neighbour, suggesting perhaps that widows were very helpful in building a reputation for trustworthiness and generosity, important for the accumulation of social capital.[38]

Interesting gendered patterns that can be observed in informal sociability of this kind suggest that the house tended to be more important as a social setting for the nurturing of neighbourly ties for women more generally. Meals, especially spontaneous suppers, could sometimes be single-sex affairs amongst women, but there were no examples of married men independently hosting supper parties for their male 'friends' at home. This may of course merely reflect the limitations of the sources, but it might also be linked to the fact that men spent more of their evening leisure time out of the house at various kinds of drinking establishments. It is worth noting, for example, that after an impromptu supper hosted by Katherine King and her husband, the men departed for the alehouse, while she stayed at home chatting with a female neighbour in the yard until around 11 o'clock when her husband returned to the house.[39] A similar pattern of separate socialising is suggested by statements made to the magistrate in connection with a case of theft. In Billericay in 1623 Anne Fford and Sara Griffin were presented to the court of quarter sessions for stealing a ' brest of pork' from William Spencer, a butcher of the same town. The women alleged that Anne Fford had gone to the Spencers' house to collect some money owed to her by Spencer's wife for a hat she had sold her. When Spencer's wife had paid for the hat she 'sent for a pott of beere and a pennie loaf and while her was fetching the same the said Anne Fford goeth for the said Sara Griffin dwelling both in the same howse to come and drink with her which she did'. While they were supping together, Spencer's

---

34 Pearson c. White (1590), LMA, DL/C/213, fos 611v–615.
35 ERO (Ch.), D/AED 1, fos 25r–26, 34r–v.
36 ERO (Ch.), D/AED 5, fos 76r–78.
37 Josselin diary, 590.
38 Carey, 'Social interactions', 211.
39 ERO (Col.), D/B5 Sb2/7, fo. 119v.

husband returned from the alehouse and fell asleep by the fire, 'being as they saw in drinke'.[40]

Vignettes like these suggest that women used the house not only for the performance of social interactions that maintained and advanced the standing of the household. The home was also the most common location for meetings with female neighbours that created and maintained a separate network, equally vital for social and material survival, which had rules and concerns of its own. The prevalence of female visiting, much maligned by male moralists, is very apparent in the sources. There are no clear examples in the records of straightforwardly social visits that were becoming popular in more affluent circles by the late seventeenth century.[41] Interactions appear to have been organised according to norms of neighbourly reciprocity. Most visits, ostensibly at least, had some purpose, whether it was to borrow or to lend or to offer some kind of practical help. Charitable visiting played a very prominent role in the lives of married and widowed women of varying social standing. It is very clear from the way that they spoke about it, and the way they acted, that the performance of kindness was a very important means by which women measured and were measured by the local society of which they were a part. For example, Margaret Stokes of Fyfield cared for widow Joan Nichols 'in hir sicknes[s] and tending upon hir even until her death' in July 1584.[42] Alice Pollard made regular visits to Elizabeth Elsinger of Toppesfield when she was feeling unwell in October 1621.[43] Anna Pulley, a rector's widow of Kelvedon, told the bishop of London's consistory court that she met her neighbour, Mistress Staines, almost 'daily' while they visited their sick neighbours.[44] A statement made by a female witness in an inheritance dispute from outside the county conveys her powerful sense of obligation to nurse neighbours in need. Agnes, wife of William Mills, continued to visit her neighbour Richard Hedworth for more than ten days before his death, despite commitments to her own family and work:

> that upon the said Friday at night around six or seven of the clock when this exa[minan]t came from shearing she went to visit Richard Hedworth. [Later that night] she came again to him and sat with him for the space of two hours after which time ... being weary with working all day went to her rest that night and rose the morning after and went to him again and did for him and afterwards went to her business.[45]

---

40 ERO (Ch.), Q/SBa 2/7.
41 Capp, 'When gossips meet', 328–9.
42 ERO (Ch.), D/AED 2, fos 114v–115.
43 ERO (Ch.), Q/SBa 2/2.
44 Staines c. Westwood (1683), LMA, DL/C/240, fo. 332v; ERO (Ch.), D/ACD 1, fos 9v–10; D/ACD 1, fo. 92r.
45 C. Issa, 'Obligation and choice: aspects of family and kinship in seventeenth-century county Durham', unpubl. PhD diss. St Andrews 1986, 191 n. 14.

The virtuous woman was not always and simply defined passively, therefore, according to patriarchal values of 'privacy' and chastity. Paradoxically, the obligation to be neighbourly offered a woman the opportunity to be honoured for her 'public' and active role as dispenser of aid within the wider community. Charitable visiting was inextricably bound up with female social status and self-worth.[46]

It has long been established that this service to the sick linked women across the social divide and gave higher-status women a degree of access to the domestic spaces of their poorer neighbours that would have been exceptional for their husbands.[47] Connections between classes were also created by the predominantly but not exclusively female sociability associated with childbirth.[48] Included amongst the guests in attendance at the 'bed feast' held by the wife of John Brown, miller and constable of Kelvedon in 1684, for example, was the wife of a gentleman, a wealthy widow and the wife of the local minister.[49] During the lying-in of Sarah, wife of Robert Jordan, a tallow chandler, she was visited on a regular basis by wives of local tradesmen, an ex-servant and tenant of her parents, as well as her aunt, Phillipa Pigeon, the wife of Daniel Pigeon, gentleman.[50] Neighbourly familiarity of this kind may help explain why elite women often tried to settle disputes that erupted between the wives of their husband's tenants.[51]

Home-based female sociability was characterised by a relative openness, encouraged to an extent by the close physical proximity of neighbours. Contact was frequent and assistance important, not only for help in sickness or old age but also in the more banal borrowing of household items such as dishes and pots. More common still was getting 'fyer' from a neighbour, to light a candle sometimes quite late after dark. The social, as well as practical importance to women of conformity to rules of neighbourly reciprocity is indicated by the fierce exchanges that could follow if assistance was denied or offers of help were refused. In 1631 Joan Brown of Hornchurch needed support from her neighbours to care for her child while she lay sick and so her nurse called at Mary Collins's house to ask for her help but found that she was out. Mary Trewell who lived nearby then offered to feed Joan's child in her place. Goodwife Collins visited Joan the next day and, angry at her lost opportunity to display generosity, scoffed that Joan and Mary were a 'cupple

[46] Heal, Hospitality, 179.
[47] On charity and female identity see ibid. 178–83.
[48] On the socially inclusive character of female visiting during lying-in see Vickery, Gentleman's daughter, 203, and Heal, Hospitality, 81. There was no absolute ban on male access after the birth of the child, although visiting appears to have been restricted to the husband and to close male relatives: Office c. Brown (1704), LMA, DL/C/248, fo. 220v; Trewell c. Collins (1632), ERO (Ch.), D/AED 8, fo. 79v.
[49] Staines c. Westward (1684/5), LMA, DL/C/237, fo. 196v.
[50] Jordan c. Jordan (1701), LMA, DL/C/254, fos 128v, 133r, 134v, 139r, 143v. Sarah's father and a 'kinsman' and neighbour of her parents also visited her regularly.
[51] Brooke c. Turnedge (1605), ERO (Ch.), D/AED 5, fos 7r–10.

of good breasts indeed' and that Trewell had had a bastard by her own father before she was married.[52]

It would be wrong, however, to assume that physical proximity and a relatively open sociability meant that visiting was unrestricted. It is clear from the depositions that while the elaborate rules of time and space that evolved over the course of the seventeenth century for the regulation of visiting at elite social levels were not applied lower down the social scale, there was a language of hospitality that visitors were expected to adhere to, which ensured that the house was not open to all and sundry. While we have seen that a culture of relative openness was important, that the multi-functional character of the early modern house made borders and boundaries difficult to control and the distinction between public and private very hard to define, it is clear that thresholds were acknowledged as important markers of transition. The open, shut or locked door had particular legal and cultural significance in this respect. Strict parameters were placed upon the rights of public officers to 'breake open' a locked door and deponents and defendants specifically justified entry into a private house on the basis that the door was open.[53] If the door was shut it seems that visitors had to knock; they were not welcome simply to walk inside. Susan Glimster was rebuked for entering her neighbour's house 'without calling or knocking', and neighbours admonished Alice Battley for visiting her sick neighbour Elizabeth Elsinger without invitation, coming 'in of her selfe w[i]thout any bodye etelinge [sic] her'.[54] The symbolic significance of the open or shut door is demonstrated powerfully by a colourful case in Stisted. A woman snubbed her neighbour by 'shutting the doore against her' after accusing her of witchcraft in the heat of an angry exchange.[55] It is interesting in this regard that women within the neighbourhood who were perceived to be overly invasive, spatially and socially, were vulnerable to accusation of witchcraft.[56] The borders of houses were important points of negotiation in early modern local society and the routes across were complex.

It would also be a mistake to assume that visiting always fostered female association and shared identity. The spatial organisation of home-based sociability was complicated in several contexts by intricate interrelations of class, age and gender. The impression from the records is that the majority of impromptu visitors entertained by married women and widows were of the same or similar marital and social status as their hosts. Occasional comments made by deponents also map out a system of spatial and social separation that

---

[52] ERO (Ch.), D/AED 8, fos 79v-80.

[53] Coke, *An exact abridgement*, 221–3; ERO (Ch.), Q/SBa 2/22; Q/SBa 2/30; Rinward c. Constable (1633), D/AED 8, fo. 135r.

[54] ERO (Ch.), Q/SBa 2/26; Q/SBa 2/2.

[55] ERO (Ch.), Q/SBa 2/56.

[56] A. Macfarlane, *Witchcraft in Tudor and Stuart England: a regional and comparative study*, London 1970, 172; A. Rowlands, 'Witchcraft and old women in early modern Germany', *P&P* clxxiii (2001), 69.

was locally understood and accepted. Mary Bird, a labourer's wife of Danbury, called as a witness to defamatory words spoken by Elizabeth Cooke against Elizabeth Davies, the wife of a husbandman of the same parish, told the court that 'she never was in company with both the said parties together otherwise than in the church & such publique places'.[57] In another case Catherine Hodges, the wife of a tanner of East Horndon, explained that although her house was under a quarter of a mile away, she was 'never at ... [the wife of one Mr Reynolds] house till Sondaye night at which tyme she and her husband went thither' to discuss the proposed prosecution.[58] Elizabeth Williams, sometime servant to Mr and Mrs Westwood of Kelvedon, reported that she once went to Mistress Staines's house but 'cannot say she was in her company'.[59] Casual remarks made by witnesses suggest that in houses large enough for spaces to be specialised, different types of visitors had different degrees of access to different rooms. Working women, who called to sell produce, were welcomed into the kitchen; a special invitation was required to enter the parlour and the sleeping spaces of women were off limits to all but the most favoured of guests. The labourer's wife Susan Glimster was severely criticised by the wife of her yeoman neighbour for entering her house 'with pretence to light a candle but being once entered might go into all the rooms'.[60]

Further research is needed to tell us how the spatial organisation of settlements affected female social relations locally. It may be that aspects of the regional topography and economy gave rise to this tendency towards more separate social and spatial interaction. One of the typical features of several Essex parishes is a 'wood-pasture' type of settlement – scattered and sprawling and so physically divided. The pressures of a market economy, stimulated by proximity to London and the importance of the cloth industry, were also especially pronounced in Essex and may also have led to more distinct social and spatial division. In the clothing village of Earls Colne, for example, it seems that as early as the sixteenth century, middling and poorer inhabitants lived in separate streets.[61] In regions characterised by more nucleated settlements, less affected by economic change, where the houses of the gentry were built in a single street alongside the houses of craftsmen and cottages of the poor, geography and economy may have preserved a more homogeneous social whole. None the less, preliminary evidence from the depositions suggests that the underlying patterns found here were not limited to a single place.[62] From the latter half of the seventeenth century women were increasingly criticised

57 Davies c. Cooke (1610), LMA, DL/C/219, fos 423v–424.
58 Reynolds c. Tyler (1636), LMA, DL/C/234, fo. 174v.
59 Staines c. Westwood (1683), LMA, DL/C/240, fo. 337v.
60 ERO (Ch.), Q/SBa 2/26.
61 A. Macfarlane, 'Historical anthropology', Cambridge Anthropology iii (1977), 16.
62 For studies of female association that focus upon conflict and difference between women of different age and class see L. Gowing, 'Secret births and infanticide in seventeenth-century England', P&P clvi (1998), 87–116; 'Ordering the body: illegitimacy and female authority in seventeenth-century England', in Braddick and Walter, Negotiating power,

for their adherence to rules of visiting that reflected a growing concern to be seen as 'civilised' and set apart from the 'vulgar' and 'uncivilised' sorts. We will also see in the next chapter that middling women as well as men were acutely aware of fine social distinctions within their own hierarchy, their position among those around them and the respect they felt to be due. Early modern neighbourhood life was characterised by interdependence and middling-sort houses were by no means impermeable to interactions with lower-status neighbours Some forms of hospitality undoubtedly reinforced ties between many different categories of women as well as men and the regular contacts made across the social scale through work and neighbourly interaction were very important. But, as Keith Wrightson has argued, recognition of the exist-ence of a range of social interactions should not obscure the varying social meaning of each encounter.[63] Vertical transactions 'had a different set of meanings ... or a multiplicity of meanings'.[64] They were often much more about patronage than mutual association, especially for the individual in the subordinate position.[65] Voluntary visits to and from middling-sort married women (and men) were for the most part confined to a select circle of social equals.

Of course, social interactions at home were not an exclusively female activity. Married women regularly entertained impromptu male visitors to their houses, whether neighbours, traders or kin. Moralists admonished women that it was their duty to entertain their husband's friends and the casual manner in which many of these encounters are described in the records indicates their banality.[66] Yet there was an underlying anxiety about propriety that meant that in some contexts hospitality could be misinter-preted as immorality and so, for women in particular, home-based sociability of this sort carried certain risks. A case that perfectly expresses these tensions is the argument that erupted in the alehouse between Mr Westwood, minister of Kelvedon, and his neighbour Mr Glascock in 1684. Westwood remarked that he had called at Glascock's house the day before but 'found him out'. Glascock assured him that 'my wife would have made you very welcome', at which point the minister easily translated affability into availability and called Mrs Glascock 'whore'.[67]

43–62, and *Common bodies*; and L. Roper, *Oedipus and the devil: witchcraft, sexuality and religion in early modern Europe*, London 1994.
63 K. Wrightson, 'The politics of the parish in early modern England', in P. Griffiths, A. Fox and S. Hindle (eds), *The experience of authority in early modern England*, Cambridge 1996, 20.
64 Ibid.
65 Mendelson and Crawford, *Women in early modern England*, 237.
66 Gouge, *Domesticall duties*, 149.
67 Staines c. Westwood (1684), LMA, DL/C/241, fo. 100v. For illuminating discussions of the problems posed for married women by expectations that they should entertain their husband's friends and the jealousy and accusations of immorality that could ensue see Foyster, *Manhood in early modern England*, 128–9, and Gowing, *Domestic dangers*, 249–51.

It is clear that interactions between men and women at home had to be negotiated carefully to conform to socially accepted boundaries of time and space. Misgivings could be aroused if men and women met unusually often, if they met at unusual times, or more importantly if they met at night.[68] Shared meals taken with a man alone could easily be misinterpreted, and secrecy was deeply mistrusted.[69] Suspicions were especially provoked if doors were locked during the day against outsiders or if the parties behaved in especially secretive ways. According to Thomas Jarry, a carpenter of Chelmsford, his misgivings about the immoral behaviour of his married neighbour Sarah Bridge began when she 'shut of her doore up that this deponent was apprehensive by reason of her doore was so shutt upp yt John Hillier ... was to have gone in at the backdoore of her the s[ai]d Bridge's house'.[70] A remark made by Thomas Skingley emphasises the potential risks to reputation posed by 'private' hospitality. When he returned home from his neighbour's churching dinner, he found the two young men and a young woman he had allowed to meet there while he was away. He immediately admonished them, asserting that they should 'not shutt the streete dore least that his neighbours should take offence at it'.[71]

Of course we are seeing only the situations where immoral activities were suspected, as a result of the records consulted. Martin Ingram has concluded that G. R. Quaife exaggerates when he asserts that any sort of casual contact between men and women alone at home was invariably sufficient grounds for prosecution for immoral behaviour. It is important to remember that these accusations, based on weak circumstantial evidence centring on casual encounters at home, seldom interested the ecclesiastical authorities. As Ingram has demonstrated, prosecutions for immodesty on the part of married (and single) women were extremely rare.[72] In almost all the instances cited above parties were acquitted and the women's reputations successfully defended. None the less the benefit of this evidence is that it exposes some of the tensions surrounding gendered patterns of use of domestic space for sociability, tensions that are often overlooked and that derive from the ambiguity of boundaries between public and private that were not stable or fixed. Houses were not enclosed private havens but highly permeable social spaces

[68] ERO (Ch.), D/AED 1, fos 34v–35; D/AED 1, fos 74v–75; Macfarlane and others, 'Records of an English village', nos 702578, 702602, ERO (Ch.) D/ABD 2, not foliated, nos 700378, 700179, D/ABD 1, not foliated; Ingram, Church courts, sex and marriage, 242–5.

[69] For cases in which shared meals were used as circumstantial evidence of immorality see Poulter c. Valentine (1615), LMA, DL/C/223, fo. 214v; Office c. Cophead and Cophead (1628), DL/C/231, fo. 63v; and Macfarlane and others, 'Records of an English village', nos 702602, 700378, ERO (Ch.), D/ ABD 2, not foliated. See also Gowing, Domestic dangers, 71.

[70] Office c. Hillier and Bridge (1727), ERO (Ch.), D/AXD 2, fo. 95v.

[71] ERO (Ch.), D/AED 5, fos 115r–117.

[72] Ingram, Church courts, sex and marriage, 242–5; G. R. Quaife, Wanton wenches and wayward wives: peasants and illicit sex in seventeenth-century England, London 1979, 48–50.

that provided the setting for a range of encounters of varying content and meaning. Domestic social interactions had 'public' meanings for women as well as for men that sometimes coincided but occasionally conflicted with patriarchal spatial norms. To understand properly the gendered constitution of social space we need to pay close attention to this intricate and dynamic interplay between the public and the private within the early modern domestic world, as well as the rules governing gender relations within the larger 'public' spaces beyond the house.

Drinking houses

It is equally problematic to map gender on to conventional notions of public and private when we turn to look at the spatial organisation of drinking houses. Boundaries, when and where one space became another, were very fluid. Alehouses, taverns and inns were commercial social spaces, but they were run out of domestic spaces and proprietors routinely used parlours, halls and kitchens to entertain their customers. This meant that the social character of these rooms could vary considerably, and sometimes illegally, between public and private patterns of use, according to different times of the day, week or year. This blurring of boundaries between economic, domestic and social space also created complex relationships between hosts and guests. The need to make a profit required the proprietor of a drinking establishment to entertain a broad range of customers of varying age, rank and gender, but in a society in which hierarchy was marked out and enforced by detailed attention to codes of dress, gesture and physical space, regulating social contact in such a fluid and dynamic social setting was complex. Clashes that came to court over seemingly small details such as where a person sat, how a person spoke and who bought drinks for whom suggest that these were decisions fraught with social difficulties. A dispute that erupted between Mr Pattinson and John Palmer in an alehouse in West Ham in 1631 provides a good example. According to witnesses Palmer 'thrust into the companie of Mr John Pattinson which rudeness he was very much troubled at'. Status had to be jealously defended even in these informal settings through minute attention to the protection of personal space.[73] The 'private rooms' within some drinking houses offered a solution for some, enabling the rich and respectable to pay for the right to exclusive use of a space, and so differentiate and distance themselves from other guests. None the less, the presence of 'private' but profit-making spaces within 'public' social arenas complicated and confused social boundaries still further.[74] Drinking houses were undoubtedly vitally important informal arenas

---

[73] Pattinson c. Palmer (1632), LMA, DL/C/233, fo. 297v.
[74] For references to private rooms see Hyde c. Rooke (1630), LMA, DL/C/233, fo. 99v, and Crooke c. Little (1683), DL/C/240, fo. 410v.

of association for the construction and maintenance of bonds of support and obligation between individuals of varying age and rank, but they were also sites that contained within them a degree of social and spatial tension.

Historians have long regarded drinking houses as important sites for the expression and affirmation of dominant gender norms in early modern society. We have seen that popular culture constructed these spaces as dangerous for respectable women, frequented primarily by dissolute and disorderly members of the female sex. It has also been assumed by modern scholars that drinking houses were predominantly male spaces whose social character was maintained and enforced by informal regulation that ranged in form from physical assault to verbal abuse and which ensured that respectable women avoided these spaces, because they tainted the reputation of those who worked or visited there.[75] Peter Clark argues that this situation only began to change after the Restoration when a small number of reputable female customers began to use the alehouse if accompanied by a male relative or other women, but even then the sexes were separated by segregated systems of seating. Clark has also used evidence of official lists of licensees to argue that, while many women were involved in commercial brewing and alehouse-keeping in the fourteenth century, the intensification of the regulation of alehouses during the early part of the sixteenth century led to the exit of women from the trade.[76] According to Judith Bennett, the prevalence of misogynistic images of the immorality and dishonesty of alewives after 1600 contributed to this process of masculinisation.[77] The following analysis will harness the evidence from the depositions to analyse the efficacy of these arguments by exploring how many women used drinking houses, which women went, why they went there and whether they went for similar or different reasons to those of men.[78] Unfortunately, the quality of the evidence does not allow us to compare patterns of use before and after the Restoration. The decline in business dealt with by the ecclesiastical and borough courts during the later seventeenth

[75] K. Wrightson, 'Alehouses, order and Reformation in England, 1590–1660', in E. Yeo and S. Yeo (eds), *Popular culture and class conflict, 1590–1914: explorations in the history of labour and leisure*, Brighton 1981, 1–27; P. Clark, *The English alehouse: a social history, 1200–1830*, London 1983. See also Griffiths, *Youth and authority*, 208, and Mendelson and Crawford, *Women in early modern England*, 211. For analyses of the central importance of the alehouse for early modern masculinity see L. Roper, *The holy household: religion, morals and order in Reformation Augsburg*, Oxford 1989, 91–3, and Shepard, 'Meanings of manhood', 179–87. For illuminating discussions of single and married women's use of the alehouse see Capp, 'When gossips meet', 331–6, and Shepard, *Meanings of manhood*, 101–3.

[76] Clark, *The English alehouse*, 79.

[77] J. M. Bennett, 'Misogyny, popular culture and women's work', *HWJ* xxxi (1991), 168–88. See also Bennett, *Ale, beer and brewsters*.

[78] The distinctions between alehouses, taverns and inns were legally defined by statute in the sixteenth century. Alehouses were described as the lower end of the social scale (existing primarily for drink, possibly lodging and to sell beer and bread to the poor). Taverns sold wine and inns were at the upper end of the social scale providing beer, wine, lodging, stabling and food: Clark, *The English alehouse*, 5.

century meant that there are simply too few cases available to make any meaningful comparison. It is also important to stress again that the limitations of the records already discussed means that the documents present some methodological difficulties. Counting references to people seen in drinking houses does not provide an absolutely accurate record of who was there. There is also a danger that the documents are not representative, because alehouses were commonly the sites of criminal disorder and so the individuals who appear as being in these spaces are often delinquent or for one reason or another suspect. None the less, the range of documentation and type of case, together with the fact that they introduce witnesses who just happened to be present and include spatial details incidental rather than central to the crux of the case, makes it a reasonably good sample that provides an effective focus for a discussion of what happened in drinking houses during day-to-day use.

In order to compare male to female presence in different types of drinking houses during the first half of the seventeenth century, every reference to individuals recorded present in these spaces has been counted in the depositions for the ecclesiastical, quarter sessions and borough courts between 1580 and 1640. Evidence for the social identity of a total of 415 individuals was obtained. This information is presented and summarised in tables 2 and 3.

Initially what is striking about the evidence presented in table 2 is the relatively large numbers of women present in drinking houses in Essex during the first half of the seventeenth century. It is important to recognise probable distortions in the proportions of men and women recorded due the overrepresentation of women in church court records. Several studies have demonstrated that female litigants dominated this legal arena by the seventeenth century. Yet it is surely significant that a large number of women were there. At least 122 women and 151 men were identified as present in alehouses between 1580 and 1640; 40 per cent of individuals recorded as appearing in these spaces were therefore women. It is also clear that women routinely visited higher-status establishments such as taverns and inns: ninety-six men and forty-six women were recorded present in these establishments between 1580 and 1640. This means that nearly 32 per cent of individuals present were women.

Admittedly, when we go on to look at which women were present and why, gender differences become more apparent. Men, more often than women, were recorded socialising in alehouses. If male and female workers in establishments are excluded from the totals of individuals present, we find that thirty-five women and eighty-seven men were present in inns and taverns, so that women comprised just over 28 per cent of individuals making social appearances in higher-status establishments during the first half of the seventeenth century. If the men and women identified as running alehouses or working as servants are removed from the totals of both groups present, then the total figures for socialising in alehouses are reduced to sixty-seven women and 118 men. In other words, men comprised 63.8 per cent of individuals socialising in alehouses whereas 36.2 per cent of social appearances were

Table 2
Social status of women in drinking establishments
in Essex, 1580–1640

wife/widow of	Alehouse		Tavern/Inn	
	number	%	number	%
gentry	0	0	7	15.2
professional	0	0	2	4.0
yeoman	6	4.9	5	10.8
husbandman	14	11.4	2	4.0
artisan	15	12.2	5	10.8
[landlady]	29	23.7	5	10.8
servant	26	21.3	6	13.0
labourer	16	13.1	0	0
unknown	16	13.0	14	30.4
Total	122		46	

Source: ERO (Ch.), D/AED 1–8; D/ABD 1–8; D/ACD 1–7; D/AXD 1–3; Q/SBa 2/1–80; ERO (Col.), D/B5 Sb2/2–8; LMA, DL/C/211–235; GL, MS 9189/1–2

Table 3
Social status of men in drinking establishments
in Essex, 1580–1640

	Alehouse		Tavern/Inn	
	number	%	number	%
gentry	3	2	12	12.5
professional	4	2.6	5	5.2
yeoman	11	7.3	9	9.4
husbandman	19	12.6	4	4.2
artisan	5	3.3	21	21.9
[landlady]	9	6	7	7.3
servant	24	15.9	4	4.2
labourer	18	11.9	7	7.3
unknown	58	33.4	27	28.1
Total	151		96	

Sources: ERO (Ch.), D/AED 1–8; D/ABD 1–8; D/ACD 1–7; D/AXD 1–3; Q/SBa 2/1–80; ERO (Col.), D/B5 Sb2/2–8; LMA, DL/C/211–235; GL, MS 9189/1–2.

female. These figures suggest that all types of drinking establishments were male-dominated social arenas, even if they were not the gender exclusive social settings described by Clark.

The superior power and ability of men to control these spaces is manifest at every turn. The risks for women of ridicule, insult and attack on their sexual reputation were real. Out of a total of 158 defamation cases brought before the ecclesiastical courts by Essex female producents between 1580 and 1640, twenty-three (14.5 per cent) involved accusations made against women in drinking establishments. To this evidence can be added the many instances when men in alehouses defamed women in their absence. Wives who were recorded as being present in drinking houses often remarked that they had been called in to drink by their husbands or that they had come to fetch their menfolk home for their meal. Of course these details may have been included to impress a legal audience, but they do suggest a male-dominated drinking culture in which men lingered far longer, more freely and frequently over their drinking than women. The length of time that men spent drinking is striking. There was a tragic outcome to the dallying of Paul Nottage of Great Waltham in Essex in the White Hart Inn where the landlord, Robert Sawell 'wilfully entertained him, excessively drinking, tippling and wantonly living' for four days, including the Sabbath. Nottage's wife, coming into the town to search for him, left her child at home 'in a chair'; the child fell into the fire, 'burned its skull until it cracked' and died an hour later.[79] Evidence of the anger that wives could arouse if they followed their husbands to the alehouse uninvited suggests that, in some contexts, men made efforts to exclude women (or more accurately their wives) altogether from these spaces. Margaret Townsend suffered severely for her rebuke of local men who lured her husband to spend his money in the alehouse. A defamatory notice was fastened to her door that led to a presentment for adultery.[80]

Close examination of the circumstances in which women appear in drinking houses also reinforces several arguments made by Clark about the social constraints on women within these spaces. Many women mentioned present were with their husbands or a male relative. Sunday was an especially popular day for these informal social gatherings, often after church. A good example is the impromptu party arranged one evening in August 1630 by Mr John Harrogate and Mr William Rooke, minister of Little Ilford, in the churchyard after evening prayer. The two men, together with Rooke's wife, Mr William Lane and his wife, a kinswoman and her maid, apparently went off to the Blue Boar Tavern in Ilford and consumed 'two pottles of wite wine mixt with a little pottle of water and six parts of sugar'.[81] In another case of defamation in 1618 Dorcas Hellawell, wife of William Hellawell painter/stainer, told court officials that she witnessed the words of defamation spoken by Francis Cruife against Barbara Chapman, whilst 'at the signe of the 3 Tunns tavern' with her 'husband & others drinkinge a pinte of wine'.[82]

It does seem that because drinking houses were imagined as spaces of sexual opportunity, a woman's reputation could be put at risk if she was seen going to an alehouse or tavern alone with an unrelated man or unaccompanied. A

[79] Grieve, *Sleepers and the shadows*, ii. 74.

[80] Emmison, *Morals*, 53; Melville, 'Use and organisation of domestic space', 246; Capp, '*When gossips meet*', 90–1.

[81] Hyde c. Rooke (1630), LMA, DL/C/233, fo. 114v.

[82] Chapman c. Cruife (1618), LMA, DL/C/225, fo. 204v; Garrett c. Everett (1620), ERO (Ch.), D/ABD 1, fo. 126v.

total of eight women, married and single, were recorded as visiting drinking establishments with unrelated men who were not suitors between 1580 and 1640. All these encounters were mentioned with reference to charges of adultery or fornication. In all other instances unaccompanied women were drawn for the most part from the poorest sections of society. A total of twenty-six (18 per cent) other women were recorded visiting drinking establishments unaccompanied. Six were poor migrant single women looking for lodgings: three of them were prosecuted for immorality; two were poor vagrant widows; four were women of unknown marital status who were also vagrants; fifteen of the women were married. Of the married women who came to the alehouse unaccompanied, one was a thief, one was probably a prostitute, while one labourer's wife came to collect a debt owed to her by a lodger, and another explained that she had come to 'seek her husband'. Four women (33.3 per cent) from the lower levels of village society, wives of poorer husbandmen and labourers, came to buy beer, bread or grain. Of those four, Alice Turnedge and goodwife Homan were verbally abused during their visit, while Alice was also physically attacked by a male customer.

None the less, when we turn to look at the social identity of the women listed as present in drinking houses, the social and spatial picture becomes more complex. The social range of men and women using drinking establishments during the period was relatively broad and surprisingly similar. Admittedly a fair proportion of the women and the men whose presence in alehouses is mentioned were from the humblest sections of society. Sixteen women (13.1 per cent) were described as wives of labourers, twenty-six (21.3 per cent) were poor widows, and eight (25 per cent) listed as present were poor migrants working as servants. Eighteen men (11.9 per cent) were listed as labourers and twenty-four (15.9 per cent) as servants. Equally the more prestigious social groups are poorly represented in the samples of male and female social appearances in alehouses, although this may be explained in part by social bias in the sources. The gentry for example tended to use other legal arenas to sue for defamation. It is nevertheless noteworthy that a relatively high proportion of women, as well as men, listed as present in alehouses were drawn from the middling ranks of local society. About 23 per cent of men were listed as yeoman, husbandmen or artisans. Of the 122 women mentioned as present in alehouses during the period, for whom occupation or husband's occupation is given, thirty-five (28.6 per cent) were the wives of established householders drawn from the 'middling-sort' of yeomen, husbandmen or craftsmen. When we turn to the higher status establishments, out of a total of twenty-six married women listed as present in inns and taverns nine (nearly 20 per cent) were described in the depositions as wives of gentlemen or 'professional' men. A further twelve (20 per cent) women who were present in inns and taverns and whose husbands' occupations can be identified were wives of middling-sort farmers or tradesmen. Looking at the men in the sample, just under half (thirty-two) of men present in inns were listed as gentlemen or professionals and around a third (twenty-three) were from the middling ranks. Some allowance should be made for distortions created by the overrepresentation of women of middling status in the records of the church courts. Even so this evidence modifies claims by Clark that the alehouse was almost exclusively the resort of respectable male householders and that these spaces were avoided by all but the poorest of women or prostitutes.

It is also clear from the depositions that there were circumstances in which women could enter these spaces more freely. It seems that alehouses and taverns were acceptable spaces for young women and men to use as part of courtship, perhaps explaining Gouge's acknowledgement that drinking houses were bearable places for young single women to be. The alehouse was an important site for apprentice and diarist Roger Lowe's courtship activities and he met his future wife Emm Potter in an alehouse during Ashton Wakes.[83] There were four instances of single women making social appearances in alehouses and taverns with a suitor. In 1608 David Bush, yeoman, visited the inn run by one Conrad Burton in Brentwood with his 'then consort' Anne when they heard William Fuller defame Burton's wife Alice.[84] In another case Stephen Elliott, labourer, told the court that he was drinking in the house of one Foncher at 8 o'clock in the morning after completing his work in Barking market, 'with a woman who was his suitor'.[85] In these limited contexts young women as well as men could behave in a relatively outgoing fashion, free temporarily from the social and spatial strictures of the household. However discipline was soon imposed forcibly if behaviour went too far. In 1595 the proprietor of an alehouse in Inworth in Essex was prosecuted for allowing 'evill rule in his house all night long on the first daye of Januarye with young men and maids togither'.[86] In similar vein in 1630 a presentment was made by the minister and churchwardens of John Strutt, and one Joseph Bridge, Joan Goodman and Amye Thorpe single men and single women. They departed 'out of the church in the tyme of the sermon in the forenoone of that Sundaye, and they went to the alehouse or taverne, which one William Chaundler keepeth, and their stayed their eating and tipplinge, both wyne and beare, until evening prayer'.[87]

Married women visited drinking houses on special occasions. Court records offer examples to confirm contemporary commentators' frequent reference to married women's carousing in alehouses after churchings and christenings.[88] In 1598 Jane Minors, for example, was presented to the archdeacon's court because she had spent the morning in the alehouse with her friends feasting and drinking 'four or five hours' and returned later in the afternoon for more drinking.[89] Use of these spaces for married women also seems to have been

[83] *Lowe diary*, 13–14, 20, 22, 23, 26, 34, 41, 43, 44, 58, 68, 79.
[84] Burton c. Fuller (1608), ERO (Ch.), D/AED 8, fo. 130v.
[85] ERO (Ch.), Q/SBa 2/21.
[86] ERO (Ch.), D/ACA 22, fo. 158v.
[87] ERO (Ch.), D/AEA 38, fo. 122v.
[88] Cressy, *Birth, marriage and death*, 201–2.
[89] Ibid.

accepted as part of a working routine. On market day, for example, women would come in to town from outlying districts and the more affluent among them would stable their horses in the inn yard while they traded. Women from a wide social range drank together before their journey home at the end of the day. In 1623 Elizabeth Wilson, a market woman of West Ham, told the ecclesiastical court how she would bring the family's produce to sell in the city and when business was done for the day she and her 'friends' would repair to the Kings Head to drink a pint of wine before they returned home.[90] Bridget Barber, wife of John Barber, of Nayland, visited an alehouse, after walking ten miles to deliver her 'dutchworke' to Colchester on market day.[91]

The interconnections of space, place and gender are also important for the understanding of patterns of female access. Women with an established reputation in a locality, who were well known to the proprietor and customers, seem to have had more freedom of movement. Several incidental references record women of middling status using local taverns and alehouses without a male relative, for whom this kind of socialising was obviously routine. For example, Mistress Waters of Blackmore was able to act as a witness in a case of defamation because she overheard William Fuller defame Alice Burton while she was sitting drinking with Richard Garrett, yeoman, and Thomas Clarke, baker, in an inn in Brentwood in 1608.[92] Another case recounts that Helen Lawrence, wife of Thomas Lawrence, seaman, witnessed an altercation in her local alehouse one afternoon in 1615 when she went for a drink before evening prayer.[93] Women like these used drinking houses in comparable ways to men – to drink, to eat, to socialise or to discuss business before the courts.[94] The regional economy may also have had some influence on patterns of use, given the importance of inns and taverns as market places for private trade in grain and cloth.[95] There were several examples of women who used drinking houses to deal in a variety of licit and illicit goods.[96] One 'Mrs. Day of Altoupe Rouding' was indicted 'for refusing to get her malt in the market place of Ongar and carrying it to an inn yard and [for having] sold it before the bell did ring'. On two further occasions she was prosecuted for selling wheat 'to the value of 5 seames' and a further six 'seames' of malt 'violently in an inn yard'.[97]

The coincidence of domestic, economic and social space was important for

---

[90] GL, MS 9189/1, fo. 74v.

[91] ERO (Col.), D/B5 Sb2/6, fos 9v–10.

[92] Burton c. Fuller (1608), ERO (Ch.), D/AED 5, fo. 130v; Wills c. Nevell (1613), LMA, DL/C/221, fo. 1403v.

[93] Poulter c. Valentine (1615), LMA, DL/C/223, fo. 212v.

[94] ERO (Col.), SB5 Sb2/6, fo. 10r; Mayle c. Mayle (1707) LMA, DL/C/249, fo. 322v.

[95] Everitt, 'The marketing of agricultural produce', 559.

[96] Wilkinson c. Witham (1600), ERO (Ch.), D/AED 4, fos 37r–38; Q/SR 349/20; Q/SR 322/106. On the use of alehouses for illicit trade see G. Walker, 'Women, theft, and the world of stolen goods', in Kermode and Walker, *Women, crime and the courts*, 81–105.

[97] ERO (Ch.), Q/SR 349/20; Q/SR 332/106.

women in other respects. In some instances, women said that they had gone to visit the alewife more as a neighbour and friend than as a paying guest. In 1618, for example, Jane Bricheley, wife of Thomas Bricheley, a chandler of Eastwick, told the court that 'being a neare neighbour' to Rose Grace, widow, who kept an alehouse in the village, she 'hath bene in the howse of the said Grace manie tymes'.[98] We also find that when Christopher Tiffin, tailor of Great Wakering, came to the alehouse of one John Rivers in 1635 to drink, he found 'Mary Hodges and the wife of the s[ai]d John Rivers sitting together' gossiping about neighbourhood affairs.[99] The importance of alehouses for the domestic economy of the rural poor adds another layer of complexity to gendered boundaries and meanings. We find for example that in April 1649 Elizabeth Page, the wife of a husbandman of Henham, told the magistrate that she visited 'Tho[ma]s Mead's alehouse' to buy bread 'of Meads wife', where she stayed drinking for a while.[100] Of course, women's explanations may have been strategic, designed to represent them in the best possible light. None the less, these testimonies do suggest a complex and dynamic spatial and social geography of drinking houses that could give rise to different understandings of the meaning and experience of these spaces between women and between men.

Evidence also confirms the continued importance of the alehouse as a workspace for women. The official lists of licensees consulted by Clark significantly under-represent female participation in these businesses. Of the total number of women present in alehouses in the first half of the seventeenth century 38.8 per cent worked there either as alewife or a servant. Half of the single women listed as present in inns and taverns were workers, while just under a quarter of women in inns and taverns were wives of the inn- or tavern-keeper who acted in some sort of managerial role or servants who worked there. The misogyny outlined by Judith Bennett, and which she and Clark argue discouraged women from the trade, is very evident in the records. Although working from court records may distort the evidence to an extent, the depositions suggest that insult and abuse went with the territory for these working women. Violent assault was another real risk, as we have seen.[101] It is equally clear that rhetoric that equated drinking houses with immorality had a material reality, especially in the larger towns such as Chelmsford or Colchester and in parishes such as West Ham nearer to London. Women who worked in or visited these establishments were undoubtedly at risk of being pimped by the proprietor.[102] Three of the twelve unlicensed victuallers presented in Chelmsford in 1567 were charged with keeping brothels. There was also a case in 1596 of a Chelmsford landlord who was prosecuted

---

98 Grace c. Spencer (1618), LMA, DL/C/ 225, fo. 175v.
99 Mircocke c. Hodges (1635), ERO (Ch.), D/AED 8, fo. 97v.
100 ERO (Ch.), Q/SBa 2/70.
101 ERO (Col.), D/B5 Sb2/9, fo. 45v.
102 Griffiths, 'The structure of prostitution', 39–56.

for 'harbouring of suspected persons of incontinent life in his house, viz. one Reynold's wife for common adultery with divers, as the common fame goeth; she keepeth a 6d. ordinary, come that listeth'.[103]

None the less, there was a wide range of drinking establishments in early modern Essex, as elsewhere in early modern England, and it would be wrong to assume that the women who worked in them, or who drank in them, were all seen in the same way. Young female servants or alewives who ran small-scale, often unlicensed, enterprises were relatively powerless and tended to be regarded as women of suspect morals. Landladies of larger, more respectable businesses, on the other hand, were more reputable.[104] Two wives of Colchester tavern-keepers, Elizabeth Coker and Susan Nire, provide examples of women at the lower end of the social spectrum. Alongside running their taverns day-to-day, these women were intimately involved in the criminal networks of the Colchester underworld and dealt regularly in stolen linen and cloth. In addition, Elizabeth Coker acted as pawnbroker and infanticidal nurse to neighbours and strangers passing through town.[105] The position of these women was profoundly different from respected and respectable figures like the wealthy widow Margaret Thunder who owned and ran an inn in Romford during the 1560s and 1570s or Francis Barfoot, who helped her husband run the Blue Boar in Ilford in 1630.[106]

Most historical discussions have tended to overlook these hierarchical distinctions, assuming instead a common space and female identity. The result has been that the complexities of the influence of gender on access to and use of these spaces have become obscured. Local knowledge was vitally important, since women could avoid alehouses and taverns known to be morally disreputable. Social distinctions between different types of drinking houses were certainly recognised by people at the time. Proprietors of respectable establishments were extremely concerned to protect their upright reputation within the community. The economic effect of scandal could be serious. In 1683 the landlady of the Chequer Inn at Hatfield Broad Oak evicted William Little and Martha Boreham from a private room they had hired, when she found that they were conducting an adulterous affair. Her servant testified that 'her mistress was very displeased and she wolde go upstairs and pull them out she wolde not have her house made a bawdy house'.[107] A case in

103 ERO (Col.), D/B5 Sb2/3, not foliated; Emmison, Morals, 22.
104 ERO (Ch.), Q/SBa 2/78; Frost c. Copsheafe (1610), LMA, DL/C/219, fos 170v–172, 256r; Copsheafe c. Frost (1610), LMA, DL/C/219, fos 250v–252.
105 For Susan Nire and her clients see ERO (Col.), D/B5 SB2/9, fos 222v, 228v, 232r, 252v, 259v, 278v. For Elizabeth Coker see D/B5 Sb2/7, fos 255v–258; D/B5 S/b 2/9, fos 92v, 198v, 203v, 235v. Coker was implicated in the shadowy activities of Richard Skeate and Lydia Downes, hanged for murder in 1639.
106 ERO (Col.), D/B5 Sb2/9, fo. 215v; M. K. McIntosh, A community transformed: the manor and liberty of Havering, 1500–1620, Cambridge 1991, 136; Hyde c. Rooke (1630), LMA, DL/C/232, fo. 198v.
107 ERO (Col.), Coke c. Little (1683), LMA, DL/C/240, fo. 410r.

Sussex provides another well-documented example. A neighbour accused Susan Willett of immorality in May 1621, standing outside her victualling house and shouting that 'she was a filthy whore' and that 'the stews was fitter for her than that place'. Willett was forced to sue for defamation because of the damaging economic impact of the insult upon her business. A witness explained that 'many of her neighbours and guests that were wont to frequent her house do now refrain from to come hither, fearing lest some discredit may happen unto them thereby'.[108]

In the earlier period religious allegiance sometimes determined patronage of drinking houses and these spaces were used for informal spiritual meetings, further complicating understanding of gendered spatial maps. In the Marian Inn of Colchester the godly apparently conducted their spiritual exercises in the 'common inns' by night.[109] The sixteenth-century Protestant radical Henry Orinel relates debating the divinity of Christ at an inn (probably the King's Head) with some servants, 'two women Gospellers' and a Dutch member of the heretical Family of Love.[110]

Defamation evidence also provides an insight into distinctions, as well as connections, between the experiences of different types of women in different drinking spaces. On the one hand the many suits of slander brought to court by middling-sort married women over sexual insults made against them in alehouses and taverns provide a stark reminder of the insecurity of these social settings for all women. Yet the fact of litigation also demonstrates that a respectable woman's reputation was not automatically rendered indefensible by presence in such places and that mechanisms were available to middling-sort women that muted the significance of the abuse that single and poorer women could do little about.[111] That some female customers were able to police these spaces informally, by aggressive objection to the unwelcome intrusion of unacceptable individuals into their company, further highlights how status and gender could come together to structure social and spatial meaning. Sometimes clashes could occur between female groups of patrons. A good example took place in an alehouse in Sussex in 1613 when some local women met to drink after evening prayer. Existing enmity between Mercy Locke and Margaret Grovett detonated a dispute in which spatial exclusion was used to powerful effect to express rejection and contempt. When Mercy tried to join the group Margaret Grovett challenged her, demanding, 'Thou wilt not sit down, wilt thou?' to which Mercy replied, 'Indeed I have forsaken much good company for your sake, but I will do so no more'.[112] In other instances women were perfectly prepared to complain about the 'uncivill'

108 Capp, 'When gossips meet', 97.
109 Collinson, The birthpangs of Protestant England, 38, 107.
110 M. Byford, 'The birth of a Protestant town: the process of Reformation in Tudor Colchester, 1530–80', in P. Collinson and J. Craig (eds), The Reformation in English towns, 1500–1640, Basingstoke 1998, 35.
111 Melville, 'The use and organisation of domestic space', 250.
112 Cited in Capp, 'When gossips meet', 212.

incursion of men into mixed social terrain. In 1633 the gentlewoman Catherine Parry was drinking with her husband and some of his friends in a private room in the Blue Boar in Ilford, when she openly protested that Mr Richard Rooke 'did rudely intrude himself into their company' and behaved in an 'uncivill manner'.[113] Another good example is a dispute in 1613 that erupted in the Black Bull tavern in Barking when a servant inquired why Anne Perse kept moving her mixed company of drinking companions repeatedly from 'room to room'. She explained that she intended to avoid the intrusion of John Nevell into their group. According to Perse his presence was unwelcome because of the immorality of his wife; she went on to call Elizabeth Nevell a 'whore'.[114]

It is noteworthy that the depositions do not offer evidence of the existence of sexually segregated seating in drinking houses of the kind outlined by Clark. Conflicts over who sat where and with whom and the presence of private rooms in inns and taverns, on the other hand, suggest an intricate internal social and spatial geography constructed around status. The drinking-house was not simply an arena for the expression and reaffirmation of dominant gender roles. It was also a space in which those divided by gender, age and status met, marked out and enforced the multiple and complex differences between them.

The street and the green

The streets, marketplaces and greens of Essex villages and towns were also important sites for popular sociability, in which different ages and social categories of women and men met and mingled. In many contexts the claims that women made on these arenas were intimately connected to their daily working lives and the material circumstances of their domestic spaces. Cramped and dimly lit domestic interiors meant that women spent a good deal of time at work in doorways where they could chat to neighbours and passers-by. In addition a good deal of 'housework' in early modern England was performed outside the house: collecting water, washing, spinning and even baking were activities that were often performed outside in the street or on the green. Women were also everywhere in Essex markets, buying goods for their family needs and selling a variety of produce and manufactured goods, loitering and gossiping with neighbours in the midst of their work.

Women, as well as men, also used these spaces for a variety of forms of informal recreation less directly related to labour. They watched public punishments and street performers and listened to preachers who provided

113 Hyde c. Rooke (1630), LMA, DL/C/233, fo. 99v.
114 Wills c. Nevell (1613), LMA, DL/C/221, fo.1120v. Amanda Vickery has also noted that genteel ladies 'enjoyed dinners' at the alehouse but 'disapproved of the promiscuous social mingling which the alehouse licensed': *Gentleman's daughter*, 203, 214.

entertainment on market day. They took walks out on the green and played mixed team games such as stoolball in the street, on the green or in the churchyard.[115] Fair days held in open spaces outside villages and towns all over Essex were another very important attraction for men and women of all ages and social classes.[116] It was apparently the custom for servants to be excused work on the day of the fair nearest to their place of work, explaining their importance as part of courtship. But there were attractions for everyone on these occasions: the meeting of friends and acquaintances, the variety of goods for sale and the amusement of the entertainments enhanced the pleasure of release from labour at least for a day. The value of the fair in the lives of ordinary people of both sexes is clear in the way it remained in their memories. When deponents and defendants were asked to identify the timing of an incident, fair day was often the nearest answer that they could give.

In practice, despite the prevalence of prescriptive and popular literature that admonished women to avoid the streets whenever possible, there was a relatively relaxed attitude to female presence out in the open spaces of local villages and towns and women were found there quite late into the evening as a matter of course. Yet this impression of inclusivity should not obscure the importance of these informal social settings for the structuring of social and gender difference. A closer investigation of use of these spaces shows the many ways they were constructed out of and in turn reflected and reinforced a set of social relations structured around hierarchies of gender, class and age.

The gender order was marked out and enforced on the streets in several ways. Official public ritual was a constant reminder to women of the pre-eminence of their gender identity and their secondary status within the political community. In Essex, as in other regions, women of all social categories were largely excluded from participation in the street processions that mapped the institutional, political, economic, social and spatial boundaries of belonging to local society. Age and status determined the participation of men. Masters and journeymen made annual parades in their respective companies, most notably in Essex the Bishop Blaise parades of the woolcombers.[117] Aldermen and councillors participated in the many civic processions staged annually to reflect and to reinforce the power of corporate institutions and offices. In some cities the wives of office-holders may have taken part. In Bristol, from 1570, the wives of former mayors and sheriffs were ordered to wear scarlet gowns on the 'solemn occasions' when their husbands did so, suggesting perhaps that they accompanied their menfolk. In Nottingham in 1629, 'the Maior, Aldermen, Councell and clothing [sic]' were ordered to pay for 'themselves and their wyefes' to attend on 'mistris Maoris' at the

---

115 Turner and Muckley c. May (1617), LMA, DL/C/ 224, fos 388v–392; ERO (Ch.), D/ACA 54, fo. 137v. On stoolball see S. Prendergast, 'Stoolball: the pursuit of vertigo?' *Women's Studies International Quarterly* i (1978), 15–26.

116 W. Walker, *Essex markets and fairs*, Chelmsford 1981; Brown, *Prosperity and poverty*, 69–71.

117 Brown, *Essex at work*, 78.

'antiente custome of going to Saint Anne well on Black-Monday' [Easter].[118] The important distinction, of course, was that on these occasions the office and authority of a man determined a woman's 'place' in the political pageant. Rogationtide processions that were made each spring through the streets and fields of local parishes to mark the material margins of place were also predominantly male parades. In some places the wives of the ruling elite may have participated in the procession. In Braintree by 1629 the wives of the ruling group known as the 'Four and Twenty' may have walked the bounds with their husbands.[119] Women were also expected to provide hospitality to participants and the wives of the 'better sort' were included as guests at the dinners that followed.[120] However in most contexts women were spectators at the celebrations. Official ritual, as Charles Phythian Adams has argued, provided a constant reminder to the community of 'its discrete and predominantly masculine identity'.[121]

Women did process along the street, but their rituals revolved around the rhythms of the life-cycle events of the family. Married women or maids held the pall at the funerals of other women. New mothers were escorted along the street by their 'gossips' to be churched. Separate bridal processions of young men and women accompanied couples to and from the ceremonial celebration of marriage.[122] But, as Merry Wiesner argues, these processional rituals asserted a female social identity that was solely determined by household and family.[123] Women could not claim a formal, political processional role, reproducible through time.

Informal street rituals, festivals and recreations also tended to reinforce gender norms. Men and women often played different games. Wrestling, 'tilting' and football were male sports; 'barley break' and 'smock-racing' were

---

[118] R. Tittler, *The Reformation and the towns in England*, Oxford 1998, 307–8; *Records of the borough of Nottingham, IV: 1625–1702*, ed. W. H. Stevenson, London 1900, 108, 140. Essex examples include the annual processions mounted every year in Colchester to mark the openings of St Dennis and midsummer fair, and the election of the mayor: Goose and Cooper, *Tudor and Stuart Colchester*, 112. In Chelmsford, the assize judge led a termly procession up the high street to the court house, attended by the sheriff and his officers: Grieve, *Sleepers*, ii. 43.

[119] For references to Rogationtide processions in Purleigh see ERO (Ch.), D/ABD 4, fo. 61v; for Tilbury see D/AED 3, fo. 74v; for Little Ilford see Hyde c. Rooke (1630), LMA, DL/C/233, fos 97r–99, 113v, 200r–203. Thanks to John Walter for the suggestion about Braintree. For discussion of the progressive social exclusivity of perambulation see S. Hindle, 'A sense of place? Becoming and belonging in the rural parish, 1550–1650', in A. Shepard and P. Withington (eds), *Communities in early modern England*, Manchester 2000, 107–8.

[120] ESRO, FBA/91/E1/1. Thanks to Deidre Heavens for this reference.

[121] C. Phythian Adams, 'Ceremony and the citizen: the communal year at Coventry, 1450–1550', in P. Clark, and P. Slack (eds), *Crisis and order in English towns, 1500–1700*, London 1982, 59.

[122] Cressy, *Birth, marriage and death*, 367.

[123] M. Wiesner, *Women and gender in early modern Europe*, Cambridge 2000, 103.

female games.[124] Hocktide and May Day were important popular festivals that ritualised separate roles for men and women, as did the informal shaming rites of charivari.[125] Street language also provided a vehicle for the expression of normative patriarchal spatial codes. Prescriptive and popular associations between 'public' spaces such as markets and streets and female immorality were manipulated to powerful effect in the language of defamation.[126] In 1610 Bridget Newton of Brentwood, speaking of Mary, the wife of John Redriffe, said, 'the puritaine his wife was occupied under a stall'.[127] Anne Poos slandered Mary Rogers in Witham in 1723, saying she 'was common and wolde lie down in the market place'.[128] Derision was part of daily experience for women in Essex as elsewhere in early modern England. The victims of public insults in the streets were overwhelmingly women. Out of forty-four defamation cases resulting from street slander taken to court during the period, female plaintiffs brought thirty-two.

The possibility of verbal assault was combined with the threat of male violence. The risk of physical attack was undoubtedly real on village and town streets at all times of day and night, especially for poor women or female servants who were required to go out alone or after dark. In November 1605, 'betweene Seven and Eight of the clocke', Thomas Kempe and Mary Campion witnessed an attack by Thomas Wilkinson on the wife of Lawrence Symonds in Morelands Lane, Colchester.[129] In 1604 Patience Dowdall, a servant in Colchester, was 'in the afternoone ... going upp the lane called parsonage lane & so into the feilde to gather sticks', when William Langley attempted to assault her sexually.[130] In 1665 Jeane Noris, servant to Mr Royston of Plaistow, complained that 'John Knight of Plaistow did by violence drage

---

[124] ERO (Col.), D/B5 Sb2/6, fo.124v; Brown, *Poverty and prosperity*, 69–71. On the gendering of games see Capp, '*When gossips meet*', 327–38, and Gowing, 'The freedom of the streets', 141. On tilting see Grieve, *Sleepers*, i. 164–5.

[125] For gender specific May-Day rituals see C. Phythian Adams, 'Milk and soot: the changing vocabulary of a popular ritual in Stuart and Hanovarian London', in D. Fraser and A. Sutcliffe (eds), *The pursuit of urban history*, London 1983, 83–104. The classic study of charivari in England is M. Ingram, 'Ridings, rough music and the "reform of popular culture" in early modern England', *P&P* cv (1984), 79–113. For the implications for gender roles see Foyster, *Manhood in early modern England*, 107–15. One episode of charivari has been identified in the Essex records. In 1681 'a great number of idell people', gathered for 'a rideinge for Bridgeman's wife beating him' at Barking. All the participants prosecuted by recognizance were men, but no details of social or marital status are included: '*Holcroft his booke*', 73.

[126] Gowing, 'Freedom of the streets', 139–40.

[127] Redriffe c. Newton (1610), LMA, DL/C/219, fo. 270v.

[128] Cox c. Poos (1702), ERO (Ch.), D/AXD 2, fo. 73v.

[129] ERO (Col.), D/B5 Sb2/3, fo. 143.

[130] Ibid. fo. 125. There were of course numerous urban highway assaults and robberies on men. For examples see ERO (Ch.), Q/SR 496/55; Q/SR 491/77; Q/SR 555/20. Samuel Pepys took evasive routes through London to avoid risk of assault or rode with a weapon drawn: J. S. Pipkin, 'Space and the social order in Pepys' diary', *Urban Geography* xi (1990), 165.

[her] … downe a lane to a well & threatned to throw her into the well if she would not let him lye with her, & tooke up her coates, which made her cry out for helpe & then he stopped her mouth with his hand'.[131]

Away from isolated or dark alleys and lanes in the bustling streets of local neighbourhoods, women's fear of violence was probably muted by the know-ledge that they could call on passers-by for help. In Colchester Edward Shep-herd, for example, went to see the cause of Patience Dowdall's cries and 'took him [William Langley] of[f] her and asked him what the cause of his being there in that manner'.[132] Fear of incurring communal condemnation might also have acted as a form of control on public violent male behaviour.[133] In these more local contexts it could be argued that women were sometimes more vulnerable inside the house than out on the neighbourhood street, where male violence was more open to public scrutiny and judgement. In 1690, for example, Sara Basse and Elizabeth Hatch made a complaint to the Colchester magistrates about their neighbour James Level whom they saw, 'in the street beat kick and unmercifully treat Mary Level his wife contrary to the peace of our sovereign lord'.[134] None the less, the threat of male violence meant that the street was imagined and experienced by women in a different way from men.

The experience and perception of open spaces also varied between the sexes because their dress, gesture and modes of address were differently ordered, although age and class consistently complicated social and spatial codes. Use of the body, as we have seen, was a critically important aspect of a system of control of all aspects of personal behaviour in early modern culture that gave tangible expression to a hierarchical ideal. There was a widespread expecta-tion amongst ordinary people, as well as the elite, that behavioural codes of this kind should be adhered to in face-to-face interactions out in public as well as in the home. Carefully ordered clothing and gesture offered a way of recognising rank and regulating the boundaries of social exchanges in these fluid ill-defined social arenas, between individuals of very different degrees of wealth and power.[135] The physical performance of status and gender out in the street carried additional weight, because it was constantly exposed to public scrutiny and needed zealous protection against insult or social slight.

Men and women were instructed to walk in different ways. The respectable adult man was advised to walk with his head erect. Women, as we have seen, were encouraged to look modestly downwards, with a 'reverend carriage and gesture'.[136] The sexes were addressed differently, most obviously by the use of

---

131 'Holcroft his booke', 56.
132 ERO (Col.), D/B5 Sb2/3, fo. 125v. Women could appeal for help from official authority: complaints by women about assault in urban areas were on the increase in this period: Shoemaker, Gender in English society, 292.
133 Foyster, Manhood in early modern England, 181–95.
134 ERO (Col.), D/B5, Sr52.
135 Wrightson, English society, 63–5.
136 Wildeblood and Brinson, The polite world, 181; Gouge, Domesticall duties, 27.

'Sir' or 'Madam' and were taught to perform different gestures on meeting. Men were expected to bow and to doff their hat or cap, while women were expected to curtsy.[137]

There was also a gender dimension in attitudes to appearance. Hair and headgear were very important for both sexes, but differently ordered. Long hair in men was condemned because it blurred gender divisions. For women, hair cut above the collar was a sign of immorality.[138] All men were expected to cover their head out in the street, even if strict rules of rank and age determined whether a man should wear a hat or cap and what type.[139] Single women, on the other hand, were meant to go bareheaded. The coif was reserved for the married; it reflected their superior status as well as their modesty and to remove the coif was a sign of moral and social disgrace.

There was not a simple dichotomy, whereby male apparel was associated with social distinctions and female clothing symbolised sexual modesty. Clothing carried clues to values as well as status for both sexes. Even though sumptuary laws had lapsed by the seventeenth century, it was expected that men and women of different social rank would be recognisable by different styles and qualities of clothing. At a more profound level it was also believed that outward appearance reflected inner moral character, as preachers incessantly insisted on modesty and moderation in dress.[140] But, as was shown in chapter 1, while this advice was applied to both sexes, it was gendered in the sense that it reflected broader cultural notions about female moral weakness and the importance of sexual reputation for women. According to male moralists, respectable women had to be much more careful over their appearance out in public, because they ran the risk of having their chastity called into question if they wore extravagant or inappropriate dress.

There is plenty of evidence to show that these warnings were widely ignored by many women (and men) in the context of an increasingly socially mobile society, the confusion created by the rise of fashion and the expanding secondhand clothing market that allowed access by inferiors to the clothing of their betters.[141] A complaint was made by the town governors of early seventeenth-century Chester that wives, widows and many maids sported white caps, kerchiefs, and great broad black hats 'whereby a single woman

---

137 Phiston, *Schoole of good manners*, sig. B2; P. J. Corfield, 'Walking the city streets: the urban odyssey in eighteenth-century England', *Journal of Urban History* xvi (1990), 154, 156.

138 Griffiths, *Youth and authority*, 229.

139 Corfield, 'Hats', 64–79.

140 Harte, 'State control of dress', 137; Davies, *The Quakers in English society*, 55–7; S. Hindle, 'Civility, honesty and the deserving poor', in H. French and J. Barry (eds), *Identity and agency in England, 1500–1800*, London 2004, 50–1, and 'Dependency, shame and belonging: badging the deserving poor, c. 1550–1750', *Cultural and Social History* i (2004), 6–35.

141 Spufford, *The great reclothing of rural England*; B. Lemire, 'Consumerism in preindustrial and early industrial England: the trade in secondhand clothes', *Journal of British Studies* xxvii (1998), 1–24.

cannot be distinguished from a married, which disordering and abusing of apparel is not only contrary to the good use and honest fashion used in other good cities and places of the realm, whereby great obloquy among strangers has and does run abroad, but also is very costly more than necessary'. To try to resolve the problem they imposed fines on all single women who dared to wear caps and on all married women who wore black hats unless they were riding or going to the country.[142] Adam Martindale noted that in rural Lancashire in the early part of the seventeenth century yeomen's daughters were beginning to chafe under the clothing restrictions of their class, daring to wear 'gold or silver laces (and store of them) about their petticoats, and bone laces or works about their linens'. He was relieved to note however that in contrast to Chester, even 'the proudest of them below the gentry durst not have offered to weare a hood, or a scarfe ..., noe, nor so much as a gowne till her wedding day. And if any of them transgressed these bounds, she would have been accounted an ambitious foole.'[143] Clothing codes for men were also apparently beginning to be ignored. In 1571 the 'Cap Act' was passed to prevent social uncertainty, to ensure that the poor dressed with deference and to allow social encounters between superiors and subordinates to be negotiated in a proper manner.[144]

Yet, despite, or perhaps because of, these transgressions, it is clear from a variety of sources that bodily regimes of behaviour did have a practical impact on gendered patterns of behaviour and experience amongst ordinary people, out in the streets of provincial villages and towns.[145] The best evidence of this comes from the anxiety generated if rules were broken. For example, there are written accounts of the ferocious attacks on Quaker men and women out in public in Essex in the second half of the seventeenth century, because of their refusal to conform to 'hat honour', their deliberate violations of modes of address and the gestures of bowing and curtsying that, according to conventional codes of behaviour, should accompany them. The minister of Abberton in Essex beat the Quaker James Potter in the street because he refused to raise his hat in respectful recognition on meeting.[146]

We also catch occasional glimpses in written records of close scrutiny of individual appearance. Men, as well as women, were watched carefully. Clergymen, as exemplars of Christian morality, were very closely studied in this respect. When parishioners searched for evidence of the moral corruption of their minister, they often referred to the ragged or dirty state of his clothing. Crushed collars were also cited as ominous indications of

[142] Cited in C. Peters, *Women in early modern England, 1580–1640*, Basingstoke 2004, 70.
[143] *The life of Adam Martindale*, ed. R. Parkinson (Chetham Society, 1845), 4, 6.
[144] Hindle, 'A sense of place', 110.
[145] S. Mendelson, 'The civility of women in seventeenth-century England', in Burke, Harrison and Slack, *Civil histories*, 115; Wrightson, *English society*, 63; Fletcher, *Gender, sex and subordination*, 265.
[146] Davies, *The Quakers in English society*, 57.

incontinence.[147] None the less, a gender dimension is apparent in the more frequent focus on modesty and propriety in relation to female dress. It seems that the notion that inappropriate or extravagant clothing denoted loss of chastity did have constraining consequences for women out in public. Female appearance was the subject of consistently close inspection and comment. According to witnesses, the moral as well as material dishonesty of Elizabeth Maskell was confirmed in their minds by her 'extravagent dress ... verie fine and choyse linnen ... far beyond the quality of such a person'.[148] Sexual censure of this kind prompted Elizabeth Shepard to refuse the present of a petticoat offered by her minister and master. 'Folkes talked enough allreadie', she explained.[149] Insults against women frequently played upon these fears. Comments on clothing were a common technique used by defamers to denigrate female sexual reputation, as well as social pretension, perfectly expressed in the oft-repeated insult that a respectable woman 'had got her fine apparel with her tail'.[150]

Additional evidence of the significance of dress and body language for the gendered organisation and differentiation of spatial experience comes from descriptions in the depositions of gestures incorporated into street fights between neighbours, when social and moral reputation came under attack. These disputes were highly ritualised performances, which the audience knew how to read and interpret. A favoured strategy was to target bodily symbols of status to denigrate the standing of an opponent. Collars and neckbands of both men and women were crushed and clothes were torn as a sign of shame.[151] In disputes between men it was common to seize the hat of an opponent, while continuing to wear one's own, to signify social superiority.[152] A common gesture in fights between women was to rip the coif off their adversary, to symbolise sexual and social disgrace. A good example is the fight between Mary Brett and the daughter of Henry Gutteridge in Leighton in Essex in 1680. According to witnesses Brett 'fell upon' her adversary 'and beate her and pulled her hood off and called her whore'.[153] Hair too had great symbolic significance. It was frequently pulled out in fights between women, simulating the symbolic punishment of the whore by the shaming shaving of her head. Eye contact was also used to insult women. When Joan Statten

---

[147] Office c. Brown (1704), LMA, DL/C/248, fos 219v–229; Brett c. Smith (1701), DL/C/247, fo. 282v.

[148] ERO (Ch.), Q/SR 80/26.

[149] ERO (Ch.), Q/SBa 2/45.

[150] Cited in Capp, 'When gossips meet', 228, 230. See also Gowing, Domestic dangers, 82–4.

[151] Shepard, Meanings of manhood, 145; Boucer c. Irnard (1710), LMA, DL/C/252, fo. 250r.

[152] Shepard, Meanings of manhood, 145.

[153] Brett c. Gutteridge (1680), LMA, DL/C/239, fo. 170v–r. See also ERO (Ch.), D/AEA 38, fo. 122v.

confronted her opponent in 1576, she shouted, 'Thou art a whore, look in my face if thou darest.'[154]

It is important to recognise, however, as the discussion has already suggested, that 'regimes' of bodily behaviour out in public were highly complex and, while gender was very prominent in the configuration of the negotiation of many social encounters, it was not always the most significant determinant of precedence or perception. Different aspects of social identity could be emphasised in different contexts at different times. The poor of both sexes were advised to 'Carry yourselves dutifully and humbly towards the rich and all your superiors.'[155] It was understood that every person of high status (man or woman) had the right to precedence out in public, as well as within the home. In the later seventeenth century, gazing at a member of the elite out in the street could be risky for all subordinate groups. The earl of Lincoln, for example, made his servants beat an apprentice to death for staring at him in the street, while the duke of Somerset had outriders to clear the roads of plebeians in case they should see him as he passed: one farmer refused to be stopped from looking over his hedge and held up his pig so that he could see him too.[156] A deferential distance had to be maintained between the rich and the poor, the married and the single, the old and the young. Touching or jostling the bodies of subordinates on the other hand was not regarded as a serious social or spatial violation.[157]

Respect for rank was owed to wives of gentlemen and the 'better sort', as well as their husbands. This meant that in some encounters, certain men (the young and the poor) were meant to defer to some women (the wealthy and the married), complicating the imagination and negotiation of social spatial maps. If a social inferior refused to show deference to a woman then she was perfectly prepared to punish such slights in court. Women sometimes prosecuted subordinate women for disrespect. A London case brought by a woman against a maidservant for verbal abuse in 1629 provides a good example. Witnesses acknowledged the right of the older woman to 'obtain satisfaction and submission'.[158] In other instances, however, a woman of rank might use the law to enforce the expression of deference by a subordinate man. During the early part of the seventeenth century in a marketplace in London a fisherman's apprentice knocked off a gentlewoman's hat and scratched her daughter's nose. His insulting gestures questioned the gentlewoman's status and her daughter's virtue. The association of the nose and genitalia was well recognised in early modern culture. The incident was all the more threatening therefore because it included a claim to judge the social order and an

---

154 Capp, 'When gossips meet', 197.
155 Hindle, 'Civility, honesty and the deserving poor', 54, citing J. Rogers, A treatise of love, London 1632, 237.
156 The journeys of Celia Fiennes, 22.
157 Bryson, From courtesy to civility, 98; Gowing, Common bodies, 52–81. See also Roodenburg, 'The hand of friendship', 166.
158 Roodenburg, 'The hand of friendship', 210.

implicit claim to equality by asserting a right to inflict disciplinary violence. The challenge to social authority was unmistakable and the gentlewoman had the apprentice indicted by the court of quarter sessions for assault and offensive words. In this kind of conflict out in public the social order was at least as important as the sexual one therefore in determining 'place'.[159]

Time also determined that different types of men and women experienced and perceived the street in different ways. Different individuals and groups used the streets differently at different times of the day and night. In early modern England, and especially in the countryside, street life for everyone was shaped and limited by light. Experience was highly seasonal. Warm summer weather and long, light evenings offered opportunities for convivial socialising between men and women in the streets until a late hour, while the cold, long winter nights confined people to their houses.[160] Even in the larger towns of Colchester and Chelmsford, there is no evidence until the middle of the eighteenth century of provision of even basic street lighting of the type found in London.[161] In early modern rural and provincial Essex, urban bright lights did not appear till much later. Rudimentary artificial lighting, supplied by rushes, tallow and expensive wax candles, meant that 'night was much more clearly contrasted with day' outside the capital, making unlit and unpaved local village streets and highways difficult and dangerous to negotiate after dark.[162] The hostile physical environment was compounded by the belief that all sorts of evil supernatural forces were abroad at night: witches, fairies, spirits, ghosts and demons. Night time was believed to be a physically, spiritually and morally 'disorderly' time, perilous and inhospitable for everyone.[163] Furthermore, because women, the young and the poor were believed to be more 'naturally' prone to disorder, these spaces were believed to be especially hazardous for them, which meant that the weight of formal and informal regulation fell most heavily upon them. Moreover, an increasingly powerful rhetoric of disorder that focused on 'night-walking', and which associated women's presence on the streets with sexual immorality, meant that the meanings surrounding men and women's use of the street at night could be profoundly different.[164]

[159] Cited in Griffiths, *Youth and authority*, 130.
[160] ERO (Col.), D/B5 Sb2/7, fos 222v, 58v, 123v respectively.
[161] On street lighting in Colchester see VCH, *Essex*, ix. 292–3; for Chelmsford see Grieve, *Sleepers*, ii. 247–9. For pre-industrial provision of street lighting see M.E. Falkus, 'Lighting in the dark ages of English economic history', in Coleman and John, *Trade, government and economy*, 254–73.
[162] For examples of curiosity aroused by lights and voices seen and heard on lanes or country roads at night see ERO (Col.), D/B5 Sb2/2, not foliated; D/B5 Sb2/3, fo. 139v.
[163] Wilson, *The magical universe*, 451; A. R. Ekirch, *At day's close: a history of nighttime*, London 2005, 7–61.
[164] Griffiths, *Youth and authority*, 209; 'The structure of prostitution', and 'Meanings of night-walking', 212–38; Gowing, 'The freedom of the streets', 14; and Mendelson and Crawford, *Women in early modern England*, 212.

Men and women of a variety of social types did use the streets and high-ways after dark. We have already come across references to individuals of both sexes visiting the alehouse at night or socialising with neighbours outside in the street in summer in the evening when the weather was fine. Maidservants were also sometimes required to go out after dark as part of their domestic duties. This made them vulnerable to violent attack, but their presence did not automatically arouse criticism from witnesses or legal officials so long as it was established that they were there for purposes of work.[165] Clearly much depended upon context and whether an individual was 'established' or not, a factor closely related to age, marital status and locality. None the less, the claims that women could make on these spaces were limited considerably by gender and complicated further by age and class.

Affluent middling-sort men and the gentry regularly walked or rode home from the alehouse at night alone, even if their journey could be hazardous. Their female counterparts, on the other hand, did not go out after dark unless accompanied by a male relative, a group of neighbours or a chaperone.[166] In 1630 Margaret Bragg, servant to Elizabeth Richardson, wife of Robert Rich-ardson, clerk of Boreham, told the archdeacon's court that 'Alice Bowles did send for Elizabeth Richardson this deponent's mistress ... and by reason it was late this deponent went to the house of the s[ai]d Alice Bowles and imme-diately after she had brought her s[ai]d mistress to the s[ai]d ... house the said Pennett Bowles went home with this deponent to her master.'[167] Gender differences are also apparent amongst the young. There is plenty of evidence to show that young men rampaged in large numbers through the streets of many provincial towns after dark in this period, making contested claims to these spaces that women did not.[168] It is noteworthy that official public policy that regulated the chronology of street life focused specifically upon the exclusion of young men from the streets at night. Several parishes in Essex imposed formal curfews on male youths. In Great Dunmow, for example, artificers and householders, together with their journeymen, apprentices and sons, were to be in their masters' or parents' homes by 9 p.m. A similar sort of curfew operated in Earls Colne.[169] Women as well as men were accused of night-walking, but the profound and linked effects of class and gender upon patterns of access to night streets are highlighted by the fact that prosecution was confined in the main to the single and poor, and authority interpreted differently the meaning of young women's presence on the street at night.

---

165 Gammon, 'Ravishment and ruin', 96.
166 For examples of elite men returning home after dark from the alehouse see Hyde c. Rooke (1630), LMA, DL/C/232, fos 86r–v, 89v, 96v, and Staines c. Westwood (1683), DL/C/240, fos 141r, 332v.
167 ERO (Ch.), D/AED 8, fo. 72v.
168 Griffiths, Youth and authority, 213; Shepard, Meanings of manhood, 96–9.
169 Emmison, Home, work, land, 328.

Male night-walkers were generally accused of disorderly drinking and theft whereas women were labelled as sexually immoral.[170]

The purpose of all these forms of formal and informal spatial regulation was to enforce conformity to a finely grained system of hierarchy that sustained order within a community based upon principles of exclusivity. For this reason it is hardly surprising that mechanisms of social and spatial exclusion were exercised most harshly out in public against the group that were perceived to threaten those values most seriously, the wandering poor Their ragged clothes, their pleading gestures and their filthy bodies all too easily marked them out as different. The whippings, the beatings and the banishments that they experienced at the hands of local and state authority, together with legal restrictions on their rights of passage, also confirmed their subordination and separation from the settled community.[171] Gender as well as class had its part to play in all of this. The movement of women was especially vulnerable to formal and informal censure of this kind, especially if they were unmarried or pregnant, because there was always a fear that bastard children and perhaps their mothers might become a charge on the parish rate.[172] Added to this, authority also regarded wandering women as morally suspect.[173] These different conceptualisations of the risks posed by the poor female wanderer may help explain why even though the general trend by 1700 was a gradual reduction in the numbers of prosecutions for vagrancy as public attitudes to the presence of the mobile poor became more relaxed, the proportion of migrant women prosecuted for this kind of 'crime' gradually increased.[174] It

[170] For male night-walkers accused of theft and disorderly drinking see ERO (Ch.), Q/SR 399/136; Q/SR 206/69; Q/SR 191/50; Q/SR 242/40, 41; Q/SR 355/106; Q/SR 274/9; Q/SR 222/60. For example of female night-walkers who were accused of sexual immorality see Q/SR 362/100; Q/SR 191/50.

[171] S. Hindle, 'Exclusion crises: poverty, migration and parochial responsibility in English rural communities, c. 1560–1660', Rural History vii (1996), 125–49. On regulation of rights of passage and passports for the poor see P. Slack, Poverty and policy in Tudor and Stuart England, London 1988, 94, 97, 99, 106. On rights of passage more generally see Corfield, 'Walking the city streets', 134. For an example of a woman using false passes see ERO (Ch.), Q/SBa 2/105.

[172] Gowing, 'Ordering the body'. For examples of harassment of unmarried women on Essex roads see ERO (Ch.), Q/SR 266/12; Q/SBa 2/37; Q/SR 419/61.

[173] Several historians have argued that a close and continuing association between female poverty and sexual and economic disorder explains the rise in prosecutions of mobile poor women during the period: Slack, Poverty and policy, 202 n. 32; P. Griffiths, 'Masterless young people in Norwich, 1560–1645', in Fox, Griffiths and Hindle, The experience of authority in early modern England, 146–86; R. B. Shoemaker, Prosecution and punishment: petty crime and the law in London and rural Middlesex, c. 1660–1725, Cambridge 1991, 178–82; Sharpe, Adapting to capitalism, 130–4; and Fletcher, Gender, sex and subordination, 277–9.

[174] Before 1600 women comprised between one quarter and one third of cases at the Essex quarter sessions courts. Of 124 vagrants presented to the Essex justices between 1564 and 1572, for example, just over a third (46) were women. But by the middle of the eighteenth century, the number of women prosecuted for these offences in Essex 'well outweighed

cannot be claimed with certainty that in the shaping of public policy gender mattered more than social and economic problems. But attending to connections between space, place, class, age and gender in these contexts allows us to see how some women were left more vulnerable to censure than others.

In conclusion we see that social space in early modern England was not organised towards the rigid patterns of segregation prescribed by popular culture and writers of prescriptive texts. Domestic sociability was a gendered domain and the drinking house was a male-dominated social space suggesting some spatial separation between the social worlds of women and men. But home-based hospitality was not always or simply a female and secondary social milieu. Men were prominent participants in domestic hospitality, reflecting its public importance for reputation within the wider community. Drinking houses were predominantly male spaces but not the gender exclusive arenas described by Clark. Women could and did use these spaces for sociability, constructing 'mental maps' of those that were respectable and safe to enter and using spatial strategies to exclude customers deemed to be 'uncivil'. That drinking houses were run out of domestic spaces created further complexities, constructing meanings and boundaries that were sometimes different for women and for men.

Patriarchal norms shaped perception and experience but they did not wholly determine them. Spaces were fluid and flexible and the influence of gender upon their organisation and use was very varied, altering according to context and to the complex and contradictory ways in which other social factors competed to define meaning. In some circumstances within the house and outside it patriarchal ideals defined the social character of space very strongly. At other times class and age were more prominent determinants of spatial experience. Some aspects of hospitality emphasised a married woman's status and power as joint governor, other situations highlighted her subordinate role as a woman and a wife. Out in the street patriarchal norms lurked in the background, shaping and constraining gender relations in these insecure public settings through ceremony, speech, bodily behaviour or more overtly through the use of physical violence. At every turn, however, patriarchy was complicated and variegated by competing claims of age, status and place that determined different experiences, perceptions and degrees of power between different types of women as well as between different types of men.

The fluid way that social space was constructed and used contrasts sharply with the early modern vision of the organisation of space within the English

men': Sharpe, *Adapting to capitalism*, 131. By this time women accounted for 65% of the commitments to the Middlesex and Westminster houses of correction for loose, idle and disorderly conduct or vagrancy: Shoemaker, *Gender in English society*, 272. Paul Slack has also found that, nationally, the proportion of women and children increased slightly at the beginning of the seventeenth century and that by the eighteenth century women were much more heavily represented among vagrants: *Poverty and policy*, 98, 202 n. 32.

parish church. It was widely believed in the seventeenth century that church-seating arrangements should reflect and reinforce a static social hierarchy in which each man and woman had a divinely ordained and unchanging 'place'. We will now go on to explore how the organisation of space reflected and reinforced this idealised vision of social and gender order within the interior of the early modern parish church.

5

Sacred Space

'To remove any from the place where they and their ancestors have time out of mind accustomed to sit will beget more brabbles, suits in law and prohibitions than either you or I would be contented to be troubled with': Archbishop Neile, 1635.[1]

The parish church was the most important arena in early modern society in which the finely grained boundaries of hierarchy were spatially, materially and symbolically mapped out. A supposedly static social and gender order was defined and displayed every week by the precise placing of parishioners in their pews. The symbolic significance of church seating for contemporaries is signified powerfully by the fact that when, in 1701, Richard Gough began to write a history of his parish of Myddle in Shropshire entitled 'Observations concerning the seats in Myddle and the Families to which they belong', he organised his study around the seating arrangements in the parish church. He listed each pew in turn and in order of social precedence and wrote a history of the families to which they belonged.[2] What happened in Myddle was fairly typical of parishes elsewhere during this period. The gentry sat in their finely furnished pews at the front while the poor sat on bare benches at the back. Women generally sat separately, segregated into their own hierarchical order. Additional spatial divisions also commonly separated the old from the young and the married from the single.

The concept of sacred space survived the Reformation, renegotiated and reformed. It was only the most zealous of Protestants who were fundamentally opposed to the localisation of the holy. The Church of England constructed a theology and architecture based upon compromise, careful to avoid ascribing holy meaning to material objects yet encouraging reverence and care for the building itself, a process intensified by Laudian developments in the 1630s.[3] Just as in the medieval church religious objects such as altarpieces or monu-

---

1 Bridgeman, *History of the church and manor of Wigan*, 377–9, cited in K. Sharpe, *The personal rule of Charles 1*, New Haven 1992, 397.
2 D. Hey, *An English rural community: Myddle under the Tudors and Stuarts*, Leicester 1974, 3.
3 J. Maltby, *Prayer book and people*, Cambridge 1998, 171; P. Lake, 'The Laudian style: order, uniformity and the pursuit of the beauty of holiness in the 1630s', in K. Fincham (ed.), *The early Stuart Church, 1603–1642*, Basingstoke 1993, 161–85; J. F. Merritt, 'Puritans, Laudians and the phenomenon of church-building in Jacobean London', *HJ* xxxi (1998), 935–60; C. Marsh, 'Sacred space in England, 1560–1640: the view from the pew', *JEH* liii (2002), 286–311. For similar arguments for Scotland see M. Todd, *The culture of Protestantism in early modern Scotland*, London 2002, 315–27; and A. Spicer, '"Accommodating of thame selfis to heir the worde": preaching, pews and reformed worship in Scotland, 1560–1638', *History* lxxxviii (2003), 405–22.

mental tombs were paid for by private patrons and imbued with temporal significance, secular and sacred meanings sat comfortably together in the pew. Hierarchical arrangements offered opportunity for social display but privilege was underpinned by religious principle. Seats were provided for parishioners for religious purposes so that they could listen attentively to the sermon, which formed the focus of Protestant worship. The most prestigious pews were those in or near to the pulpit and the chancel, the sanctified stage of the priest under Catholicism and an important focal point for post-Reformation Christians. Church attendance was not universal in early modern society but most parishioners of whatever gender, age or rank took part in the same service, said the same words and participated in the same rituals every week. The vision was one therefore of divinely ordained inequality but also of neighbourly reciprocity, of enduring hierarchy but also of harmony. The spiritual and the social were inextricably intertwined.

Of course society had never been quite as this vision suggested, but the records of the ecclesiastical courts provide plentiful evidence to show that ideology became even more distant from reality during the late sixteenth and seventeenth centuries. The parish church was in fact an arena of constant contest and negotiation in early modern England, as parishioners struggled to define and redefine its shifting social and sacred spatial meanings. Fiercely fought struggles over place were a persistent feature of local parochial life, reflecting tensions within a society still wedded to a language and ideology of static hierarchical social relations, while at the same time undergoing broad structural social, cultural and economic change which generated significant social mobility.

Historians have generally studied conflicts of this kind in order to understand complex and often obscure issues related to the impact of structural economic change upon local social relations. However more recent scholarship has started to recognise the significance of space within the parish church for analysis of gender. Historians such as David Underdown, Susan Amussen, Christine Peters and Margaret Aston have examined the subject of seating in terms of social and gender order, social change and gender segregation.[4] Mendelson and Crawford, and most recently Laura Gowing and Bernard Capp, have also explored the significance of separate seating for female culture, female civility and female social space.[5] Yet despite this varied work, we are still faced with a number of important questions that need to be addressed in order to appreciate properly the gendered significance of space

---

[4] M. Aston, 'Segregation in church', in Sheils and Wood, *Women in the Church*, 237–94; D. Underdown, *Revel, riot and rebellion: popular politics and culture in England, 1603–1660*, Oxford 1985, 29–33; Amussen, *An ordered society*, 137–44; and C. Peters, *Patterns of piety: women, gender and religion in late medieval and Reformation England*, Cambridge 2003.

[5] Mendelson and Crawford, *Women in early modern England*, 210; Mendelson, 'Civility of women', 115, 116; Gowing, *Common bodies*, 55–59; Capp, *'When gossips meet'*, 54, 188, 221.

within the parish church, questions which need to be tackled at a local and regional level. Most basically we need to have more detail about the impact of the Reformation upon gendered spatial organisation. We also need to find out what kinds of women were involved in spatial conflicts, of which type and why? What meaning did they hold for women, and were those meanings different from those of men? The purpose of this chapter is to address these issues by exploring the structure of social spatial contests within Essex parish churches that involved women during the seventeenth-century. The analysis begins by exploring the internal spatial reorganisation of Essex parish churches that accompanied the Reformation. It then turns to look at the way in which laywomen contested these official spatial definitions through their interventions in disputes over pews. The chapter aims to show that the parish church was a social as well as a sacred space rich in symbolism and meaning, but those meanings were not simply ascribed by male parochial officials. The construction and organisation of social and sacred space within the parish church was a highly dynamic process, and was a product of the interplay between official authority and the actions and attitudes of local laywomen as well as laymen.

A history of sitting in church

Margaret Aston has shown that sexual segregation was practised in Christian churches from as early as the third century AD, that it was common although not universal during the Middle Ages, and that space was also divided according to age and vocation.[6] She has concluded that segregation came to be the accepted form of organisation for worship in part because of general notions about the relative status of men and women as well as ancient ideas about the impurity of the female body, although by the thirteenth century the principal preoccupation of ecclesiastical authority was the sexual distraction

---

[6] The pioneering study of customs of sexual segregation in church is Aston, 'Segregation in church'. See also K. Dillow, 'The social and ecclesiastical significance of church seating arrangements and pew disputes, 1500–1740', unpubl. DPhil diss. Oxford 1990. Local studies of church seating that explore the subject of segregation of the sexes include D. Dymond, 'Sitting apart in church', in C. Rawcliffe, R. Virgoe and R. Wilson (eds), *Counties and communities: essays on East Anglian history presented to Hassell Smith*, Norwich 1996, 213–24; N. Evans, 'A scheme for re-pewing the parish church of Chesham, Buckinghamshire, in 1606', *The Local Historian* xxii (1992), 203–7; A. Flather, 'The politics of place: a study of church seating in Essex, c. 1580–1640' (Friends of the Department of English Local History, paper 3, Leicester 1999). Several studies written over one hundred years ago, as a result of the then contemporary controversy over pews, deal with the subject, in particular A. Heales, *The history and law of church seats, or pews*, i, London 1892; W. J. Hardy, 'Remarks on the history of seat-reservation in churches', *Archaeologica* liii (1892), 95–106, and 'Notes on the division of sexes, and the assignment of seats in public worship, in the primitive Church', *The Ecclesiologist* xxix (1868), 100–5. For examples of pre-reformed churches divided according to status see Peters, *Patterns of piety*, 23.

that 'promiscuous seating' might produce.[7] Segregation was common practice, organised according to Durandus in two main ways, either by placing the
women behind the men who were positioned nearest to the east, or dividing
the nave according to gender, often but not always placing men on the south
side and the women on the north. Both of these arrangements, he asserted,
reflected the patriarchal principle that 'the husband is the head of the wife'.[8]
Christine Peters has found that these gendered spatial rules were by no means
universally applied in English parish churches, leading her to the conclusion
that in England the nave was seen as a 'unified space'. We will see that in
Essex systems of seating were also very variable; yet while meaning is always
problematic to establish it is difficult not to conclude, with Aston, that
segregation was the accepted arrangement at least in part because of ancient
assumptions about the secondary and subordinate status of the female sex.[9]

These ideas are suggested, for example, by the arrangement of seating in
the chancel, the most sacred part of the medieval Church because of its association with the ministration of the sacraments. According to a thirteenth-
century episcopal statute, laymen as well as laywomen were to be excluded
from the chancel during divine service.[10] But privileges of rank soon began
to override ecclesiastical injunction and by the fourteenth century it became
common for prominent places in the chancel to be granted to men of high
distinction, principally patrons of the church or prominent landowners in the
parish. In Essex in 1511, for example, the will of Robert Fabyan, the chroni-
cler and citizen and draper of London stated that, 'If it happen me to decesse
at my mansion called halfstedys, then I will that my corps be buried atweene
my pewe and the high altar, wt in the quire of the parisshe churche of All
Hallowen of Theydon Garnon in the shyre of Essex.'[11] Other examples include
fifteenth-century 'stalls' at Castle Hedingham, Shalford and Newport.[12]

Local celebrities were very occasionally permitted to place their wives in
these privileged seats in the east end in the chancel. Widows were also occasionally granted this honour. The widowed Lady Wyche had a seat in the
chancel as early as 1468.[13] In 1584 Anne Bridges, widow, was one of eight of
the parish elite of Chelmsford who openly displayed their superior position
in the social hierarchy when they separated themselves from the rest of the
congregation on Sundays and at their own expense built a partition between
the chancel and the body of the church, with seats for themselves in front of
the chancel.[14]

But these rare exceptions aside, faculty evidence and court records from

---

7   Aston, 'Segregation in church', 244–5.
8   Ibid. 241; Peters, *Patterns of piety*, 22.
9   Peters, *Patterns of piety*,. 22.
10 Aston, 'Segregation in church', 245.
11 Cited in Heales, *History and law of church seats*, 63.
12 J. C. Cox, *Bench ends in English churches*, London 1916, 98.
13 Heales, *History and law of church seats*, 175.
14 Grieves, *Sleepers*, i. 130.

Essex suggest that during this earlier period permission to sit in the chancel was generally restricted to men. In 1611 Edmund Bragge, a gentleman of Great Burstead in Essex, and his wife Judith, were licensed to build two pews in their parish church. One, measuring 8ft by 3 ft, was in the chancel, for use by Edmund, his male friends and householders. The other, 9ft by 3ft, was on the north side of the church in the nave and was for Judith, her family, female companions and friends.[15] In 1602 Robert Cammocke, gentleman of Layer Marney, applied for permission 'for the putting of twoe smalle seates into one' in the body of the parish church for the use of his wife, 'or for any other gentlewomen whoe shall accompanie her'. Mr Cammocke sat in the chancel of the church.[16] A story recounted by William Roper in the 1590s suggests that Sir Thomas More sat in the choir while his wife Alice sat in the nave. Apparently when service at the church was ended it was necessary for one of his gentlemen 'to come to my Ladie his wives pue dore, and saie unto her, Madame, my Lord is gone', presumably because she could not see him leave.[17]

Women's access to the medieval parish church was therefore predominantly confined to the less sacred, less privileged space of the nave. Even here gender shaped experience albeit in complex and variable ways. Several historians have asserted that women tended to be grouped together on the north side of the church while men stood on the south side, as Durandus described.[18] This lateral division, they suggest, was part of a more general association of women with the north side of churches. Images of female saints were often placed on the north side of the altar while male saints were located to the south. Rood screen representations of the Virgin Mary were consistent in their northern associations and lady chapels were generally situated on the northern side of the chancel. Eamon Duffy has also commented on the tendency for these chapels to be cared for and maintained by the women of the parish.[19]

Peters argues persuasively that too much should not be made of these divisions for our understanding of the influence of gender upon sacred spatial organisation. In several churches women stood or sat behind the men on the same side of the nave not always according to an east–west orientation, and while male and female gilds emphasised gender distinctions they were organised in similar ways. The Virgin Mary was a powerful model for Christian men as well as women and in their bequests women did not favour female

[15] LMA, DL/C/340, fo. 33v.
[16] LMA, DL/C/338, fos 68v–69r.
[17] Cited in Heales, *History and law of church seats*, 69; Aston, 'Segregation in church', 246.
[18] For the association of women with the northern side of churches see Aston, 'Segregation in church', 280, and Gilchrist, *Gender and material culture*, 134–6.
[19] E. Duffy, *Stripping of the altars: traditional religion in England, 1400–1580*, London 1982, 11–52, 155–206; J. C. Cox, *Churchwardens' accounts from the fourteenth century to the close of the seventeenth century*, London 1913, 37, 143–4.

saints more than male ones. Furthermore, by the late fifteenth century in England, the significance of rood screen images gave way to the prominence of the Passion, as depictions of the Last Judgement were transferred to the east wall of the nave above the chancel arch and became the focal point for the congregation.[20] What is clear, none the less, is that men and women were, for the most part, divided for worship in the pre-reformed church.

There were continuities as well as changes to these arrangements after the Reformation. The chancel became more accessible to women. Peter's arguments about the lack of pre-Reformation preoccupation with female impurity are convincing. But it is difficult not to concur with Margaret Aston that these alterations were connected, at least in part, to the fact that under Protestantism the chancel was not considered to be any more sacred than any other part of the church and so ecclesiastical authority was no longer anxious about the presence of 'impure vessels' in this part of the building. It remained a privileged place for persons of high rank. But repudiation of the sanctity of the mass and the transformation of the altar into a communion table which could be moved into the nave, reduced the sacred significance of the east end and, by the early part of the seventeenth century, it became more acceptable and more common for elite women to sit in seats in the chancel to hear divine service. For example, in 1618 Margery Lawson, widow of Fobbing, was granted a licence to sit in a seat in the chancel of her parish church,[21] while in July 1638 Sara Aylett, wife of Giles Aylett, yeoman of Great Sutton, was also given permission to sit in a seat in the chancel of the church while she remained resident in the parish.[22] At Halstead, the right of Dorothy Etheridge, wife of John Etheridge, vicar, to sit in the chancel of the parish church to hear divine service, was confirmed in 1628.[23]

Furthermore, as Protestant churchmen began to think out the principles that should govern the organisation of a building now used for Prayer Book worship, new gendered spaces were created within the body of the nave.[24] It became established that different parts of the church were to be used for different services. The font was generally placed at the west end near to the church door, 'to signify that baptism was the entrance into the church mystical', and certain pews were assigned nearby for the christening party, often dominated by women of the parish.[25] A special pew was also provided for the churching of married women after childbirth, although there was considerable negotiation and confrontation during the period about where that seat should be placed.

These controversies were by no means sterile debates. John Walter's

---

[20] Peters, *Patterns of piety*, 21.

[21] LMA, DL/C/339, fo. 6v.

[22] LMA, DL/C/ 343, fos 38v–39.

[23] LMA DL/C/ 342, fos 54v, 58r.

[24] G. W. O. Addleshaw and F. Etchells, *The architectural setting of Anglican worship*, London 1947, 65, 84.

[25] Ibid. 67; Cressy, *Birth, marriage and death*, 166–70.

recent work has shown that clashes over the ordering of sacred space were central to the confessional politics of the period.[26] Debates over the site of the churching ceremony were related to important factors such as local custom, the convenience and importance of the service to the woman and to the congregation and, more broadly, the meaning and significance of the cere- mony itself. In the pre-reformed Catholic service the priest met the woman in the church porch and she was only admitted after she had been sprinkled with holy water. The rubric of 1549 ordered that the 'woman shall come into the church, and there shall kneel down in some convenient place, nigh unto the church door', while the 1552 Prayer Book ordered that women should kneel down 'in some convenient place nigh unto where the table standeth'. When Queen Anne of Denmark, wife of James I, was churched in 1605, for example, she made her offering at the altar.[27]

David Cressy has argued that in the end details of religious worship often appear to have been 'locally negotiable and locally variable according to custom, to local contest between different religious groups and to the discre- tion of ecclesiastical authority'.[28] It is certainly clear that in many churches in Essex a special churching pew stood in the nave. A seat survives in Ashen, for example, which until recently had always been by the church door, with an inscription written in red, dated 1620, which reads, 'This hath been the churching the mearrying stoole and so it shall be still'.[29] When, in 1620, the churchwardens of Rickling were presented to the archdeacon's court in Colchester and asked, 'Have they a seat for the churching of women?' they replied: 'there is a seate in their church which for a long time hath been appoynted to that use and that nowe of late there are certaine parishioners of the parish which doe sitt in the same seate'. They were ordered by the court to 'admonish the parishioners to forsake the said seates and to leave it to the use above or else to present them to the next court'.[30] Later in 1629 Mr

[26] J. Walter, '"Abolishing superstition with sedition"? The politics of popular iconoclasm in England, 1640–1642', *P&P* clxxxiii (2004), 79–123.

[27] Cited in Addleshaw and Etchells, *Architectural setting*, 84.

[28] D. Cressy, 'Purification, churching and thanksgiving in post-Reformation England', *P&P* cxli (1993), 106.

[29] Ashen was the home of the renowned Puritan lecturer and teacher Richard Blackerby from 1605 to 1628. One of his most famous pupils was Samuel Fairclough, who lived with him for a while in Ashen, married his daughter and then went on to become minister of nearby Kedington under the patronage of 'one of the top branches amongst our Suffolk cedars', Sir Nathanial Barnardiston: P. Collinson, *The religion of Protestants: the Church in English society, 1559–1625*, Oxford 1982, 164; T.W. Davids, *Annals of evangelical non-conformity in the county of Essex*, London 1863, 289. Sadly, court records do not survive for the archdeaconry of Middlesex for that period and no record of any incident can be found in the records of the court of the bishop's commissory or consistory court relating to Ashen at that date. However it is interesting to speculate about the local struggles that lay behind the inscription in a parish split between Blackerby, his famous pupil and the pluralist Arminian minister, William Jones.

[30] ERO (Ch.), D/ACA 42, fos 107v, 113r.

Purcas of Great Yeldham was in trouble with the 'greater and better sort' of parishioners because he 'did demolish pull down and carry away one ancient seat which stood in the parish church in the upper end thereof on the south side next before the minister' desk being antiently viz for fifty years or more ... commonly used for marriages, churching of women and christenings'.[31]

These variations probably persisted for three reasons. Calvinists in particular objected to kneeling at the altar, which they argued smacked of 'popish purification'.[32] Secondly, it was simply more convenient for the minister to take the service in the nave during Morning and Evening Prayer.[33] Thirdly, the new mother was certainly more visible to the rest of the congregation. This was very important to the woman herself. This ceremony was a public affirmation of her re-entry into the community after childbirth, a celebration of her status as a mother, the time when she was the centre of attention at least for the day.[34] There were always some women who objected, but the work of Jeremy Boulton has demonstrated the strength of the attachment to the ceremony amongst most married women. In Southwark in the 1630s, 93 per cent of mothers were churched after the delivery of a child.[35] According to the Essex records churching pews were not constructed after the Restoration but it is clear that in other parts of the country they continued to be put up well into the eighteenth century. They were part of an elaboration and clarification of the mapping of the interior of churches, which was of permanent but differing importance to men and women.

The major innovation and addition to the interior of the nave after the Reformation was the introduction of seating for the whole congregation. There is written and visual evidence to suggest that fixed seating was provided in the nave of several medieval churches, predominantly, although not exclusively, for women, especially the old and frail, and that individuals claimed rights to seats or 'places'. But it was not until around 1600 that sitting in church became typical rather than exceptional for the whole congregation. In the new religion of Protestantism, although the celebration of holy communion remained an important and central ritual for the expression of the Christian community, Scripture and sermon were preeminent.[36] It was most important that the minister was heard as well as seen reading the lesson, reading the prayers and preaching the sermon. A static congregation was required to

31 ERO (Ch.), D/ABC 4, fo. 29v. In 1616 the minister of Terling and his wife obtained permission to erect two pews, 'not having a convenient seat and there also wanting a convenient seat for women who came after childbirth to give God thanks'. They offered 'to build a seat in a void place for themselves and for such women as accompany them, possibly 5 or 6 times a year': LMA, DL/C/341, fo. 209v.

32 Cressy, 'Purification', 104.

33 Addleshaw and Etchells, Architectural setting, 84.

34 Ibid. 106–46.

35 P. Crawford, Women and religion in England, 1500–1720, London 1993, 55; Boulton, Neighbourhood and society, 196–7.

36 A. Hunt, 'The lord's supper in early modern England', P&P clxi (1988), 49.

listen as well as to look. Movement around the church became a real problem and the best way of stopping it was to secure everyone safely in a seat.

While it is difficult to generalise about arrangements across the country, evidence from the ecclesiastical courts suggests that in Essex at least sexual segregation remained the most common arrangement in parish churches and continued to be so well into the seventeenth century. Reformers, at least at first, continued to believe that it was prudent and proper for women to be placed separately from men to hear divine service and the nave continued to be a predominantly segregated space, at least until the middle of the seventeenth century. The rubric of the 1549 prayer book stated that 'So many as shall be partakers of the Holy Communion, shall tarry still in the quire, or in some conveniente place nigh the quire, the men on the one side the women on the other side.'[37]

In Great Bentley in 1604, for example, the churchwardens were ordered to place 'men on one side and women on the other side without any interruption according to their states and conditions'. In 1609 John Newton of Chapple was presented to court by the churchwardens because he 'refused to sitt in any pewe save where the gentlewomen sitt'.[38] As the judgement of a dispute over the ordering of seating in Earls Colne in 1617 declared, 'it is more decent for men to sit by [t]hemselves and women by [t]hemselves then so confusedly, men and women together or both on one and the same syde of the churche'.[39]

Some women's seats were placed on the northern side of the nave. A full description of seating in the church of North Benfleet in Essex, for example, made between 1585 and 1595, 'at the time of the amending or new making of the stools or seats', records male householders placed on the south side of the church and their wives on the north side.[40] A similar arrangement applied in the parish churches of Earls Colne, Saffron Walden, St Botolph's, Colchester, and Great Sutton.[41] There were, nevertheless, parishes where women were seated on the south side, for example in Theydon Garnon, Halstead and Little Sampford.[42] Margaret Aston has suggested that where women were seated on the south side of churches, it may have been because the lady altar had been situated on the south side of the church, as for example outside the county at St Lawrence in Reading.[43] Yet there were other inconsistencies. In

[37] Cited in Aston, 'Segregation in church', 281; Peters, *Patterns of piety*, 154.
[38] ERO (Ch.), D/ACA 29, fo. 44v; D/ACA 32, fo. 80v. Further references to wives' pews include Rickling (1629), D/ABC 4, fo. 29v; Theydon Garnon (1616), LMA, DL/C/ 341, fo. 22v; Layer Marney (1602), DL/C/338, fos 68v–69r; Chelmsford (1593), Grieve, *Sleepers*, i. 153; Great Burstead (1611), DL/C/ 340, fo. 33v; Great Waltham, DL/C/341, fos 153v–155; Great Sutton (1638), DL/C/343, fos 38v–39r.
[39] LMA, DL/C/341, fos 39v–40.
[40] Emmison, *Morals*, 144.
[41] LMA, DL/C/ 341, fos 39v–40.
[42] Ibid. fo. 22v; DL/C/343, fos 54v, 58r; DL/C/341, fo. 126v.
[43] Aston, 'Segregation in church', 280.

Chelmsford the lady altar had been situated to the north of the altar, but the women were seated in the south isle, suggesting that universal rules did not and perhaps had long since not applied in the relationship between gender and space within the parish church.[44] There were also instances where some women sat behind men on the same side of the nave, as for example in North Benfleet, where maidservants sat behind men servants on the same side of the church. None the less in most churches in Reformation Essex men and women did sit separately to hear the gospel of grace.[45]

While gender remained an important distinction between parishioners, access to and experience of sacred space was always closely linked to questions of social status. Seating within the post-Reformation church was not only used to segregate male and female groups; it also reflected and reproduced divisions created by the status hierarchy. By the end of the sixteenth century, the power to place parishioners in their pews lay firmly in the hands of the churchwardens, with the consent of the Ordinary of each diocese, and sometimes with the assistance of 'the better sort' or the vestry of each parish. After around 1570 these local elites were regularly ordered to allocate places to men and women according to their 'degrees, estates, qualities and conditions'.[46] In practice this proved to be extremely problematic, not least due to the variety of ways in which seats were allocated. Churchwardens could not interfere with pews in the chancel: disposal of these seats lay in the hands of the parson. Certain seats in the nave were also unavailable for allocation. Some were held prescriptively and exclusively of the churchwardens, in the right of a house, following the customary arrangements described by Richard Gough.[47] Other exclusive seats were held by a title gained by the grant of a licence or faculty from the bishop. These could be granted for a variety of reasons, including long-term residence in the parish but 'without any seate fitte and conveniente'[48] or because the applicant had built or repaired the seat at great personal expense.[49] Unless clauses were added stipulating that

---

[44] Grieve, *Sleepers*, i. 69, 153. David Dymond also found that in Stowlangtoft and West Walton in Suffolk women sat on the south side, but he gives no details about the original position of the lady chapels in these churches: 'Sitting apart in church', 213–24. In Chesham, Buckinghamshire, women sat on both sides of the church but in an inferior position towards the west end of the nave: Evans, 'A scheme for re-pewing', 205.

[45] Ulrich, *Goodwives*, 54.

[46] By common right the actual disposal of seats in a church belonged to the Ordinary; and the churchwardens acted in virtue of a commission from the chancellor of the diocese; in a few instances, the right belonged to the churchwarden by immemorial custom: Heales, *History and law of church seats*, 117–18; Dillow, 'Pew disputes', 44, 87–9.

[47] R. Gough, *The history of Myddle*, ed. D. Hey, London 1981. Essex examples include the faculties granted to Alexander Maskall of Woodham Walter, LMA, DL/C/340, fos 34v–36, and to John Sorrell and John Sams of Great Waltham, DL/C/341, fo. 153v.

[48] This had very flexible application. Claims varied upwards from four to forty years and sometimes residence was merely described as 'for divers yeares last past'. For examples see LMA, DL/C/ 341, fo. 27v; DL/C/343, fo. 180v; DL/C/342, fo. 127v.

[49] In 1612, for example, a faculty was issued to John Gilberd of Woodford in Essex, 'for

a faculty was only to endure whilst a person was resident in a parish or in a particular house, these pews were regarded as a piece of personal property and an inheritable asset.[50] Certain pews were exclusively attached to public office,[51] and the allocation of seats could be further disrupted, especially in market towns, by the spread of systems of seat rents charged for a month, a year or for life.[52] Some parishes, such as Shenfield, made the situation even more complicated by having different monthly rates.[53] Above all, the distinctive socio-economic and cultural pressures of the late sixteenth and seventeenth centuries especially complicated and confused customary hierarchies as wealth became increasingly at odds with social status. The intention in pew allocation was to define a fixed social hierarchy, but the reality was that communities were always changing.[54]

What is clear from the cases of conflict over the placement of people in church is that seats were significant symbols of social status in seventeenth-century England.[55] Contemporary clerics were well aware of the temporal

which seat he had constructed and built at his own expense and to the ornament of the church': LMA, DL/C/340, fo. 12v.

[50] Heales, *History and law of church seats*, 113. In Chelmsford the rules of inheritance were clear. When a 'room' or seat became vacant by an occupant's death or departure from the parish, the surviving occupants or their successors chose who should fill it, all newcomers paying 6s. 8d. towards church repairs. A male heir, provided he was a householder of 'honest condition and behaviour', inherited the seat free of charge. Similar rules applied to the regulation of wives' pews, although the husbands of newly admitted wives, excluding daughters-in-law of sitting occupants, paid 3s. 4d.: Grieve, *Sleepers*, i. 153.

[51] For seats assigned to the ruling group of Braintree, known as the 'Four and Twenty' see W. E. Quinn, *A history of Braintree and Bocking*, Lavenham 1981, 49; for Chelmsford aldermens' seats see Grieve, *Sleepers*, i. 151.

[52] Heales, *History and law of church seats*, 113. Dillow has concluded that the spread of systems of seat rents was not as extensive as previously thought. It was confined in the main to market towns and did not expand much beyond the middle of the seventeenth century: 'Pew disputes', 99–116. Evidence of systems of seat rents in Essex include monthly rents at Little Baddow (1612), LMA, DL/C/338, fo. 22v; Great Baddow (1616), DL/C/340, fo. 116v; Theydon Garnon (1620), DL/C/341, fo. 22v. For yearly rentals of £8 in Braintree in 1620 see *Early Essex town meetings: Braintree, 1619–1636, Finchingfield, 1626–1634*, ed. F. G Emmison, London 1970, 7; for life-time rentals in Chelmsford see Grieve, *Sleepers*, i. 151.

[53] ERO (Ch.), D/AEA 28, fo. 147v.

[54] For the classic discussion of the impact of demographic and economic change on systems of social stratification in early modern England see Wrightson, *English society*, ch. i.

[55] For analysis of the symbolic social significance of church seating see Underdown, *Revel, riot and rebellion*, 9, 30–3; Amussen, *An ordered society*, 137–44; Dillow, 'Pew disputes', 204–24; and Hindle, 'A sense of place', 106, and 'Civility, honesty and the deserving poor', 41–2. For a critique of emphasis upon social competition and social control within these analyses see C. Marsh, '"Common Prayer" in England, 1560–1640: the view from the pew', *P&P* clxxi (2001), 66–92; 'Sacred space in England, 1560–1640, 286–311; and 'Order and place in England, 1580–1640: the view from the pew', *Journal of British Studies* xliv (2005), 3–26.

ambition that led to aspiration to high places and large pews. In 1622 Bishop Corbett of Norwich wrote to his clergy that 'stately pews are now become tabernacles, with rings and curtains to them. ... I will not guess what is done within them ... but this I dare say, they are either to hide some vice, or to proclaim one; to hide disorder, or proclaim pride'.[56] Their power as a symbol of status is illustrated by a remark made by the earl of Huntingdon in 1638 in allegations made over an intrusion into his pew: 'in all my time, which is thirty years since the decease of my grandfather ... I was never so confronted nor such an indignity offered to be put on me'.[57]

Sacred and social spatial meanings were inextricably linked in this respect. The seats at the east end of the church within or near to the chancel were the most sought-after places amongst the rich and respectable. Bare benches were provided at the west end, sometimes marked in red, 'for the poor'.[58] Seats at the east end of the nave or in the chancel were the largest and most elaborate in the church, sometimes converted from chantry chapels after their dissolu-tion, as for example in Lavenham and Kedington just over the county border in Suffolk. It is important to remember, as A. D. Mackinnon has pointed out, that status was signified by space as well as place within the chancel or the nave.[59] John Carpenter of West Ham, for example, explained to the bishop of London's consistory court in 1672 that 'the ordinary sort of people of the said parish sitt in the said church severall of them in a pew together, but there are some of the better sort as esq[uire] Meile & Mr. Shirly, who have each of them a particular pew for himselfe and family'.[60] In Hackney in 1692 it was explained that only 'Mr Justice Tylson, Col[onel] Cash, Mr Holworthy, have particular seats belonging to themselves and their families'. Other parish-ioners, including several 'persons of quality and plentifulle estates', shared pews with members of at least six other families.[61]

The symbolic social importance of seating meant that the power given to churchwardens and 'the better sort' of the parish at the end of the sixteenth century to place their fellow parishioners in their pews was politically signifi-cant. It came at a time when 'the increase of governance' under Tudor and early Stuart monarchs had already considerably extended and concentrated the political power of the middle and upper ranks of local society through their monopoly of local legal and administrative office-holding. It also came at a time when social, cultural, religious and economic change meant that 'social boundaries were being re-drawn and proper respectable society being

[56] Cited in Heales, History and law of church seats, 181.
[57] CSPD, 1639, 337.
[58] Hindle, 'Civility, honesty and the deserving poor', 41. No examples of this inscription have been found in Essex, but marks in red 'for the poor' can be seen at St Edmund Sarum and at Croft in Yorkshire: Cox, Churchwardens accounts, 187, and Bench ends, 36.
[59] A. D. Mackinnon, '"According to the custom of the place I now live in": life and land in seventeenth-century Earls Colne, Essex', unpubl. PhD diss. Melbourne 1994, 96.
[60] Hancock c. Carter (1672), LMA, DL/C/238, fo. 201v.
[61] March c. Northy and others (1699), LMA, DL/C/246, fo. 389v.

newly and more tightly defined'.[62] These men now had the power to define
and to enforce the boundaries of belonging to a local community and those
seats which remained free and common to all could be allocated according to
their own conceptions of status and reputation.

Being a householder was the fundamental basis of a right to a seat in
church for an adult male. His precise position then depended on a locally
variable, complex combination of criteria, which reflected the varying attitudes of parish elites towards the appropriate social distribution of seating.
Consideration could be given to any one or a combination of several factors
including residence in a particular house, levels of wealth, the amount paid
by an individual in rates to the church, appointment to public office, moral
reputation, religious affiliation or, more problematically, merely the workings
of systems of local patronage.[63]

What is clear is that the status of a man was judged differently from that of
a woman. Gender, as well as rank, determined the placing of married female
parishioners at prayer. The important difference for women was that their
position in relation to one another was almost entirely determined by their
relationship to their husband. Outside the household, married women had no
formal status in their own right other than being someone's wife. This position
was reflected in and reinforced by systems of seat allocation in church. Women
could not claim seats independently, but only through their husband's position in the parish. Faculty applications, for example, were typically made by a
husband on behalf of his wife or jointly by a married couple. It was the man, as
household head, in whom the title to a seat was invested.[64] In 1618 Mr John
Baker of Little Sampford, for example, was granted a faculty for 'a principall
or cheef seate or pewe in the Church' for the exclusive use of his wife Mistress
Elizabeth Baker and her children, in part because he had 'lately purchased the
Lordship called and knowne by the name of the manor of Giffords als Stanley'
and because his father had been 'one of the cheefest men in that towne'.[65] In
1628 Dorothy Etheridge, wife of John Etheridge, was assigned a pew on the
south side of the chancel of the parish church of Halstead on the basis that
her husband was the vicar of the parish and 'intendeth for the most part to
live and reside w[i]th his family upon the said vicaradge'.[66]

It is also apparent that married women placed by churchwardens were
arranged according to perceptions of the status of their husbands. In St Peter's
West Cheap in London women were seated 'according to their husband's
antiquity and bearing of office'. In Eccles in Lancashire, women's place in

---

62 Slack, *Poverty and policy*, 23–4.
63 For a comprehensive study of systems of allocation of church seats for men see Dillow,
'Pew disputes', 96–129. For a preliminary analysis of the policies and politics involved in
the allocation of seats by Essex churchwardens during the first half of the seventeenth
century see Flather, 'The politics of place', 26–42.
64 Dillow, 'Pew disputes', 137.
65 LMA, DL/C/340, fo. 126v.
66 LMA, DL/C/ 341, fo. 58v.

church depended on their husband's rating assessment.[67] At Braintree in Essex in 1620 the wives of members of the famous ruling company of 'Four and Twenty' were seated in a huge pew on the south side of the church, and they moved places as the seniority of their husband's position changed.[68] Discussion of pew disputes in later sections of this chapter will show that women's role in the gendering of sacred space was not passive, and that they exercised a degree of informal dominance and control over place and behaviour in their own area of the church. Yet disputes also demonstrate that at a formal, legal level a woman's position in church was essentially dependent on that of her husband, father or master. In one intriguing case in 1598, for example, it seems that Margaret, wife of John Parke of Barking, was forced to suffer social humiliation because of the moral more than material failings of her spouse. She was presented by the churchwardens, 'for wilfully refusing to be placed in such a pew as was by our discretions thought meet for her, but will have a pew of her own choice'. She argued, 'For so much as her husband is charged towards her Majesty's service [probably meaning the subsidy assessment] as greatly as others, she thinketh she ought to have as good a seat as they, for so her husband willed her to sit.' The court however dismissed her plea. John Parke had been a persistent offender against moral order for quite some time. He had been presented at the bishop's visitation in 1595 for adultery with Margaret while his first wife Sara was still alive.[69]

Seating plans typically list husbands and wives sitting on opposite sides of the church but at an equal distance from the altar.[70] Admittedly Kevin Dillow found that in certain parishes, especially in the overcrowded churches of central London, wives' seats did not always directly correspond with those of their husbands.[71] He also points out that some women claimed seats in the right of men other than their husbands. Sara Aylett, for example, the wife of Giles Aylett, yeoman of Great Sutton, derived her right to sit in a seat moved from the chancel to the front of the north side of the church from her father-in-law, sometime vicar of the parish, who had built and furnished the pew.[72] Ann Gooday sat in a seat in Braintree church 'at the appointment of her father in law',[73] and some of the rented seats in Chelmsford church were paid for by fathers-in-law. Married women might also sometimes claim seats in the right of their fathers, as, for example, did the daughters of a Mr Denham of Laindon in 1618.[74]

[67] Dillow, 'Pew disputes', 137.
[68] Quinn, *Braintree and Bocking*, 122.
[69] ERO (Ch.), D/AEA 18, fo. 226v; D/AEV 3, 62; H. Shawcross, A *history of Dagenham in the county of Essex*, London 1904, 148. For further examples of seating cases that pivoted around moral reputation see Marsh, 'Order and place in England', 12.
[70] For North Benfleet see Emmison, *Morals*, 131–2; for Stowlangtoft, Suffolk, see Dymond, 'Sitting apart in church', 213–24.
[71] Dillow, 'Pew disputes', 131; Marsh, 'Order and place in England', 11.
[72] LMA, DL/C/ 341, fos 39v–40v.
[73] ERO (Ch.), TA/242 7, 34.
[74] LMA, DL/C/218, fo. 223v.

But I would argue that, these anomalies aside, evidence suggests that parishes tried, as far as possible, to arrange married women in a ranking system based upon, and parallel to, that of married men. That this was an important principle is indicated by the fiercely fought public and legal battles waged by men over the position of their wives in church. It is very obvious from this evidence that the seats of married women were significant symbols of the status of their husbands and their households. In 1598, for example, Thomas Pickering, the rector of Hadstock, appeared in person at the archdeacon's court to protest about the placing, 'in disordered manner', of the 'wife of one Jellybrond' in his wife's pew in the parish church. Jellybrond was a disorderly fellow who had been convicted of assault the previous year. The rector clearly considered the presence of goodwife Jellybrond to be a slight on the status of his wife, 'a gentlewoman born of good friends and parentage'. But he also interpreted it as a political attack by the churchwardens on his own reputation and that of his household. He explained to the court that the new arrangement had been made 'upon a revengeful mind'.[75] Instance disputes, clashes between parties over claims to a seat, very often involved fiercely fought struggles between men over the title to a seat for their wives. In Braintree in 1584 Richard Goodday of the Temple, gentleman, sued Joseph Mann of the same parish, for displacing his wife Anne out of a pew she had previously shared with Mann's wife. The court concluded that because Anne Goodday's 'husband is a gentleman student in the Inns of court we think it meet that his wife be placed in some convenient higher pew fit for her calling'.[76]

The detailed dispute that occurred in Chelmsford in 1624 shows the political and social importance of this issue. The quarrel involved two of the 'chiefe parishioners', Richard Freeman and John Wallinger. They were both lawyers, but there had always been tension between the two families. Wallinger was the younger man but head of an old established town family. The Wallingers had appeared in Chelmsford in the 1390s and during the sixteenth century played a leading role in the town's affairs. They served regularly as churchwardens and overseers of the poor and also in high office as governors of the town.[77] Mr Freeman was a newcomer. He had only come to Chelmsford in the 1590s, but he was clearly doing well, having purchased Guy Harlings, one of the largest properties in the town in 1616 for £550.[78] He represented a considerable challenge to the Wallingers, professionally, socially and politically.

Before 1624 Wallinger's wife had shared a pew with the wife of Matthew Rudd, another member of 'the better sort'. Rudd was the owner of the Saracen's Head and other property in the town. However, in January 1624 Mr Wallinger made a bid for social and political predominance by applying to

75 Emmison, *Morals*, 132.
76 ERO (Ch.), TA/42, 3.
77 Grieve, *Sleepers*, i. 128–9.
78 Ibid. ii. 7.

the bishop of London for a faculty giving his wife and children the exclusive right to sit in the 'foremost' of the womens' pews on the south side of the church, built for their wives by his father Thomas Wallinger and his uncle John Reynolds in 1593. Wallinger claimed in his application that the arrangement with Mistress Rudd was 'only on sufferance'. Although confirmed by the consistory court, the faculty was revoked in February when the churchwardens, Matthew Bridges and Nicholas Sutton, issued an order placing Mrs Knightsbridge next to Mrs Wallinger in the pew. Mrs Knightsbridge was the wife of John, gentleman, attorney of Common Pleas, and another rising star in the Chelmsford ruling elite.

Contention over the Wallingers' bid for symbolic social precedence culminated in a clash between Mr Freeman and Mr Wallinger on Sunday 21 March 1624. Both men were in the chancel discussing parish business with the other 'chiefe parishioners' when they 'fell into some speech' about Wallinger's faculty. Mr Freeman said that Wallinger had used false information in his application, an accusation that Wallinger fiercely denied. Both men were presented to the bishop's commissary court by the churchwardens for 'using brawling words in the church'. Wallinger confessed that, 'in the heat of blood rashly and unadvised' he had called Freeman a liar. Freeman also confessed that he, 'being much moved by the said uncivil and disgraceful words ... did rashly and unadvisedly' tell Wallinger in the chancel that 'he was a jack and a base fellow in giving him the lie'. Both men were barred from church until they had made 'humble submission' at court. Mr Wallinger lost his battle to establish superior symbolic status over his social and political rivals and soon after Mrs Knightsbridge joined Mrs Wallinger in her pew.[79] But the case provides powerful proof of the local political and social significance of married women's seats as symbols of the power and prestige of their husbands and their households.

The arrangement of widows was more complex. The position, especially of wealthy widows, was in many ways comparable to that of male heads of household. When seats were held in the right of a house, for example, it might be a widow, as head of a household, in whom a title to a seat was invested. Joyce Smith, widow and gentlewoman of Dagenham, was placed in a pew at the east end of the nave next to the chancel because she had recently bought a house called Hydes 'and there is a pew belongs to the house so bought by her'.[80] The widowed mother of Stephen Bussard, sometime parishioner of St Botolph's Colchester, had been granted title to a pew she had built in the parish church to be 'used and innioyed by her or her ffarmers of a farme wh[i]ch shee then helde'. Mistress Lambert and Mistress Maynard, both widows, had also built pews in the church.[81] It is also clear, as Dillow acknowledges, that a widow, as head of the household, could retain control of

[79] Ibid. ii. 31.
[80] Comyns c. Elkyns (1705), LMA, DL/C/248, fo. 401v.
[81] STAC 8/63/1; Stephens c. Bussard (1614), ERO (Ch.), D/ACD 2, fos 51v–54.

prescriptively-held men's and women's seats on the death of her husband.[82] In 1616 Mary Archer, widow of Theydon Garnon in Essex, was granted a faculty giving her title to the seat once occupied by her husband.[83] Inheritance of a prescriptively-held seat was not always automatic. Some faculty applications were granted as a kind of restoration of rights to a seat to the widow of the previous occupant.[84] But where widows' claims to privately-held seats were contested, judges frequently found in their favour, as for example with Mary Archer and Margery Lawson of Fobbing.[85] Outside the county, there are also cases of widows successfully defending similar claims in the higher courts of Star Chamber and High Commission.[86] These rich and powerful women had to face the responsibility of running a large estate as well as the possibility of remarriage. On both counts maintenance of symbolic status within the community was of vital importance.

It must be acknowledged that such similarities with men could be outweighed by significant differences. Where churchwardens allocated seats, a widow's right to retain her place continued to be derived from the status of her late husband. In 1699 'Mrs Northey wife of William Northey esq, Mrs Vernattie, wife of Constantine Vernattie esq, Mrs Eastwick and Mrs Lane widdows' defended their claim to a seat in the middle aisle of St John's church, Hackney, on the basis that they were all 'persons of considerable estates' and that their husbands had 'served all offices in the parish'.[87] Dorothy Comyns, widow of Richard Comyns, gentleman of Dagenham, defended her right to continue to sit in the foremost seat of the middle aisle of the church, in part because her husband left 'an Estate in the s[ai]d parish of 150 or near two hundred pounds the yeare which the widow and children now enjoy' and also because 'Richard Comyns was in his lifetime a Captaine of the Malitia [sic] in the county of Essex'.[88]

Widows and married women typically shared the same seats. In 1616, for example, the chancellor to the bishop of London defended the right of the recently widowed Mistress Anne Archer to continue to occupy the same seat as Mistress Carleton and Mistress Mitchell.[89] Widow Alice Sandford shared her seat in St Botolph's church, Colchester, with the wives of several aldermen. The private pews for women in Chelmsford church, built in 1593, were occupied by the wives of John Reynolds, Thomas Wallinger, John Pake, Robert Wood and Richard Long and two widows, Anne Bridges and Elizabeth

[82] Dillow, 'Pew disputes', 140–1.
[83] LMA, DL/C/341, fo. 22v.
[84] LMA, DL/C/342, fo. 209v; DL/C/342, fo. 20v.
[85] LMA, DL/C/339, fo. 6v; ERO (Ch.), D/AMW 3/143, will dated 1618; LMA, DL/C/341, fo. 22v.
[86] Report of cases in the courts of Star Chamber and High Commission, ed. S. R. Gardiner (Camden Society n.s. xxxix, 1886), 243–4.
[87] Marsh c. Northey et al. (1699), LMA, DL/C/246, fo. 384v.
[88] Comyns c. Elkyns (1705), LMA, DL/C/248, fos 393v–410v.
[89] LMA, DL/C/341, fo. 22v.

Long.[90] Just over the county border, in Stowlangtoft in Suffolk, a seating plan of the church, dated 1614–18, placed widows next to married women in the same pew.[91]

While widows and married women frequently shared the same seats, age as well as status had its part to play when decisions were made about the ordering and allocation of pews for women and for men. Nicholas Alldridge found that in the parish church of St Michael's Chester 'older parishioners could rely on a certain tribute being paid to their seniority. Freemen placed in the third row of the church had an average age of about forty-nine, while those in the fifth, sixth and seventh rows were progressively younger'.[92] Pew disputes from outside the county indicate that age was considered to be a significant factor in decisions over precedence of place. In 1618 Sir Robert Swift of Doncaster denied Thomas Mountney's claim to a seat in the parish church because he was 'of the meanest rank of gentleman' and 'not above twenty four years old'.[93] The rearrangement of seating in Earls Colne in 1617 took into account the right of aged people, in this instance women who were hard of hearing, to sit nearer the pulpit than the young. Similarly, when in 1600 a man named Clerk of Old Meade in Henham

> being of good reckoning and aged, thick of hearing, and so likewise his wife, being in one of the highest pews or seats whereby through distance of place he cannot well hear the sermon and service desireth that he may be placed in some convenient place or pew near the pulpit or seat of the minister.

A sympathetic judge ordered a letter to be written to the churchwardens accordingly.[94]

It is equally clear from court evidence that a strong belief existed in the impropriety of unruly children and servants intruding into the seats of older parishioners. In 1604 one of the reasons given by the churchwardens of Great Bentley for their request to undertake a comprehensive reorganisation of seating in their church was that, 'the people sit confusedly without order, the youth prevent the married people of their seates, wherefore we crave by cause of this sort to place the parishioners'.[95] At Earls Colne in 1617 anxiety was expressed by some of the 'better sort' of parishioners that aged women and church elders were placed, 'lower than maids and yonge women who bore no charge ... aboute the mainteynance of the church'.[96]

Ancient traditions of separation of young and old, married and single,

---

[90] Grieve, *Sleepers*, i. 153.

[91] Dymond, 'Sitting apart in church', 9.

[92] N. Alldridge, 'Loyalty and identity in Chester parishes, 1540–1640', in S. J. Wright (ed.), *Parish, church and people: local studies in lay religion*, London 1988, 95–6.

[93] Cited in Dillow, 'Pew disputes', 166.

[94] LMA, DL/C/341, fos 39v–40; Emmison, *Morals*, 135.

[95] ERO (Ch.), D/ACA 29, fo. 44v. For 'Captain Ffarr's maid's pew' at Great Burstead see D/AEV 7, fo. 8v.

[96] LMA, DL/C/341, fos 39v–40.

therefore continued to be enforced within the separate male and female hier-archies of the reformed Church of England. The young and the unmarried were typically seated separately. Servants generally stood at the back of the church or were seated in their own pews.[97] At North Benfleet in Essex men sat in the first four seats on the south side of the church and their male serv-ants sat in the three seats behind them, in order of their master's social prece-dence. The third and fourth seats on the north side, behind two women's seats, were also allocated to male servants. Maidservants were similarly placed behind their mistresses on the north side and in the rear two seats at the back of both sides of the church.[98] In Layer Marney the maidservants of the wife of Robert Cammocke sat behind her pew at the front of the nave before the pulpit and just behind the pew of Mistress Tuke.[99]

Many parishes also set aside seats or areas of the church for children. Some were placed on portable 'hanging' or flap seats in the middle aisle of the church. The daughter of Mistress Hayward of Burnham was in trouble with the court in 1616, 'For that she being a young mayde doth sitt in the pew with her mother to the great offence of many reverent women.' She had been admonished by the vicar 'to sitt at her mother's pew dore'. She had obeyed at first, but 'now sittes againe with her mother'.[100] In Chelmsford, the grammar school master had a pew at the end of the south aisle, where his scholars and other children sat on long forms.[101] At the west end of Kedington church, just over the county border in Suffolk, there were two blocks of seats rising in tiers, that were used by the children, and that date from the start of the eighteenth century. The boys sat in the seats in the north aisle and the girls occupied those in the south aisle. Facing each of these blocks was a seat for the teacher in the back row of the ordinary pews, so made that during the service he faced the children and not the east end.[102]

It is also clear that there was a ranking system even amongst the young. Private seats were built for the exclusive use of children of the elite. In 1591 Mr Edward Makin paid for a little bench to be built in Chelmsford church alongside Mr Wallinger's pew for the use of his own children and the children of the occupants of Mr Wallinger's pew, and a similar children's bench beside Mr Robert Wood for his children.[103] The sons of Mr Riches, Mr Harvers and Mr Dunkins of West Ham sat in a pew in the chancel of their church.[104] The churchwardens' accounts of Harwich record payment for the construction of a pew for the sons of burgesses in 1672.[104] In Puddletown in Dorset in 1637:

97   Griffiths, Youth and authority, 197.
98   Emmison, Morals, 131; Dillow, 'Pew disputes', 144.
99   LMA, DL/C/338, fos 68–9.
100   ERO (Ch.), D/AEA 29, fo. 284.
101   Addleshaw and Etchells, Architectural setting, 93.
102   Grieve, Sleepers, i. 153.
103   Hancock c. Carter (1672), LMA, DL/C/236, fos 198v–210v.
104   ERO (Ch.), T/P 162/9.

Men's daughters of the best rank and estate and also the maids that are to attend their ladies and mistresses were placed in that part of the fore-alley that is at the back of their mothers and mistresses. All other maids, tenants, daughters and maidservants sat in all the north alleys and lower alleys against their own mothers or dames seats.[105]

While the Protestant system of beliefs and values therefore generated significant changes in the meaning and use of space in English parish churches, the custom of seating continued to reflect and reinforce ancient assumptions about social inequality. Images and rituals were rejected for pulpits and pews, but traditional distinctions of sex, age and status continued to be defined and displayed every week by the seating arrangements in the parish church. Rich and poor, young and old, women and men, were reminded of the separateness of their social identity every time they walked into the church.

There is none the less evidence to show that these deep-seated traditions of segregation were slowly, but significantly, challenged by the new religion of Calvinism during the period. Christine Peters has pointed out that the rubric ordering segregation was removed from the Prayer Books of 1552 and 1559. There is also evidence of an opinion amongst the laity that gender order was best maintained by the placing of wives next to their husbands in family pews and that this was the established arrangement in many northern churches by the sixteenth century.[106] It may well be that Protestant insistence on the central importance of the household as the basis of all religious, social and moral discipline and stability gradually began to alter attitudes about the propriety of sexual segregation. There is certainly evidence to show that in Essex practices were beginning to change and it gradually became more common for husbands and wives to sit together in church, although, unlike in the north, change was patchy geographically, chronologically and socially.

In Essex, as elsewhere, family pews were first adopted by the upper ranks of local society.[107] Whatever the spiritual principles that underpinned these altered arrangements, there is little doubt that their enthusiastic adoption by the gentry was linked to the opportunity that family pews offered for social display. Large and elaborate seats occupied by a dutiful and decorative wife, with rows of disciplined, deferential children and servants seated behind, provided powerful visual propaganda. They were a public demonstration of social and political power and prestige in a culture where display of the magnificence of a household was central not only to codes of honour amongst the gentry, but also to the practice of local politics.[108]

From around 1590 increasing numbers of the more eminent members of

---

[105] Dillow, 'Pew disputes', 146.
[106] Peters, *Patterns of piety*, 171, 172.
[107] Larger seats could separate men and women who sat at the 'higher' end while their husbands sat lower down: Marsh, 'Order and place in England', 11.
[108] Fletcher, *Gender, sex and subordination*, 137.

the parish began to apply to the ecclesiastical courts for licences or faculties to build private pews for themselves and their households.[109] The earliest recorded grant made by the diocese of London was in 1594, but the numbers steadily increased so that by 1616 there was an average of five applications a year from aspiring Essex men of the middling or better sort.[110] As Victor Skipp has remarked they were another sign of the growing affluence of the landed classes. The great rebuilding and reclothing of England during the early part of the seventeenth century also coincided with the great re-pewing of the English parish church. For an English gentleman, or aspiring gentleman, it was not just his home that was his castle. It was also his family pew.[111]

Seats belonging to the top people of the parish were often magnificently furnished; several had fireplaces and many had separate entrances. One even had a dog kennel.[112] It also became fashionable to roof and curtain the pew, as, for example, at High Ongar in Essex. This meant, as Swift so caustically observed, that they came to look like four-poster beds:

> A bedstead of the antique mode
> Compact of timber many a load
> Such as our ancestors did use
> Was metamorphosised into pews
> Which still their ancient nature keep
> By lodging folk disposed to sleep.[113]

The doors and locks that were frequently fitted indicate a powerful sense of private ownership even though locks could occasionally be troublesome. In 1615 Mr Edmund Bragg of Great Burstead was presented to the archdeacon's court because, 'by casinge his wyves pue dore to be locked, the congregation is often troubled by noyse in unlockinge the same againe in tyme of Devyne service, by his servant a long time temperinge of the lock'.[114] Many

---

[109] In 1618 Robert Wiseman of Stondon was given permission to hold a pew, 'for yourselfe only, your children and your family and such as you bring with you': LMA, DL/C/342, fo. 120. For further examples of family pews see DL/C/342, fo. 114v, Alexander Maskell of Woodham Walter; DL/C343, fos 202v–203, Henry Mildmay of Great Baddow; DL/C/342, fo. 212v, William Bentley of Langham.

[110] Faculty applications were generally made after the seats had been built so that although they provided a useful new source of income for the church, many people clearly did not bother with legal formalities to avoid inconvenience and expense. In Bishop Wren's Visitation Articles of 1636, for example, churchwardens were asked, 'Hath any private man or men of his owne authority erected any pewes or builded any new seats in your church?': Heales, History and law of church seats, 96, 114.

[111] V. Skipp, Crisis and development: an ecological case study of the Forest of Arden, Cambridge 1978, 81; Heales, History and law of church seats, 114.

[112] Cox, Bench ends, 37–8.

[113] Cited ibid. 32.

[114] ERO (Ch.), D/AEA 26, fo. 109v. For further references to locks and doors of pews see Grieve, Sleepers, i. 151; LMA, DL/C/341, fo. 22v.

of these large family pews were also very high.[115] Some have argued that high pews were sometimes constructed for principled reasons, so that Puritans could hide behind them and avoid what they believed to be popish liturgical gestures such as bowing at the name of Jesus or turning east for the Gospel or Creed.[116] None the less comfort and privacy were no doubt also important considerations. One gentleman of Haverstock in Essex expressly stated that he had extended the height of the pew in 1616 to 'breake and kepe of the winde that cometh out of the Chancell'.[117]

These large and high pews were criticised throughout the period because they obstructed ordinary parishioners' view of the pulpit and, as we have seen, because separation of the sexes was the preferred arrangement in many parishes.[118] However hostility intensified in the 1630s when, under Bishop Laud, ecclesiastical authority began to demand that parishes make alterations and improvements to their church furnishings. One specific feature of this policy was a dislike of seats or pews that in any way interfered with the dignity or visibility of the altar, in particular high family pews erected in the chancel or near to the pulpit or communion table. This was related to a renewed reverence for the east end of the church and a revival of ancient opposition to the presence of women in the chancel, for fear of physical defilement. Bishop Wren made sure that in Fen Drayton in Cambridgeshire 'ye women be not placed in ye chancel but removed into convenient seates in ye church'.[119] Numerous directives were issued in the 1630s ordering the lowering, removing or moving of seats from these prestigious positions, and several historians have documented the fiercely fought battles between civic and ecclesiastical authority that ensued, especially in cathedral cities, due to the great offence given to men and women of high rank who had become accustomed to sitting together in the chancel of the church. At Durham the seats of the mayor and corporation, the wives of the dean and prebendaries and of other gentlewomen were removed from the cathedral choir at the

---

115 Mr Coyse of North Ockendon was reported to the archdeacon's court in 1599 for constructing a 'noisome pew ... by reason of the height', and Mr Gurney of Stifford was in trouble with the authorities in 1612 because his pew was ' built 6 foote high'. Both men were ordered to 'take down the head of the pewe ... at their own expense': ERO (Ch.), D/AEA 19, fo. 223v; D/AEA 27, fo. 20v.

116 Heales, History and law of church seats, 168.

117 LMA, DL/C 341, fo. 22v.

118 ERO (Ch.), D/AEA 19, fo. 223v; D/AEA 27, fo. 20v.

119 Aston,'Segregation in church', 250. For examples of hostility to Laudian preaching on female impurity see J. White, The first century of scandalous, malignant priests made and admitted into, by the prelates in whose hands the ordination of ministers and government of the church hath been OR A narration of the causes for which the parliament hath ordered the sequestration of the benefices of severall ministers complained of before them for vitiousness of life, errors of doctrine, contrary to the articles of our religion, and for practising and pressing superstitious innovations against law for malignancy against parliament, London 1643, 50–2, and The Suffolk committees for scandalous ministers, 1644–1646, ed. C. Holmes (Suffolk Records Society xiii, 1970), 35. For an earlier example see Byford, 'The birth of a Protestant town', 41.

king's command. Laud gave similar orders at Gloucester, York and Salisbury, with Charles's full support, and Bishop Wren issued identical instructions for the removal of seats in Norwich Cathedral.[120]

According to Dillow these policies were only patchily implemented in rural parishes and smaller towns.[121] It is therefore noteworthy in this regard that in Essex the Laudian ideal of a nave filled with straight pews, of a uniform height of about 3 ft, all facing towards the east end and allowing clear visibility of the altar led to a total of thirty-six orders for the lowering, moving or removing of the more pretentious pews belonging to the gentry between 1633 and 1638. In addition, a reinforcement of ecclesiastical discipline prompted several orders to initiate the costly and contentious issue of a general reseating, which included a reinforcement of sexual segregation. No presentments of married couples for 'promiscuous sitting together', similar to those that were made in Cambridgeshire, have been found in the records of the Essex courts, but during the visitation to Essex in 1638 by Archdeacon Edward Layfield, Laud's nephew, orders were given to the parishes of Stamford Rivers, Bobbingworth, Stow Marie, Dengie and Loughton to 'place the parishioners the men on the one side of the church and the women on the other side of the church'.[122] Furthermore, while records do not reveal disciplinary cases instigated by the bishop against the gentry over their refusal to adjust the height or placing of their pew, similar to those in York and Durham, there is evidence of anger at the disruption caused by these policies amongst parishioners otherwise 'very forward to settle others in obedience'.[123] When Mr Bentley of Langham was presented by reason of the height and position of his pew in 1635 and 1636, for example, he appeared in person at court, obviously furious, shaking a faculty from the bishop under the nose of the judge and declaring, 'he should not be troubled in the courts about it'.[124] In a society organised and governed on the basis of respect for custom these policies attacked and offended the very people on whom the administration of order depended, perhaps explaining why several bishops were reluctant to enforce them. Their seriousness is indicated by the fact that when Laud found against Sir John Corbet of Adderly in Shropshire in a seating dispute in 1637, Corbet became an opposition member of the Long Parliament.[125]

After the Restoration, the Arminian Bishop Wren of Ely continued to

---

[120] C. Hill, *Economic problems of the Church: from Archbishop Whitgift to the Long Parliament*, Oxford 1996, 179; M.E. James, *Family, lineage and civil society: a study of society, politics and mentality in the Durham region, 1500–1640*, Oxford 1974, 123–5; Sharpe, *Personal rule*, 395–400; Collinson, *Religion of Protestants*, 144–5.
[121] Dillow, *Pew disputes*, 175.
[122] Aston, 'Segregation in church', 290; ERO (Ch.), D/AEV 7, fos 1v, 2v, 3r.
[123] R. A. Marchant, *The Church under the law: justice and discipline in the diocese of York, 1540–1640*, Cambridge 1969, 77; James, *Family, lineage and civil society*, 122–3; LMA, DL/C/241–343; DL/C/322–3; Dillow, 'Pew disputes', 185.
[124] ERO (Ch.), D/ACA 51, fos 74,143,149; LMA, DL/C/343, fo. 212.
[125] Hill, *Economic problems of the Church*, 179, 180, 182.

oppose the 'promiscuous' habit of mixed seating: 'Doe men and women sit together in those seates, indifferently and promiscuously, or as the fashion was of old, do men sit together, upon one side of the church and women upon the other?'[126] These directives give the distinct impression, nevertheless, that the tradition of separating 'ordinary' men and women in church was becoming outmoded, although evidence from the courts indicates that patterns of change were locally and socially very variable. Margaret Aston has suggested, probably correctly, that change occurred first in parishes in or near the capital. But in Hackney, a parish very close to the centre of the city, segregation still remained the accepted arrangement in 1699, in part because of shortage of space. According to John Thinn, gardener,

> The said parish of Hackney is much increased since ye year 1671 both in buildings and with Inhabitants and that within ye said time there hath been severall fair, handsome and great houses now built and inhabited by good persons of ffashion and quality ... that if every person of quality and plentifull estates who are parishioners and Inhabitants in the said parish should obtain ffaculties or be placed with their ffamilies in particular pews or seats exclusive to others, the church would or could not accommodate half the parishioners ... it has been customary to place severall gentlemen with the males of their family together in one seate and the wifes or widdowes with the ffemales of their family in another seat.[127]

Ancient and customary systems of separation continued, especially in some rural communities throughout the seventeenth century and beyond. Segregated seats are mentioned in presentments made by churchwardens from Stapleford Tawney in 1626, White Colne in 1637 and Goldhangar in 1638. In Kelvedon Hatch in 1684 the 'better sort' of the parish continued to sit separately to take communion. Robert Dent, gentleman, explained to the bishop of London's court that 'there being no rayles about the Communion Table' communicants received the sacrament in their pews, 'the men cheife Communicants did usually receive it by themselves in one Pew and the cheife of the women by themselves in another'. It was also customary for the men to receive the bread and wine before the women.[128]

It is interesting to note that religious radicals perpetuated the Anglican custom of seating their members separately at their meetings. In Quaker meetinghouses similar to the one established in Earls Colne in 1674, there was a women's meeting room and gallery. The arrangement of seating within the main meetinghouse also divided the men from the women, although it is not known if they were arranged into any sort of status hierarchy. Methodist men and women also sat separately.[129]

126 Aston, 'Segregation in church', 290.
127 Marsh c. Northy et al. (1699), LMA, DL/C/246, fo. 384v.
128 Staines c. Westwood (1684), LMA, DL/C/241, fo. 41v.
129 Cited in Mackinnon, 'Life and land', 117; Hufton, The prospect before her, 416.

Over time, most Anglican churches appear to have evolved a combination of mixed and single-sex pews. In several places social status determined the distinction between gender-specific and mixed seating. In Chesham, Buckinghamshire, in 1606, only six women sat with their husbands, all in the superior pews. A further 169 women sat in single-sex pews. As we have seen, at Hackney, as late as 1699, only the most prominent men of the parish sat with their wives, while 'the meaner sort' sat in segregated seats. The same sort of arrangement operated in Great Baddow in 1638, in Chelmsford in 1634 and in West Ham in 1672.[130] In the large town church of Beccles in Suffolk, as late as 1672 the principal inhabitants sat with their wives in their own special seats, but the other female parishioners, including married women, sat apart from men.[131]

In other parishes, allocation of single-sex seating was determined predominantly by marital status. Nicholas Alldridge found that at St John's Chester in 1638 prominent parishioners sometimes, but not always, had separate pews for their wives. In addition, young single men were seated separately from single women, but upon marriage they moved with their wives to mixed pews. As early as 1524, when the churchwardens of St Christopher-le-Stocks in the City of London allotted pews to parishioners, single men and women were separated, but married couples sat together.[132] At Earls Colne, by 1660, it had become accepted that families would sit together in church. But clear distinctions were made between married and single parishioners in that parish, as they were in Ashdon in 1631 and Great Braxted in 1628. Servants and young people of both sexes continued to be seated separately in many parishes right up until the first half of the twentieth century.[133]

Gender and the politics of place

While women and men did not challenge the customary system of seating, and the values of hierarchy that it ratified, during this period, individual women as well as men were perfectly willing to contest their place within the system if they believed that it did not properly reflect their rank or degree. Recent attempts by historians to explain why women were prominent in these kinds of controversies during the late sixteenth and seventeenth centuries have focused on two largely complementary interpretations. David Underdown has argued that explanations lie in the social and economic context of the period.

---

130 ERO (Ch.), D/AEV 7. A faculty was granted in 1634 to Matthew Rudd of Little Baddow for a pew in Chelmsford church for himself, his wife and his children: LMA, DL/C/343, fo. 17v, and to Henry Mildmay of Moulsham in 1632: DL/C/343, fos 134v–135r; the rest of the congregation sat in segregated seating: Grieve, *Sleepers*, ii. 31; for West Ham see Hancocke c. Carter (1672), DL/C/236, fos 198v–210.
131 Evans, 'A scheme for re-pewing', 205.
132 Hardy, 'Remarks', 101–2.
133 Mackinnon, 'Life and land', 99–100.

He and Susan Amussen have used detailed social and economic analysis of disputes to demonstrate that contests over seats in church were predominantly 'symbolic struggles for power and status'. They argue that there was an increase in this type of litigation, especially amongst the middle and better sort of people, during the later sixteenth and early seventeenth centuries and that this was symptomatic of social strain generated by demographic, economic and social structural change. Parishioners struggled to maintain a system of seating in church that mirrored a supposedly static social hierarchy, but the reality was that population growth and social mobility meant that order was always changing. Disputes reflect the tensions that this redefinition of the social hierarchy could produce. Underdown argues that in the context of harshening economic conditions for the lower orders, disputes involving women reflected their economic, social and political marginality, making them vulnerable targets for presentment by churchwardens.[134]

Kevin Dillow to some extent supports Underdown's suggestions. In his fine study of seating disputes over a wide variety of jurisdictions, he argues that gendered patterns of litigation can be explained by the way in which most seats were allocated to women. He makes the important point that there were many more female defendants in disciplinary disputes brought to punish disobedience or physical disruption than female litigants in instance causes, disputes between parties where a place in a seat was at stake or a whole seat was claimed. This gendered pattern of litigation, he suggests, 'may well reflect their [women's] reliance on churchwardens for the provision of their seats'.[135] Instance causes predominantly focused on disputes over the title to an exclusive seat in church. Most of these seats were held in the right of a house. Since the title to the seat was invested in the head of the household and most heads of households were adult males, it was men, mainly of minor gentry status, who were involved in this sort of litigation, whether the seat belonged to a man or a woman. As we have seen, in seventeenth-century Essex there were several cases in the records where men sued other men for the seats of their wives and these cases demonstrate that the seats of married women were important symbols of the status of their husbands and their households.[136]

It is clear from the information presented and summarised in table 4 that in Essex, as in other regions, married women rarely appeared in court as plaintiffs or defendants in instance suits: they made up only around 14 per cent of litigants involved in these party and party disputes.[137] We can see that

---

134 Amussen, An ordered society, 137–44; Underdown, Revel, riot and rebellion, 29–33.

135 Dillow, 'Pew disputes', 208.

136 For examples see Godwin c. Rogers (1600), ERO (Ch.), D/ACA 24, fo. 339v; Lacy c. Kemp (1616), D/ACA 39, fo. 125v.

137 The proportions of female plaintiffs and defendants vary slightly from Dillow's findings. In the records of the seven jurisdictions he studied, a greater number of women appeared as defendants in instance causes than as plaintiffs. In Essex, with fewer cases, numbers were almost the same: 'Pew disputes', 7–8.

Table 4
Gender, social and marital status of litigants
in instance seating causes, 1580–1720

	Plaintiffs			Defendants		
	man	woman	married couple	man	woman	married couple
gentleman	10	2 (w)	1	10	1 (w)	2
yeoman	3	1 (m)	0	2	0	0
husbandman	0	0	0	0	1 (m)	0
artisan	0	0	0	0	0	0
uss	1	0	0	2	0	0
Total	14	3	1	14	2	2

uss = unknown social status
(m) = married
(w) = widowed.

Sources: ERO (Ch), D/AED 1–8; D/ABD 1–8; D/ACD 1–7; D/AXD 1–3; D/AEA 12–44; D/ACA 9–55; D/ABA 1–12; Q/SBa 2; Q/SR 5–560; T/A 42; LMA, DL/C/211–58; GL, MS 9189/1–2. An impression of the wealth and status of litigants has been obtained through a careful examination of a variety of sources including common law records, wills and ship money assessments The attribution of status is based on the system of social stratification devised by Hunt, *Puritan moment*, 21.

widows, on the other hand, did on occasion take independent action. As female family governors, the position, especially of a wealthy widow, resembled that of any male head of a household, and so when seats were held in the right of a house, for example, it might be a widow, as head of a household, in whom a title to a seat was invested. Furthermore where widows' claims to privately-held seats were contested, judges frequently found in their favour, as for example with Mary Archer and Margery Lawson of Fobbing.[138] Mistress Eadon, wealthy widow of South Hanningfield, was prepared to sue Mr John Pascall for taking away a pew that belonged to her farm, 'Giffords', and erecting a new pew in its place. Pascall was ordered by the archdeacon to dismantle his pew and make good the repairs.[139]

The unique and often complex position of widows notwithstanding, evidence summarised and presented in table 5 provides considerable support for Kevin Dillow's argument that women were far more likely to appear as defendants in office causes. Detailed examination of the records has identified a total of 104 office-promoted seating causes relating to Essex parishioners presented to the ecclesiastical courts between 1580 and 1640. Thirty-three disciplinary cases, just under a third, involved female defendants. In Essex, as

---

[138] LMA, DL/C/339, fo. 6v; ERO (Ch.), D/AMW 3/143, will dated 1618; LMA, DL/C/341, fo. 22v.
[139] ERO (Ch.), D/AEA 23, fo. 157.

Table 5
Social and marital status of female defendants
in office seating causes, 1580–1640

Status	Married	Single	Widowed	ums	Total
gentry	2	0	0	0	2
yeomanry	1	1	1	0	3
'small farmer'	9	2	0	0	11
artisan	2	1	1	0	4
uss	11	0	0	2	13
Total	25	4	2	2	33

uss = unknown social status
ums = unknown marital status

Source: ERO (Ch.), D/AED 1–8; D/ABD 1–8; D/ACD 1–7; D/AXD 1–3; D/AEA 12–44; D/ACA 9–55; D/ABA 1–12; Q/SBa 2; Q/SR 5–560; T/A 42; LMA, DL/C/211–258; GL, MS 9189/1–2.

in most other regions, disciplinary presentments died out after the Restoration.[140]

Evidence from Essex also tends to confirm the conclusions of David Underdown and Susan Amussen about the social distribution of this sort of dispute. An impression of the wealth and status of female defendants has been obtained through a careful examination of a variety of sources including common law records, wills and ship money assessments. This information is presented and summarised in table 5. It shows that the majority of women involved in this sort of litigation were from the middling sort and lesser gentry. There were some differences between men and women. The social distribution of female defendants was lower than that of men. Only 8 per cent (two) women were of gentry status compared to 27 per cent (twenty) men.[141] Of the women presented to court for disciplinary offences related to seating disputes, just under half (18) can be identified as members of the middling sort compared to 35 per cent of men. The twenty-two male and thirteen female defendants whose social status is unknown were more likely to be of lower social rank and not so easily identifiable.

Closer examination of the social identity of defendants makes it more difficult to accept Underdown's suggestion that women's involvement in this form of dispute represented their more marginal status. First of all, most defendants were men. Authority did not especially target women. Second, 76 per cent

[140] In Dillow's seven jurisdictions, including the diocese of London, office cases died out or declined markedly in numbers after the Restoration: 'Pew disputes', 193–4.
[141] This is explained in part by the regular presentment of gentlemen heads of households for the construction or alteration of private pews without proper permission from the bishop. For examples see ERO (Ch.), D/AEA 20, fo. 32v; D/AEA 27, fo. 20v; D/AEA 35, fos 15v, 45r; D/AEA 36, fo. 4v.

(twenty-five) female defendants were married. Only two defendants can be identified as widows, two as daughters, one as a sister and one as a servant. Admittedly this may reflect the limitations of the sources. The poor and the vulnerable, as Underdown suggests, may be amongst those whose status is unknown and who suffered social humiliation at the hands of churchwardens in a dignified but powerless silence.[142] But these cases do not provide proof of any sort of rigorous repression of marginal or masterless women.

Some women were from the poorer sort of households. The wife of husbandman George Hockley was one of several humble female parishioners presented to court, 'that she will not take her place according to an order out of this court by the churchwardens and the Minister'. The Hockleys rented a smallholding of around four acres in the village.[143] In 1638 Anne Biggs of Goldhangar was presented to court 'for refusing to be placed in the church by the churchwardens'. Her husband Edward was not rated in the ship money assessment of 1637. According to William Hunt's scheme of social stratification, Biggs was therefore likely to have been an agricultural labourer or a poorer artisan, possibly a weaver.[144] In 1605 the wife and the daughter of Bartholomew Bradford, a carpenter of Great Leighs, were presented for refusing to be placed according to order. The household had clearly been suffering for some time from pressures and problems generated by poverty. Several members of the family had been presented to court over the previous two years for petty theft of wheat and barley.[145] These women had clearly fallen on very hard times. As they suffered the humiliations and depravations of life on the margins of poverty, a seat in church was vitally important to them. It was a sign that they still belonged within the boundaries of 'respectable' local society.

But many more women presented to court for disobedience or disruption were married to men of some significance in local society. Marian Halstead of Lawford, for example, was presented to court in 1607 'for sitting in a stool in Lawford church unseemly and unfitting for her degree and years'.[146] When the churchwarden Thomas Cole 'requested and desyrered [her]to remove herself ... she proudly and stubbornly said to Mr Cole I will not out of this stole'.[147] Some measure of the wealth and status of the Halsteads can be gleaned from the fact that Marian's father-in-law, Christopher, had served as a juror at the court of quarter sessions.[148] Her husband was rated at 4s. 7d. in the ship money assessment in 1637, suggesting that he was probably a small farmer

142 Underdown, Revel, riot and rebellion, 33.
143 ERO (Ch.), DDDFC 130; D/ACA 42, fo. 56v.
144 ERO (Ch.), D/ACA 1, fo.100v; T/A 42, 21. This attribution of status and those that follow, drawn from ship-money assessments, are based on the system of social stratification from ship money assessment, devised by Hunt, The Puritan moment, 21.
145 ERO (Ch.), D/AEA 23, fo. 174v; Q/SR 162/50, 51, 73, 74, 75.
146 ERO (Ch.), D/ACA 29, fo. 363v.
147 Ibid.
148 ERO (Ch.), Q/SR 129/11.

or prosperous artisan.[149] Another defendant's husband, William Potter, was rated at 3s. in the ship money assessments suggesting the household was of solid middling status.[150] Mary Spillman of Great Leighs was another female defendant presented in 1605 for disobedience. Her husband James described himself as a 'husbandman' in his will of 1607. He held 'ffreeland' in the parishes of Great Leighs, Terling and Fairstead.[151] Rose Aiger, wife of John Aiger of Feering, provides another example. She was presented to the arch-deacon's court at Colchester in 1638, for her 'disorderly sitting in the church in a seat that is not appoynted for her rank or to the forme of the commission granted for the placing of the parishioners both men and women'. The wife of George Mott, of the same parish, was presented for the same offence at the same time.[152] John Aiger and George Mott were both assessed at 2s. in the ship money assessment.[153] Acts of defiance could sometimes reach severe proportions. In 1612 the wife of Robert Sturgeon, a tanner of Great Sutton, 'being quietly admonished by the minister to take her place according to an order taken by Mr Chancellor did notwithstanding the admonishment of the minister, on Sunday 20th brake down the order, disturb the congregation by her rude and disorderly behaviour and force the minister to brake off in time of prayers'.[154] Official authority would not and could not tolerate such disobedience and disruption by women or men. All these defendants were admonished by the court to take their place in the pew assigned to them by the churchwardens.

But these women were not marginal to the 'moral community'. They were likely to have been significant actors within local society, well integrated into local networks of sociability, work and worship. Indeed I would argue that the participation of all these women in this type of controversy indicates that the neighbourhood, socially and materially, was central to their existence. As such, the place they occupied in it was vitally important to them. The ferocity with which they fought to defend their symbolic status demonstrates a profound concern for local public opinion and a strong commitment to the church and to local society.[155]

Turning now to why presentments occurred, evidence suggests that, like disputes involving men, those involving women had a variety of contextual causes. Some presentments were probably related to moral offences. In Mount Bures in 1593, for example, Margaret Potter, wife of William, was presented

149 ERO (Ch.), T/A 42, 168.
150 Ibid. 234.
151 ERO (Ch.), D/AEA 23, fo. 202v; D/ABW 36/72.
152 ERO (Ch.), D/ACA 34, fos 156v, 160v.
153 ERO (Ch.), T/A 42, 236.
154 ERO (Ch.), D/AEA 27, fo. 35v.
155 For the significance of disputes for the strength of local ties see J. Bossy (ed.), *Disputes and settlements: law and human relations in the west*, Cambridge 1987. For similar, but sometimes contradictory, arguments about the significance of disputes for the strength of communal ties see Marsh, 'Common Prayer', 72–3, and 'Order and place in England', 3–8, 14–26.

to the archdeacon for refusing to take her place. She had previously been indicted for adultery with John Badcok a married man.[156]

Other conflicts had their roots in religious differences. There is an interesting cluster of cases related to use or misuse of the seat set aside for the churching of women after childbirth. As we have seen, to most female parishioners the ceremony was an acceptable and enjoyable part of the liturgy but to zealous Protestants it was 'heretical, blasphemous knavery'.[157] Where cases did appear in court they usually signified doctrinal differences and divisions in the community between the godly and their more moderate neighbours. Local confrontations that focused on these seemingly small details were far from trivial matters to the people of the time. Each small-scale incident was a significant local struggle for control of sacred space born out of conflicting but deeply held convictions about religious belief and practice.[158] Laywomen as well as laymen played an active part in these contests.

Thus in 1593, for example, the wife of John Damion 'went to church to give thanks disorderlie in her petticoate ... and satt in her usual pew far from the minister and not wherein the right seate her husband maintaining her herein'.[159] The same year Dorothy Mastell was presented by Mr Cole the rector of St Peter's Colchester because 'not churched ... she went abroad and thrust herself in the pewe wherein Mr Cole satt after he had churched George Mowles wife'.[160] In 1615 the moderate Protestant churchwarden of St Giles, Colchester, Robert Osborn, presented Ellen Brettle, wife of the godly John Brettle, because she 'thrust both the women and the church wardens in the stole where women used to be churched in'.[161]

These issues took on heightened political significance in the 1630s when, under the direction of Archbishop Laud, ecclesiastical authority attempted to enforce the wearing of the veil and the churching of women at the altar. To Laudians these details were not only adding to the honour and ornament of God's house, they were also vital to salvation through sacramental grace. To the godly they signalled surrender to popery and eternal damnation. Thus the wife of Edward Firmin was presented for 'refusing to come neere the communion table according to the Rubricke in the booke of common prayer to give thanks for her safe deliverance in childbirthe'.[162] We also find that the wife of Samuel Taylor of Saffron Walden 'refused to give god thanks for her

---

[156] ERO (Ch.), D/ACA 21, fo. 160; Q/SR 112/10. William Potter was rated at 3s. in the ship-money assessments: T/A 42, 234.
[157] Cited in Cressy, Birth, marriage and death, 37.
[158] J. Walter, 'Confessional politics in pre-Civil War Essex: Prayer Book, profanation and petitions', HJ xliv (2001), 667–701, and '"Abolishing superstition with sedition"?', 79–123.
[159] ERO (Ch.), D/ACA 21, fos 55v–6.
[160] Ibid. fo. 90v.
[161] ERO (Ch.), D/ACA 39, fos 27, 34, 45. Osborn prosecuted his predecessors for building a new seat in place of the midwife's and churching pew (fos 7, 13, 37, 85). Thanks to R. Dean Smith for biographical details.
[162] ERO (Ch.), D/ACA 54, fo. 113v.

safe deliverance in childbirth at the rayles neere the communion table'.[163] In 1638 Elizabeth Cram was presented 'for being churched without a vaile' and in 1637 Mary Judd of Haverstock was brought before the archdeacon's court, for coming to be churched, 'without a vaile or kerchief to the ill example of others'.[164] Episodes like these point to a willingness by godly women to challenge male ecclesiastical authority when episcopal policy clashed with their beliefs about proper religious practice. In doing so these women cast themselves as custodians of the settings of ceremonies closely associated with female knowledge, female fellowship and female sacred space.

It seems safe to conclude with Dillow, Underdown and Amussen that most other disputes were primarily about the defence of the status and honour which a place within a pew symbolised. But while the central role of social competition is acknowledged, the complex and gendered dimensions of these causes should not be overlooked. It is important to recognise that women had their own objectives in these actions, and that these were, on occasion, different from men's. There were, for example, probably personal reasons for married women's involvement in disputes over place. Since women's seats were significant public symbols of status in early modern local society, and men were willing to go to the trouble of instigating costly and lengthy litigation to defend the symbolic social position of their wives, it is no surprise that women themselves were prepared actively to protect the only public emblem of status they possessed. These actions also had a practical purpose, closely connected to married women's work and household position, and thereby to feminine codes of honour and self-worth.

It is well established that married women were seen to have a particular 'public' role in the protection of the reputation and resources of their household. In the domestic context this could involve violent resistance to attempts by officials to 'rescue' members of the family or to distrain goods or taxation. At other times it might mean participation in negotiation and confrontation with male officials who controlled the market in food or in opposing the damaging actions of market traders and middlemen. In the parish church, the arena where the social hierarchy was most clearly defined and displayed, it was exemplified by the willingness of married women to challenge or to resist decisions made by churchwardens and clergy which would reduce the symbolic status and reputation of their households. The ultimate aim of the women in all these interventions was the same. It was to protect the income and social standing of their household.

As we have seen throughout this study, early modern England was a society where reputation was of economic, social and personal importance and depended on public recognition and symbolic and spatial representation. Details of dress, gesture and forms of address were obsessively ordered. Seemingly small matters such as a person's place in a public procession or, most

---

163 ERO (Ch.), D/ACA 51, fo. 228v; see also fo. 237v.
164 ERO (Ch.), D/AEA 41, fo. 181v.

important, his or her seat in church, were powerfully protected. They were part of a 'shared system of meanings', which underpinned order and stability in a strictly hierarchical, but vastly unequal society.[165] The actions and gestures involved in struggles over a seat in church were read and understood as a deliberate defence against symbolic humiliation, which might cause an individual or a household significant social or material harm through loss of neighbourhood credit. Their effectiveness lay in their public performance in the arena in which hierarchy was most visibly defined and displayed.

Such interpretations take us some distance from explanations of these causes in terms of local elite campaigns directed against a vulnerable or marginal female population. They suggest that the actions of these women were bound up with their own cultural perceptions of female responsibility, female authority and female social and sacred space. This becomes even more apparent when consideration is given to causes which came to court as disciplinary disputes, but which clearly involved tensions between women. As we have seen, women were less likely than men to fight over rights to a place in church through a disputed faculty cause in the official sphere. Disputes between women over claims to a place typically came to the attention of the ecclesiastical court when one or both parties were sued for causing a disturbance in church. These incidents took different forms. They could range in severity from spontaneous scuffles to more serious assaults. In 1596 goodwife Keeble of Great Holland was presented to court, 'that when Mistress Woody took her seat above goodwife Keeble in the place where she used to sit, she punched the intruder with her elbow'.[166] More subtly, perhaps, Judith Brett of Pleshey was presented in 1637 for disturbing Elizabeth Soame in her seat, 'by plucking flowers out of her hatt and throwing them on the ground in a scornefull and disgracefull manner'.[167]

Other incidents were more calculated and more carefully planned. There are cases outside the county of deliberate mockery of a person's status by inversion of the expected social and gender order.[168] In Hutton Cranswick in Yorkshire in 1581 Robert Skelton, 'did see Edward Seval, a beggarly fellow having but one eye being full of lice and very loathsome sit in the stall in controversy straight before the face of ... Alice Warner with his face against her mocking and mowing at her and deriding of her so that she could not in a quiet manner serve God'.[169] The disregard of social rules of gender and status, the placing of a man of mean status in a woman's seat, the staring into her face and the disrespect for her personal space were deliberate gestures designed to disgrace.

Disputes could involve acts of exclusion, a symbolic casting out of the victim to try and reduce their reputation by subjecting them to humiliation

---

165 Wrightson, *English society*, 37–65.
166 ERO (Ch.), D/ACA 23, fo. 26v.
167 ERO (Ch.), D/ABA 8, fo. 198v.
168 Hill, *Economic problems of the Church*, 177.
169 Dillow, 'Pew disputes', 222.

and loss of face. A controversy that came before the courts as a disputed faculty cause, involving women of higher status, provides an example. In 1616 Anne Archer, widow of Henry Archer, gentleman and lord of the manor of Hemnalls in Theydon Garnon, made a formal complaint to the bishop of London's consistory court. Until her husband's recent demise she had sat in the uppermost place in the foremost pew in the nave of the parish church, together with her neighbours Mistress Carleton and Mistress Mitchell. But recently she had arrived at church to find that 'without the consent and against the will of the said Anne Archer and without any lawful authorisation ... Mistress Carleton had ... sett a locke on the door wherein the said Mistress Archer was to sitt and by that meanes kept her out'.[170] The Archers, Carletons and Mitchells were all members of the parish elite, although the Carletons were of slightly higher status in terms of wealth and landholdings than the Archers and Mitchells.[171] The Carletons and the Mitchells had interests in lands that formed part of the manor of Theydon Garnon, and the Carletons had a turn in presentations to Theydon Garnon rectory.[172] Mistress Carleton was taking advantage of Anne Archer's social vulnerability as a new widow to assert a perceived precedence of symbolic status. However, the bishop's chancellor defended Mistress Archer's title to her former seat and her status, reputation and property were protected.

Another, more serious, incident involved the wives of two gentlemen of Layer Marney. On Sunday 23 July 1598 Frances Cammock arrived at church to find that a lock had been fixed to the door of her pew by Elizabeth, wife of Peter Tuke esquire. Mistress Cammock, her daughter Martha and servant, Robert Beridge, were then threatened when they tried to enter the pew. Mistress Tuke and her manservant: 'beat and ill-treated the said Frances, Martha and Robert and tore a lawn apron which the said Frances wore, and violently witheld the said Frances from her pew, so that the said frances with her children, household and servants were not able to hear divine service quietly and peacefully without peril of death'.[173]

The tearing of Frances's apron was as significant as the violence inflicted here since, as we have seen, damaged or dishevelled clothing was recognised by contemporaries as a symbolic sign of dishonour. This incident was the beginning of a long contest over space and place within the church between the two leading families in Layer Marney.[174] Peter Tuke, esquire and justice of the peace, was lord of the manor of Layer Marney. The Cammocks were also an old-established local family. They were tenants of the Tukes, but also held lands in Layer Breton, Little Birch, Messing and Maldon. Elizabeth was

170 LMA, DL/C/341, fo. 22v.
171 PRO, E 179 112/617, lay subsidy 1629. George Carleton assessed at £7 lands, Anne Archer, widow, at £6 lands and Francis Mitchell at £2 lands. ERO (Ch.), T/A 42, fo. 278, ship money assessment 1637. The Carletons and the Archers were both assessed at £2.
172 VCH, Essex, iv. 264.
173 ERO (Ch.), Q/SR 143/73.
174 LMA, DL/C/338, fos 68v–69.

the daughter of Robert, the third Lord Rich, and had heroically eloped with Thomas Cammock whilst he had been in service to her father. This marriage had complicated the local hierarchy of status, since the Cammocks were now related to the peerage within the county.[175]

Some of these conflicts were merely transient tussles generated by petty jealousy, malicious gossip, or more simply the desire to defend one's place in a congested and ill-defined area.[176] Others were connected to enforcement of the hierarchy of age as well as rank in the determination of social precedence. The case of Marian Halstead, who 'displeased her betters' by refusing to sit in a seat in Lawford church set aside for the young, has already been mentioned.[177] Another single woman, Isabel Pragle, was presented in 1588 'for intruding herself into an pewe among grave women'.[178] Elizabeth Beere and Elizabeth Grove, were admonished for 'intruding' themselves 'into married women's places'.[179] An interesting case in Leicestershire involved a maidservant from the vicar's household defending her right to sit in a pew occupied by the unmarried daughter of the manorial lord, suggesting intricate distinctions between age, status and 'place'.[180]

It is probable however that the maidservant was instructed by her master to sit in the seat, and it would be highly unlikely that she would sue independently, suggesting that this dispute, like many others, could be deployed as weapons in wider conflicts, endemic in the day-to-day life of early modern face-to-face local societies. Several of the quarrels appear to have originated within a female social domain. A clash between Mrs Palmer and Mrs Cowper from Grundisburgh, just over the county border in Suffolk, provides an example. Officials in court were told that on a Sunday during divine service:

> Mrs Cowper went beyond Mrs Palmer but sat up close to her whereupon Mrs Palmer rose and sat in Mrs Cowper's lap then Mrs Cowper did use her best endeavours to remove her off and when she did so remove her the said Mrs Palmer did after that set upon Mrs Banyards arm or some part thereof and very near to her all the time of the sermon and during that time and especially while Mrs Cowper reached to lift up her scarfe and which (being out of order) Mrs Palmer did shove and in a manner punch the said Mrs Cooper and said 'be quiet'.[181]

Again the gestures incorporated into these incidents symbolised more than resentment at the discomfort at overcrowded seats. As we have seen, married

---

[175] Emmison, *Disorder*, 186; P. Morant, *The history and antiquities of Essex*, i, Colchester 1768, 323.
[176] For examples and details of disputes between men see Flather, 'The politics of place', 42–54.
[177] ERO (Ch.), D/ACA 29, fo. 363v.
[178] ERO (Ch.), D/AEA 13, fo. 184v.
[179] ERO (Ch.), D/ACA 42, fo. 42v.
[180] Capp, 'When gossips meet', 217.
[181] ESRO, FAA/3/6, fos 20r–21.

women expected and were generally accorded respect for their personal space and to jostle or touch their bodies was regarded as a serious social slight. The depositions also reveal that the incident was symptomatic of long-term social tensions between Mrs Palmer and several of her female neighbours. Two women witnesses deposed that Mrs Palmer was 'contentious with her neighbours of a very turbulent spirit and given to suit contention upon several causes'.[182]

The details of this case provide some support for Christopher Marsh's recent argument that disputes might sometimes have been as much about maintenance of communal harmony as inter-personal competition. According to Marsh it is important to emphasise that the orderly arrangement of parishioners at prayer symbolised hierarchy within community, a simultaneous acceptance of both values. Disciplinary presentments by churchwardens of people who refused to adhere to communal conceptions of order were not necessarily about power and control. They could be a function of a widespread adherence in early modern society to ideals of harmony and communal unity of effective if not actual equals before God, encapsulated in the concept of 'common prayer'.[183] Mrs Palmer was clearly one of those individuals who did not always adhere to communal values of consensus, and her female neighbours, as well as male officials, were perhaps prepared to identify and to informally discipline women like her who offended these neighbourly norms.

In similar vein, although more unusual and serious, is the case of Parnella Abbott, a widow of Greenstead. During her prosecution for witchcraft in 1599 it became clear that an altercation in church involving Parnella and Jane Dyson was the second serious breach of neighbourly relations between the two women, and was interpreted as the occasion for witchcraft. According to John Dyson, a labourer and Jane's husband, he had been present at home when, 'the sayd Parnell did misuse his wife'. About a fortnight after,

> this examinant's wyf going into Grenstead church with her yonge childe the sayd Parnell was sett there in the stole before his wife cam in and the sayd examinant's wyf thrusting in by her with the said childe the same child was presently taken shaking and quaking in fearful manner and languishing long after and leaving ytself afterwards thee said child dyed and she believeth was done by the sayd Parnell.[184]

Laura Gowing has shown that in a culture where women's words, actions and access to the law were limited by 'a whole host of prescriptions', slander litigation provided 'a way of shifting personal semi-public disputes into the official

---

[182] Ibid. fo. 21v.
[183] Marsh, 'Common Prayer', 66–92; 'Sacred space in England, 1560–1640', 286–311; and 'Order and place', 2–26.
[184] ERO (Col.), D/B5/ Sb2/5, fo. 85v.

sphere'.[185] These cases suggest that women may have used disputes over seats in church in a similar way, either to defend personal reputation or to damage the neighbourhood credit of a female rival. This would have been especially important to middling women who were likely to have been involved in some sort of trade. They might also represent unofficial efforts by women to retain some measure of communal harmony, by disciplining women who disrupted deeply held ideals of Christian unity. None the less these cases emphasise that while communal consensus may have been the ideal, the mechanisms by which it was achieved involved spatial strategies designed to humiliate, to differentiate and to separate those who deviated from communal social norms.

This argument is reinforced by striking examples of women's involvement in disputes that go beyond interpretations in terms of tensions entirely within 'the female domain'. It is now recognised that married women claimed an informal power to police and to punish sexual misconduct. It seems that struggles over seats could sometimes grow out of this sense of communal authority and responsibility. A good example is a pew dispute in Hursley, Hampshire, between Elizabeth Eyers and Robert Hellier which was, according to witnesses, part of an ongoing conflict. A cucking stool had already been placed outside Hellier's house and cuckold's horns hung over his door.[186]

A dispute at Colchester between the wife of William Rogers, yeoman and keeper of Colchester gaol, and the wife of the 'chirugion', Marcel Godwin, provides another example. One Sunday in 1600 after divine service in St Giles' church, Rogers's wife came to Godwin's wife and her daughter sitting in their pew, 'and with vehemency bade them come out, or else I will pull you out'. Later in the churchyard Goodwife Rogers accused Mistress Godwin of being a 'gossip and flirt', and the wife of William Pydd completed the insult by calling her a 'butcher's curr, butcher's dog and crouchback'.[187] The Godwins were already involved in a very public conflict with the officials of the parish and their wives over a disputed paternity suit. Earlier that year, Alice Bradley, servant of Widow Swetyng, had given birth to an illegitimate child. During the delivery Goodwife Pydd had pressured Alice to name the father and she had accused George, son of Marcel Godwin. But on examination before the borough court, George Godwin denied the charges, and his father supported his testimony.[188] In the context of a parish-based system of poor relief under severe strain due to depression in the cloth industry and growing problems of poverty, this question of paternity had implications for the economic as well as the moral welfare of the community. The prospect of another newborn infant being charged to the parish was extremely unwelcome. When officials

[185] L. Gowing, 'Language, power and the law', in Kermode and Walker, *Women, crime and the courts*, 43
[186] Dillow, 'Pew disputes', 222.
[187] ERO (Ch.), D/ACA 24, fo. 339v; D/ACW/7/125; Assize calendar 35/57/T/32; 35/59/T19.
[188] ERO (Col.), D/B5 Sb2/6, fos 1v–2, 5v, 7v.

failed to make George Godwin financially and legally responsible for his actions, the wives of the parish were prepared to intervene informally to exclude symbolically and to shame the household that threatened the good name, material well-being and good order of their neighbourhood. Although the public confrontation was fought out within the female sphere, its purpose was larger and more pervasive. The wives of the parish intended to put pressure on the men of the Godwin family to conform to community demands by challenging the single most important symbol of status, credit and political prestige that the household possessed.

Another dispute suggests female involvement in local religious factional conflict. In 1638, for example, the court was asked to make a judgement 'touching the differences between [Mistress Guyon] and the wife of Edward Potter about their sitting in the church'. The court ordered that 'Mrs. Guyon shall have the upper hand and sitt next the arch & [Potter's wife] admonished to give her place'.[189] Mistress Guyon was the wife of Robert Guyon, the rector of White Colne, who was charged with 'scandalous' life and doctrine in 1644, and soon after sequestered from his living. Two members of the Potter family were amongst the group of 'godly' parishioners who deposed against Guyon, claiming that their rector was 'distempered in his braine'.[190] The altercation between the two women was likely to have been a deliberate attempt by Potter's wife to denigrate and humiliate Mistress Guyon, as part of a wider and longer local campaign of disruption directed by a group of dissatisfied parishioners against an unpopular minister.

In conclusion, therefore, we see that the early modern parish church was a highly dynamic space and the influence of gender upon patterns of control over the construction and maintenance of its social and sacred meanings was complex. The social organisation of space within the parish church affirmed a hierarchical system that rendered women subordinate. At the same time it also divided and privileged the married from the single, the old from the young and the 'better sort' from the poor. Keenly conscious of these fine social distinctions which defined place within their own symbolic social hierarchy, married women of the middling and better sort were prepared to intervene on occasion to enforce and occasionally to modify the system according to their own definitions of what constituted social and sacred order. In doing so, middling-sort married women, as well as men, became engaged at an informal level in the ordering of sacred space, the local politics of social relations and the wider negotiations of ecclesiastical power.

The notable absence from the records of disciplinary disputes involving women after 1660 suggests that the social role of the parish church, at least for a certain section of female local society, changed as systems of segregation gradually died out. Reformation reverence for the institution of marriage meant that over time it became common practice for husbands and wives

189 ERO (Ch.), D/ACA 53, fo. 108v.
190 BL, MS Add. 5829, fo. 24v.

to sit together in church, even if initially this was only amongst the elite. Eventually gender-specific seating was generally only assigned to the young and the unmarried. This age-specific system of segregation reflected and reinforced the lower position of servants and children in the social order. It also expressed the higher position in the social hierarchy of the wife and mistress. At the same time family pews expressed and enhanced the patriarchal power of the husband over his wife as well as his household. Space in the reformed church reflected and reproduced a system that rendered women subordinate. The disappearance of a separate social and spatial terrain meant the loss of probably the best public location for developing altercations with female adversaries. A focal point of middling-sort married women's social lives, over which they had had some informal control, had been lost.

Conclusion

This study has explored how individual women and men interpreted patriarchal notions of gendered space in the course of daily life. It has shown that space was vitally important for the marking out and maintaining of the hierarchy that sustained social and gender order in early modern England. It was not simply a passive backdrop to a social system that had structural origins elsewhere. The way people used space reflected, and in turn had effects back upon, the way social relations were expressed, reaffirmed, challenged or changed. In the sixteenth and seventeenth centuries status and gender were displayed, physically and spatially, every moment of the day. A person's place at table, the bed on which they slept, the pew that they occupied in church, their dress, gesture, posture and modes of address made systems of social and gender order visible and real. All were minutely measured to make sure that individuals were accorded the appropriate respect required to sustain a social system based upon principles of hierarchy and locality, deference and difference. However, the spatial and social system that was mapped out was highly complex, dynamic and varied according to context. Contradictions within, as well as between, prescription and practice created inconsistencies. Time, context and the intersection of gender with other social factors, such as age and status, also complicated social and spatial codes.

Conduct writers often defined gender in spatial terms, but their discussions displayed significant tensions and contradictions about where precisely to draw the boundaries between male and female space. While attempting to establish the irrational and inferior character of femininity that rendered women unfit for activities outside the home, advice manuals also acknowledged the limits of this patriarchal model for the practice of marital roles. It was acknowledged that men worked at home and women performed productive and 'public' activities outside when necessary. Women were expected to be competent assistants in their husbands' businesses, to buy and sell produce at the market, to be good neighbours and dutiful parishioners. These tensions between competing expectations of female behaviour meant that attitudes to women's use of space were very flexible. Presence in almost any space could be justified so long as it could be demonstrated that it was part of their work or their domestic duties.

Inconsistencies within patriarchal spatial models also enabled women to explore alternative social and spatial identities. For instance, while male moralists repeatedly restated the necessity for women to stay at home in order to protect their chastity, advice writers also emphasised women's obligation to be neighbourly. Paradoxically, female conformity to conventional codes thus provided them with a way of contesting patriarchal norms, constructing female status in terms of 'public' and communal action rather than private and passive subordination.

In part because of these complexities, the influence of patriarchal precepts upon the everyday organisation and use of space was very uneven. In some circumstances ideology was very prominent. Normative notions of propriety, for example, fundamentally shaped access to the drinking house, even if processes of inclusion and exclusion sometimes varied along lines of status and to a lesser extent age, as well. As a consequence, sociability could be patterned differently between the sexes, even if it was not mutually exclusive. Out in public, although men and women intermingled, experience was not equal. Female access was restricted and differentiated by time, ceremony, speech and bodily behaviour, although experience was complicated consistently by distinctions of age and status. Most seriously, in dysfunctional households men invoked patriarchal prerogatives of domestic spatial control to justify violence or confinement of women within their own homes.

In other contexts, however, normative notions were far les influential, or even irrelevant. For instance, the model of separate spheres influenced the working activities and locations of men and women, but it did not wholly determine them. Precepts were always complicated and counterbalanced by the demands of practical necessity. Women and men had to be adaptable to any circumstance that they encountered and were relatively unconstrained by patriarchal notions of propriety or hierarchy when it came to decisions about the organisation of space for work.

Understanding of the social construction of space also requires recognition that gender was not the only, or always the most prominent, social factor that determined spatial meaning. Anomalies in the patriarchal spatial system were created by the widely held belief in early modern England that principles of social and spatial order were not simply underpinned by the gender hierarchy. Distinctions of age, marital and social status had to be taken into account as well. Conflicts within the gender system were created by these principles, because they placed some women (the older and the married) in positions of precedence over some men (the young and the poor). As a consequence, differences in spatial experience were sometimes more pronounced between different categories of women and men than between them. For example, within the household, law and ideology invested overall authority in the husband and master, but advice literature delineated a complex pattern of domestic authority that delegated considerable power to the mistress. Her superior position in the household hierarchy in relation to other subordinates of both sexes, was defined and displayed spatially, by the degree of power and control that she wielded over the use of the house and its rooms, the seating arrangements at table, the quality and quantity of food that she ate and the bed and room in which she slept. Systems of dress, gesture and modes of address also demanded display of deference to married women by the young and socially inferior of both sexes, reflecting and reinforcing complex (and often conflicting) forms of authority within the local community as well as in the home.

We see, therefore, that women as well as men occupied a variety of positions within the hierarchies that ordered early modern society, and performed a multiplicity of roles in a variety of spaces that enhanced and inhibited their ability to exercise agency, depending on the context. For example, normative notions of gendered propriety shaped patterns of use of domestic space for sociability, especially where entertainment of the opposite sex was concerned. In other circumstances, however, home-based hospitality offered the opportunity for female agency. In non-conforming households, for instance, women's role in domestic management and responsibility for the organisation of domestic commensality could empower them, in semi-public ways, as custodians of clandestine worship. Within the church, seating arrangements materially represented and reinforced the secondary status of the female sex. The orderly arrangement of pews according to rank, on the other hand, meant that as wives, married women had an important public role in the representation and defence of the superior symbolic position of their households within the hierarchy of social status. More generally, their accepted role as parishioners gave married women of the middling sort an informal role in local negotiations and confrontations with neighbours and official ecclesiastical authority over the ordering and meaning of space within the most important 'public' arena in which social hierarchy was defined and displayed.

Understanding of the dynamic, complex, uneven and unstable influence of patriarchy upon the organisation, imagination and experience of space, has important implications for approaches to gender relations in early modern England. It helps to bridge interpretative oppositions between studies that stress the exercise of exclusionary patriarchy and interpretations which emphasise that patriarchal theory coexisted with a more permissive reality that offered considerable scope for female agency.[1] Space reflected and reinforced the whole range of these interpretations in different contexts at different times, exposing the contradictions and varieties within the early modern social and gender system created by inconsistencies within patriarchal ideology itself, as well as between ideology and social practice.

Focus on space also raises additional doubts about the utility of the separate spheres analogy and particularly the use of binary oppositions of male/female and public/private to describe gender relations and their changes in this period. The model of 'separate spheres' still plays an important structural role in arguments about long-term changes in gender relations in early modern society. Discussions have suggested that developing concepts of gender difference, from a hierarchy to notions of incommensurability, were associated with the spatial separation of the sexes, whereby women were progressively margin-

---

[1] For discussions that emphasise male domination see Stone, *The family, sex and marriage*, and J. M. Bennett, 'Feminism and history', *G&H* i (1989), 251–72. For proponents of the second interpretation see Capp, *'When gossips meet'*; Gowing, *Domestic dangers*, and *Common bodies*.

alised and enclosed within the private sphere of the home.[2] New research is beginning to dismantle these accounts and to recover a more complex reality, as well as chronology, within patterns of continuity and change.[3] A further corrective to these arguments is provided by consideration of the shifting dynamic of spatial experience.

The boundary between public space and private space was very blurred in seventeenth-century England. 'Private' domestic spaces had 'public' functions. Commercial businesses were run out of rooms or shops attached to 'private' houses. Economic necessity, together with norms of neighbourly reciprocity, meant that domestic spaces had to be highly permeable arenas, constantly open to intrusion by neighbours, customers or paying guests. Putatively 'private' activities had public qualities. A central feature of domestic sociability was its preoccupation with 'public' matters. Moreover, space could become more or less private, or more or less public, depending on the context. Rooms within drinking houses, for example, could sometimes be used by patrons and at other time set aside for the sole use of family members.

Space was not static but fluid and highly dynamic. Its meaning was constantly shifting. Short-term, gendered use of space could alter according to the time of day or the season of the year, through to specific occasions such as childbirth. Festive time was also important. Special celebrations, for instance churchings, could overthrow an underlying pattern of gendered space, not least in the alehouse. At other times, notably out in the street at night, space could become more male configured. All of these shifting dynamics were complicated by the intersection of gender with other aspects of social identity. The presence of interlocking factors of time, status and age that enlarged the scope for some women, by the same token meant that other women, who lacked some or all of these advantages, were more constrained.

Recognition of these complexities requires a revision of interpretations of the gendered meaning of changes in the organisation of space over time. The clearest transformation that took place was a move towards integration rather than separation of the sexes within the parish church. Family pews began to replace systems of segregated seating amongst the more affluent, married members of the parish by the seventeenth century. Paradoxically, it was spatial integration of the sexes that reflected and reinforced a new emphasis on the family and principles of patriarchy. As a consequence an important 'public arena' for the negotiation of disputes between female adversaries, over which middling married women had had some informal control, had been lost.

In most other contexts, however, patterns of continuity and change were more complex and their meaning dynamic and contradictory. During the late seventeenth century more affluent middling householders reorganised their

---

[2] Laqueur, *Making sex*.

[3] Gowing, *Common bodies*, 17–29; K. Harvey, 'The substance of sexual difference: change and persistence in representations of the body in eighteenth-century England', *G&H* xiv (2002), 202–23. See also studies listed in ch. 4 n. 2 above.

houses in order to create specialised spaces for different functions. The multi-functional hall was replaced by a kitchen and service rooms used for cooking, along with a parlour used for entertaining. Bedrooms were also built upstairs. However, interpretations of the meaning of these developments that rely on conventional, dichotomous models of public/private and male/female to argue for a progressive sharpening of the division between male and female space and a corresponding decline in female status fail to capture the complexity of the influence of gender upon changes in spatial patterning. Room use was not set in stone. Almost all spaces remained accessible to everyone and continued to be multifunctional; their social character changed according to use at different times of the day. In general changes in the way that domestic space was used and organised reflected and reinforced a sharper difference in the distribution of privileges between individuals of different rank more than between men and women. In houses large enough to have more than one room for eating and separate bedrooms for servants, there was an increasing spatial separation between servants and their masters and mistresses for the everyday activities of eating and sleeping. The presence of closets and studies that could be locked also suggests an increasing desire and ability on the part of both household governors to separate themselves from their servants (or their spouses), if they so wished.

The intersections of gender, normative literature, time and other elements of social identity were so subtle that they complicate and undermine meaningful generalisation about the consequences of patterns of continuity and/or change in the organisation of space, for the distribution of power between the sexes. They emphasise the inadequacy of earlier analysis of gendered power relations and their changes, framed around a binary model of public/private, male/female, which failed to address these complexities within the construction and experience of gender and authority. Male and female status and power cannot be defined simply because it was so complex. It is not the purpose of this study to minimise the influence of patriarchy within early modern society, but it does suggest that its articulation was often uneven and contradictory. What is required is further research into the spaces where we see individual men and women, on a daily basis, negotiating the tensions created by the complementary and competing definitions of masculinity and femininity that existed in tandem with patriarchal codes. We also need further investigation into the interplay between gender and other social factors, to see how ordinary women (and men) negotiated, contested and occasionally challenged the terms of their subordination.

Bibliography

Unpublished primary sources

Chelmsford, Essex Record Office

Archdeaconry of Colchester
D/ACA 1–55   Act books, 1540–1666
D/ACD 1–7   Depositions, 1587–1641
D/ACV 5   Visitation, 1633
D/ACW/7/125 Will, 1605

Archdeaconry of Essex
D/AEA 12–44 Act books, 1580–1665
D/AED 1–10   Depositions, 1576–1630
D/AEV 3   Visitations, 1591–1603
D/AEV 7   Visitation, 1638

Archdeaconry of Middlesex
D/AMW 3/143 Will, 1618

Bishop of London's commissary in Essex and Hertfordshire
D/ABA 1–12   Act books, 1612–70
D/ABC 1–8   Causes, 1618–65
D/ABD 1–8   Depositions, 1618–42
D/AXD 1–3   Depositions, Essex and Colchester, 1631–1740

Estate and family records
DDDFC 130   Deed of Snoden Farm, Debden, 1618

Maldon Borough Records
D/B/3/1/5–10   Court books, 1557–1623

Quarter sessions records
Q/SBa 2   Quarter sessions bundles: main series, 1621–89
Q/SBb   Quarter sessions bundles: later series, 1727
Q/SR 5–560   Quarter sessions rolls, 1580–1714

Transcripts.
T/A 42   Calendar of Essex ship money assessments, 1637
T/A 427/1–7 Calendar of Essex lay subsidy roll, 1524 (PRO, E 179/108/151)
T/P 162/9   Harwich churchwardens' accounts, 1672

Colchester, Essex Record Office

Colchester borough records
D/B5 Sb2/2–9 Books of examinations and recognizances, 1573–1687
D/B5 Sr52   Quarter sessions roll, 1690

Ipswich, East Suffolk Record Office

Archdeaconry of Suffolk
FAA/3/6   Allegations and depositions, 1660–3

London, British Library
MS Add. 5829

London, Guildhall Library
MS 9189/1   Bishop of London's consistory court depositions, 1622–4, 1627–8

London, Metropolitan Archive

Bishop of London's consistory court
DL/C/13,14,16, 20 Act books, instance, 1605–9, 1609–11, 1613–16, 1634–7
DL/C/211–58   Depositions, 1586–1740
DL/C/322–43   Act books, office, 1629–40
DL/C/338–43   Vicar general's books, 1601–40

London, The National Archive

Public Record Office
E 134   Court of Exchequer
E 179   Lay subsidy rolls, various dates.
REQ 2/26–424   Court of Requests
STAC 8   Court of Star Chamber proceedings, James I

Microfiche

'Records of an English village: Earls Colne, 1400–1750', ed. A. Macfarlane and others, Cambridge 1980–1

Published primary sources

The autobiography and personal diary of Dr Simon Foreman, the celebrated astrologer, from A.D. 1552 to A.D. 1602, ed. J. O. Halliwell, London 1895
Autobiography of Thomas Wythorne, ed. J. Osborn, Oxford 1961
The autobiography of William Stout of Lancaster, 1665–1752, ed. J. D. Marshall (Chetham Society, 3rd ser. xiv, 1967)
Calendar of state papers, domestic series, of the reign of Charles I, 1625–1649, ed. J. Bruce and W. D. Hamilton, Nendeln 1967

The complete works of Samuel Rowlands, ed. S. J. Herrtage, Glasgow 1880

Cox, J. C., *Churchwardens accounts from the fourteenth century to the close of the seventeenth century*, London 1913

The description of England by William Harrison 1587, ed. G. Edelen, London 1968

The diary of John Manningham of the Middle Temple, 1602–1603, ed. R. P. Sorlien, Hanover, NH 1976

The diary of Ralph Josselin, 1616–1683, ed. A. Macfarlane, Oxford 1976

The diary of Roger Lowe of Ashton-in-Makefield, Lancashire, 1663–74, ed. W. Sachse, London 1938

The diary of Samuel Pepys, ed. R. C. Latham and W. Matthews, London 1970

Early Essex town meetings: Braintree, 1619–1636, Finchingfield, 1626–1634, ed. F. G. Emmison, London, 1970

Emmison, F. G., *Elizabethan life: disorder*, Chelmsford 1971

———— *Elizabethan life: morals and the church courts*, Chelmsford 1973

———— *Elizabethan life: home, work and land*, Chelmsford 1991

Eyre, A., 'A dyurnall or catalogue of all my actions', in *Yorkshire diaries and autobiographies in the seventeenth and eighteenth centuries*, ed. C. Jackson (Surtees Society lxx, 1877)

The farming and memorandum books of Henry Best of Elmswell, 1642, ed. D. Woodward, London 1984

Fuller, T., *The holy state and the profane state* (Cambridge 1624), ed. M. Walten, New York 1938

Gough, R., *The history of Myddle*, ed. D. Hey, London 1981

The illustrated journeys of Celia Fiennes, ed. C. Morris, London 1982

The justicing notebook of Henry Norris and the Hackney petty sessions book, ed. R. Paley (London Records Society, 1991)

The life of Adam Martindale, ed. R. Parkinson (Chetham Society, 1845)

Morant, P., *The history and antiquities of the county of Essex*, Colchester 1763

The notebook of Robert Doughty, 1662–65, ed. J. Rosenheim (Norfolk Record Society, 1989–91)

The Pepys ballads, ed. W. G. Day, Cambridge 1987

Records of the borough of Nottingham, IV: 1625–1702, ed. W. H. Stevenson, London 1900

Report of cases in the courts of Star Chamber and High Commission, ed. S. R. Gardiner (Camden Society n.s. xxxix, 1886)

The Rev. Oliver Heywood BA, 1630–1702: his autobiography, diaries, anecdote and event books, illustrating the general and family history of Yorkshire and Lancashire in three volumes with illustrations, ed. J. H. Turner, Brighouse–Bingley 1881–5

The Roxburghe ballads, ed. W. Chappell and J. Ebsworth, London 1866–99

A series of precedents and proceedings in criminal causes, extending from the years 1475 to 1640: extracted from the act books of the diocese of London, ed. W. H. Hale, Edinburgh 1847; intro. R. W. Dunning, Edinburgh 1973

Sermons by Hugh Latimer, ed. G. E. Corrie (Parker Society xxii, 1844)

Smith T., *De republica anglorum: a discourse on the commonwealth of England*, ed. L. Alston, Cambridge 1906

Suffolk committees for scandalous ministers, 1644–1646, ed. C. Holmes (Suffolk Records Society xiii, 1970)

'Thomas Baskerville's journeys in England, Temp. Car 11', HMC, *The manuscripts of his grace the duke of Portland: preserved at Welbeck Abbey*, ii, London 1893

Two East Anglian diaries, 1641–1729: Isaac Archer and William Coe, ed. M. Storey
(Suffolk Records Society xxxvi, 1994)
'William Holcroft his booke': local office-holding in late Stuart Essex, ed. J. A. Sharpe,
Chelmsford 1986

Contemporary books and articles

Allestree, R., The ladies calling, Oxford 1693
Anon., Certain sermons or homilies appointed to be read in churches in the time of
Queen Elizabeth, London 1687
Anon, Tittle-tattle: or, the several branches of gossipping, London 1603
Becon, T., The worckes of Thomas Becon which he hath hitherto made and published,
with diverse other newe bookes added to the same, heretofore never set forth in print,
divided into the tomes or parts and amended this present [sic] of our Lord 1564;
perused and allowed, according to thorder appointed in the Quenes maiesties injunc-
tions, London 1564
Cleaver, R., A briefe explanation of the whole booke of the proverbs of Saloman,
London 1615
Coke, Sir E., An exact abridgement in English of the eleven books of reports of the
learned Sir Edward Coke, knight, late lord chiefe justice of England, and the councell
of estate to his majesty, King James, London 1651
De Courtin, A., The rules of civility; or, certain ways of deportment observed amongst
all persons of quality upon several occasions, London 1685
De Vives, Juan Luis, A very fruitfull and pleasant booke, called the instruction of a
Christian woman, made first in latin, by the right famous cleark M. Lewes Vives,
and translated out of Latin into Englishe, by Richard Hyde, London 1585
Dekker, T., Lanthorne and candle-light, London 1608
Dod J. and R. Cleaver, A godlie forme of householde government: for the ordering of
private families, according to the direction of Gods word, London 1612
Gataker, T., Marriage duties briefely couched togither, London 1620
——— A good wife's God's gift: and a wife indeed: two marriage sermons, London
1623
Gouge,W., Of domesticall duties: eight treatises, London 1622
Griffith, M., Bethel: or, a forme for families, London 1663
Heales, W., An apologie for women, London 1609
Hieron, S., 'The dignitie of the Scripture, togither with the indignitie which the
vnthankfull world offereth thereunto', in All the sermons of Samuel Hieron,
minister of Gods word, at Modbury in Devon, London 1614
Jackson, A., The pious prentice, or the prentices piety, London 1640
Leigh, D., The mother's blessing, London 1627
Locke, J., Two treatises of government, ed. P. Laslett, Cambridge 1988
Markham, G., Cheap and good husbandry, London 1653
Mayo, R., Present for servants, London 1693
M. R., The mother's counsel; or, live within compasse: being the last will and testament
to her dearest daughter, London 1630
Phiston, W., The schoole of good manners, London 1609
Rich, B., My ladies looking glasse: wherein may be discerned a wise man from a fool, a
goode women from a bad, London 1616
Rogers, D., Matrimoniall honour, London 1642

Smith, H., A preparative to marriage, London 1591

Stubbes, P., The anatomie of abuses: contayning, a discoverie, or briefe summarie of such notable vices and imperfections, as now reigne in many Christian countreyes of the worlde: but (espectiallie) in a verie famous Ilande called Ailgna: together, with most fearefull examples of Gods judgementes, executed vpon the wicked for the same, as well in Ailgna of late, as in other places, elsewhere, London 1583

Tuke, T., A discourse against painting and tincturing of women: wherein the abominable sinnes of murther and poysoning, pride and ambition, adultery and witchcraft, are set foorth and discovered, London 1616

Walker, A., The holy life of Mrs Elizabeth Walker, London 1690

Whately,W., A bride-bush or a wedding sermon: compendiously describing the duties of married persons: by performing whereof, marriage shall be to them a great helpe, which now finde it a little hell, London 1617

White, J., The first century of scandalous, malignant priests made and admitted into, by the prelates in whose hands the ordination of ministers and government of the church hath been OR A narration of the causes for which the parliament hath ordered the sequestration of the beneficies of severall ministers complained of before them for vitiousness of life, errors of doctrine, contrary to the articles of our religion, and for practising and pressing superstitious innovations against law for malignancy against parliament, London 1643

Wolley, H., The compleat servant-maid, London 1685

Secondary sources

Addleshaw, G. W. O. and F. Etchells, The architectural setting of Anglican worship, London 1947

Alcock, N., 'Physical space and social space', in M. Locock (ed.), Meaningful architecture: social interpretations of buildings, Aldershot 1994, 207–30

Alldridge, N., 'Loyalty and identity in Chester parishes, 1540–1640', in S. J. Wright (ed.), Parish, church and people: local studies in lay religion, London 1988, 85–125

Amussen, S. D., An ordered society: gender and class in early modern England, Oxford 1988

—— '"Being stirred to much unquietness": violence and domestic violence in early modern England', Journal of Women's History vi (1994), 70–89

Archer, I., Pursuit of stability: social relations in Elizabethan London, Cambridge 1991

Ardener, S., 'Ground rules and social maps for women: an introduction', in S. Ardener (ed.), Women and space, London 1981, 11–34

Aston, M., ' Segregation in church', in Sheils and Wood, Women in the Church, 237–94

Baer, W. C., 'Housing the poor and mechanick class in seventeenth-century London', London Journal xxv (2000), 13–39

Bailey, J., Unquiet lives: marriage and marriage breakdown in England, 1660–1800, Cambridge 2003

Barker, H. and E. Chalus (eds), Gender in eighteenth-century England: roles, representations and responsibilites, Harlow 1997

Barley, M. W., 'Rural building in England', in Thirsk, Agrarian history of England and Wales, iv. 590–685

Beattie, J. M., *Crime and the courts in England, 1660–1800*, Oxford 1986

Ben-Amos, I. K., 'Women apprentices in the trades and crafts of early modern Bristol', *C&C* vi (1991), 227–63

Bennett, J. M., 'History that stands still: women's work in the European past', *Feminist Studies* xiv (1988), 269–83

—— 'Feminism and history', *G&H* i (1989), 251–72

—— 'Misogyny, popular culture and women's work', *HWJ* xxxi (1991), 168–88

—— 'Women's history: a study in continuity and change', *Women's History Review* ii (1993), 173–84

—— *Ale, beer and brewsters in England: women's work in a changing world*, Oxford 1996

—— and A. Froide (eds), *Single women in the European past, 1250–1800*, Philadelphia 1999

Boddington, A., 'Raunds, Northamptonshire: an analysis of a country churchyard', *World Archaeology* xviii (1987), 411–25

Borsay, P., 'All the town's a stage', in P. Clark (ed.), *The transformation of English provincial towns, 1600–1800*, London 1984, 229–58

Bossy, J. (ed.), *Disputes and settlements: law and human relations in the west*, Cambridge 1987

Botelho, L. and P. Thane (eds), *Women and ageing in British society since 1500*, Harlow 2001

Boulton, J., *Neighbourhood and society: a London suburb in the seventeenth century*, Cambridge 1987

Bourdieu, P., *Outline of a theory of practice*, Cambridge 1977

—— 'Social space and the genesis of classes', in P. Bourdieu, *Language and symbolic power*, Cambridge 1991, 229–51

Braddick, M. J. and J. Walter, 'Grids of power: order, hierarchy and subordination in early modern society', in M. J. Braddick and J. Walter (eds), *Negotiating power in early modern society: order, hierarchy and subordination in Britain and Ireland*, Cambridge 2001

Bremmer, J. and H. Roodenburg (eds), *A cultural history of gesture*, Oxford 1991

Breward, C., *The culture of fashion*, Manchester 1995

Brown, A. F. J., *Essex at work, 1700–1815*, Chelmsford 1969

—— *Poverty and prosperity: rural Essex, 1700–1815*, Chelmsford 1996

Brown, F., 'Continuity and change in the urban house: developments in domestic space organisation in seventeenth-century London', *Comparative Studies in Society and History* xxviii (1986), 558–90

Bryson, A., *From courtesy to civility: changing codes of conduct in early modern England*, Oxford 1998

Burke, P., *History and social theory*, Cambridge 1992

—— B. Harrison and P. Slack (eds), *Civil histories: essays presented to Sir Keith Thomas*, Oxford 2000

Butler, J. M., *Gender trouble: feminism and the subversion of identity*, London 1991

Byford, M., 'The birth of a Protestant town: the process of Reformation in Tudor Colchester, 1530–80', in P. Collinson and J. Craig (eds), *The Reformation in English towns, 1500–1640*, Basingstoke 1998, 23–47

Capp, B., 'The poet and the bawdy court: Michael Drayton and the lodging-house world in early Stuart London', *Seventeenth Century* x (1995), 27–37

—— 'Separate domains? Women and authority in early modern England', in Fox, Griffiths and Hindle, *The experience of authority in early modern England*, 117–45

—— 'The double standard revisited: plebeian women and male sexual reputation in early modern England', *P&P* clxii (1999), 70–100

—— *'When gossips meet': women, family, and neighbourhood in early modern England*, Oxford 2003

Carlson, E., 'The origins, function, and status of churchwardens', in M. Spufford (ed.), *The world of rural dissenters, 1520–1725*, Cambridge 1995, 164–207

Charles, L. and L. Duffin (eds), *Women and work in pre-industrial England*, London 1985

Chartier, R. (ed.), *A history of private life*, III: *Passions of the Renaissance*, London 1989

Chaytor, M., 'Household and kinship: Ryton in the late sixteenth and early seventeenth centuries', *HWJ* x (1980), 25–60

Clark, A., *Working life of women in the seventeenth century*, London 1919, 3rd edn, 1992

Clark, P., *The English alehouse: a social history, 1200–1830*, London 1983

Coleman, D. C. and A. H. John (eds), *Trade, government and economy in pre-industrial England: essays presented to F. J. Fisher*, London 1976

Collinson, P., *The religion of Protestants: the Church in English society, 1559–1625*, Oxford 1982

—— 'The role of women in the English Reformation illustrated by the life and friendships of Anne Locke', in P. Collinson, *Godly people: essays on English Protestantism and Puritanism*, London 1983, 57–76

—— 'Elizabethan and Jacobean Puritanism as forms of popular religious culture', in C. Durston and J. Eales (eds), *The culture of English Puritanism, 1560–1700*, Basingstoke 1996, 32–57

—— *The birthpangs of Protestant England: religious and cultural change in the sixteenth and seventeenth centuries*, London 1998

Corfield, P. J., 'Dress for deference and dissent: hats and the decline of hat honour', *Costume* xxiii (1989), 64–79

—— 'Walking the city streets: the urban odyssey in eighteenth-century England', *Journal of Urban History* xvi (1990), 132–74

Cowan, B., 'What was masculine about the public sphere? Gender and the coffee-house milieu in post-Restoration England', *HWJ* li (2001), 127–57

Cox, J. C., *Bench ends in English churches*, London 1916

Crawford, P., 'Attitudes to menstruation in seventeenth-century England', *P&P* xci (1981), 47–73

—— 'Public duty, conscience and women in early modern England', in J. Morrill, P. Slack and D. Woolf (eds), *Public duty and private conscience in seventeenth-century England*, Oxford 1993, 57–76

—— *Women and religion in England, 1500–1720*, London 1993

Cressy, D., 'Purification, churching and thanksgiving in post-Reformation England', *P&P* clxi (1993), 106–46

—— *Birth, marriage and death: ritual, religion, and the lifecycle in Tudor and Stuart England*, Oxford 1997

Davidoff, L. and C. Hall, *Family fortunes: men and women of the English middle class, 1780–1850*, London 1987

Davids, T. W., *Annals of evangelical non-conformity in the county of Essex*, London 1863

Davidson, C., *A woman's work is never done: a history of housework in the British Isles, 1650–1950*, London 1982

Davies, A., *The Quakers in English society, 1655–1725*, Oxford 2000

Davies, K. M., 'Continuity and change in literary advice on marriage', in R. B. Outhwaite (ed.), *Marriage and society: studies in the social history of marriage*, London 1981, 58–80

Davis, N. Z., *Society and culture in early modern France*, Stanford 1975

—— *Fiction in the archives*, Oxford 1987

Deetz, J., *In small things forgotten: the archaeology of early American life*, New York 1977

Doggett, M. E., *Marriage, wife-beating and the law in Victorian England*, Columbia 1993

Dolan, F., *Dangerous familiars: representations of domestic crime in England, 1550–1700*, New York 1994

Douglas, M., *Natural symbols: explorations in cosmology*, London 1973

—— *Purity and danger: an analysis of the concepts of pollution and taboo*, London 1979

Duffy, E., *Stripping of the altars: traditional religion in England, 1400–1580*, London 1982

Dymond, D., 'Sitting apart in church', in C. Rawcliffe, R. Virgoe and R. Wilson (eds), *Counties and communities: essays on East Anglian history presented to Hassell Smith*, Norwich 1996, 213–24

Eales, J., 'Samuel Clarke and the "lives" of godly women in seventeenth-century England', in Sheils and Wood, *Women in the Church*, 365–75

Earle, P., 'The female labour market in London in the late seventeenth and early eighteenth centuries', *EcHR* xlii (1989), 328–53

—— *The making of the English middle class: business, society and family life in London, 1660–1730*, London 1989

—— *A city full of people: men and women of London, 1650–1750*, London 1994

Ekirch, A. R., *At day's close: a history of nighttime*, London 2005

Ellis, J., '"On the town": women in Augustan England', *History Today* xlv (1995), 20–7

Erickson, A. L., *Women and property in early modern England*, London 1993

Evans, N., 'A scheme for re-pewing the parish church of Chesham, Buckinghamshire, in 1606', *The Local Historian* xxii (1992), 203–7

Everitt, A., 'The marketing of agricultural produce', in Thirsk, *Agrarian history of England and Wales*, iv. 552–62

Falkus, M. E., 'Lighting in the dark ages of English economic history', in Coleman and John, *Trade, government and economy*, 248–73

Fissell, M., *Vernacular bodies: the politics of reproduction in early modern England*, London 2004

Flather, A., 'The politics of place: a study of church seating in Essex, c. 1580–1640' (Friends of the Department of English Local History, paper 3, Leicester, 1999)

Fletcher, A., *Gender, sex and subordination in England, 1500–1800*, London 1995

Foreman, A., *Georgiana, duchess of Devonshire*, London 2001

Fox, A., P. Griffiths and S. Hindle (eds), *The experience of authority in early modern England*, London 1996

Foyster, E. A., *Manhood in early modern England: honour, sex and marriage*, London 1999

────── 'At the limits of liberty: married women and confinement in eighteenth-century England', *C&C* xvii (2002), 39–62

Fraser, A., *The weaker vessel: women's lot in seventeenth-century England*, London 1984

Friedman, A.T., *House and household in Elizabethan England*, London 1989

Garrard, R., 'English probate inventories and their use in studying the significance of the domestic interior, 1500–1700', *AAG Bijdragen* xxiii (1980), 53–77

Gent, L. and N. Llewellyn (eds), *Renaissance bodies: the human figure in English culture, c. 1540–1660*, London 1990

Giddens, A., *Central problems in social theory*, London 1979

────── *The constitution of society*, Cambridge 1984

Gilchrist, R., *Gender and material culture: an archaeology of religious women*, New York 1994

Glassie, H., *Folk housing in middle America: a structural analysis of historic artefacts*, Knoxville 1975

Goody, J., *Cooking, cuisine and class: a study in comparative sociology*, Cambridge 1982

Goose, N. and J. Cooper, *Tudor and Stuart Colchester: an extract from The Victoria history of the county of Essex, IX: The borough of Colchester*, edited by Janet Cooper, Oxford 1994, repr. Chelmsford 1998

Gould, P. and R .White, *Mental maps*, London 1986

Gowing, L., 'Language, power and the law', in Kermode and Walker, *Women, crime and the courts*, 26–47

────── *Domestic dangers: women, words and sex in early modern London*, Oxford 1996

────── 'Secret births and infanticide in seventeenth-century England', *P&P* clvi (1998), 87–116

────── 'Ordering the body: illegitimacy and female authority in seventeenth century England', in Braddick and Walter, *Negotiating power*, 43–62

────── 'The freedom of the streets: women and social space, 1560–1640', in P. Griffiths and M. S. R. Jenner (eds), *Londinopolis: essays in the cultural and social history of early modern London*, Manchester 2000, 130–53

────── 'The haunting of Susan Lay: servants and mistresses in seventeenth-century England', *G&H* xiv (2002), 183–201

────── *Common bodies: women, touch and power in seventeenth-century England*, London 2003

Graves, C. P., 'Social space in the medieval parish church', *Economy and Society* xviii (1989), 297–322

Grieves, H., *The sleepers and the shadows: Chelmsford: a town, its people and its past, I: The medieval and Tudor story*, Chelmsford 1988; *II: From market town to chartered borough, 1608–1888*, Chelmsford 1994

Griffiths, P., 'The structure of prostitution in Elizabethan London', *C&C* viii (1993), 39–56

Griffiths, P., 'Masterless young people in Norwich, 1560–1645', in Fox, Griffiths and Hindle, *The experience of authority in early modern England*, 146–86

—— Youth and authority: formative experiences in England, 1560–1640, Oxford 1996

—— 'The meanings of nightwalking in early modern England', Seventeenth Century xiii (1998), 212–38

Guillery, P., The small house in eighteenth-century London, London 2004

Gullickson, G. L., Spinners and weavers of Auffay: rural industry and the sexual division of labour in a French village, 1750–1850, Cambridge 1986

Guyford, J., Public spirit: dissent in Witham and Essex, 1500–1700, Witham 1999

Hall, H., Society in the Elizabethan age, London 1902

Hammer, C. I., 'A hearty meal? The prison diets of Cranmer and Latimer', Sixteenth Century Journal iii (1999), 653–80

Hanawalt, B., Growing up in medieval London: the experience of childhood in history, Oxford 1993

Hardwick, J., The practice of patriarchy: gender and the politics of household authority in early modern France, University Park, PA 1998

Hardy, W. J., 'Notes on the division of sexes, and the assignment of seats in public worship in the primitive Church', The Ecclesiologist xxix (1868), 100–5

—— 'Remarks on the history of seat-reservation in churches', Archaeologica liii (1892), 95–106

Harte, N. B., 'State control of dress and social change in pre-industrial England', in Coleman and John, Trade, government and economy, 132–65

Harvey, K., 'The substance of sexual difference: change and persistence in representations of the body in eighteenth-century England', G&H xiv (2002), 202–23.

Hassell-Smith, A., 'Labourers in late sixteenth-century England: a case study from north Norfolk', C&C iv (1989), 11–52, 376–94

Heal, F., Hospitality in early modern England, Oxford 1990

Heales, A., The history and law of church seats, or pews, i, London 1892

Hewitt, M. and I. Pinchbeck, Children in English society, I: From Tudor times to the eighteenth century, London 1969

Hey, D., An English rural community: Myddle under the Tudors and Stuarts, Leicester 1974

Hill, B., Women, work and sexual politics, Oxford 1989

Hill, C., Economic problems of the Church: from Archbishop Whitgift to the Long Parliament, Oxford 1996

Hindle, S., 'The shaming of Margaret Knowsley: gossip, gender and the experience of authority in early modern England', C&C ix (1994), 391–419

—— 'Exclusion crises: poverty, migration and parochial responsibility in English rural communities, c. 1560–1660', Rural History vii (1996), 125–49

—— 'A sense of place? Becoming and belonging in the rural parish, 1550–1650', in A. Shepard and P. Withington (eds), Communities in early modern England, Manchester 2000, 96–114

—— 'Civility, honesty and the deserving poor', in H. French and J. Barry (eds), Identity and agency in England, 1500–1800, London 2004, 38–59

—— 'Dependency, shame and belonging: badging the deserving poor, c. 1550–1750', Cultural and Social History i (2004), 6–35

Hitchcock, T., 'Sociability and misogyny in the life of John Cannon, 1648–1743', in T. Hitchcock and M. Cohen (eds), English masculinities, 1660–1800, London 1999, 25–43

Hodgkin, K., 'Thomas Wythorne and the problem of mastery', *HWJ* xxix (1990), 20–41

Hoskins, W. G., 'The rebuilding of rural England, 1560–1640', *P&P* iv (1953), 44–59

Houlbrooke, R., *The English family, 1450–1700*, London 1984

Hufton, O., 'Women and the family economy in eighteenth-century France', *French Historical Studies* ix (1975), 1–22

——— *The prospect before her: a history of women in western Europe*, I: *1500–1800*, London 1995

Humphries, J., 'Enclosures, common rights and women; the proletarianisation of families in the late eighteenth and early nineteenth centuries', *Journal of Economic History* l (1990), 17–42

Hunt, Alan, *Governance of the consuming passions: a history of sumptuary law*, London 1990

Hunt, Arnold, 'The lord's supper in early modern England', *P&P* clxi (1998), 39–83

Hunt, M., 'Wife beating, domesticity and women's independence in eighteenth-century London', *G&H* i (1992), 10–29

——— *The middling sort: commerce, gender, and the family in England, 1680–1780*, London 1996

Hunt, W., *The Puritan moment: the coming of revolution in an English county*, London 1983

Ingram M., 'Ridings, rough music and the "reform of popular culture" in early modern England', *P&P* cv (1984), 79–113

——— *Church courts, sex and marriage in England, 1570–1640*, Cambridge 1987

——— '"Scolding women cucked or washed": a crisis in gender relations in early modern England?', in Kermode and Walker, *Women, crime and the courts*, 48–80

——— 'Sexual manners: the other face of civility in early modern England', in Burke, Harrison and Slack, *Civil histories*, 87–110

——— 'Child sexual abuse in early modern England', in Braddick and Walter, *Negotiating power*, 63–84

Jack, S. M., *Towns in Tudor and Stuart Britain*, Basingstoke 1996

James, M. E., *Family, lineage and civil society: a study of society, politics and mentality in the Durham region, 1500–1640*, Oxford 1974

Johnson, M., *Housing culture: traditional architecture in an English landscape*, London 1993

——— *An archaeology of capitalism*, Oxford 1996

Jones, A. J. and P. Stallybrass, *Renaissance clothing and the materials of memory*, Cambridge 2000

Jordonova, L., *Sexual visions: images of gender in science and medicine between the eighteenth and twentieth centuries*, London 1989

Kent, S., *Domestic architecture and the use of space: an inter-disciplinary cross-cultural study*, Cambridge 1990

Kermode, J. and G. Walker (eds), *Women, crime and the courts in early modern England*, London 1994

King, P., 'Customary rights and women's earnings; the importance of gleaning to the rural labouring poor', *EcHR* xliv (1991), 461–76

Klein, L., 'Gender, conversation and the public sphere in early eighteenth-century England', in J. Still and M. Worton (eds), *Textuality and sexuality: reading theories and practices*, Manchester 1993, 100–15

—— 'Gender and the public/private distinction in the eighteenth century: some questions about evidence and analytic procedure', *Eighteenth-Century Studies* xxix (1995), 92–109

Kussmaul, A., *Servants in husbandry in early modern England*, Cambridge 1981

Lake, P., 'Feminine piety and personal potency: the "emancipation" of Mrs Jane Ratcliffe', *Seventeenth Century* ii (1987), 143–65

—— 'The Laudian style: order, uniformity and the pursuit of the beauty of holiness in the 1630s', in K. Fincham (ed.), *The early Stuart Church, 1603–1642*, Basingstoke 1993, 161–85

—— *The boxmaker's revenge: 'orthodoxy', 'heterodoxy' and the politics of the parish in early Stuart London*, Stanford 2001

Laqueur, T., *Making sex: the body and gender from the Greeks to Freud*, Cambridge, MA 1990

Laslett, P., *The world we have lost*, London 1971

Lawrence, A., *Women in England, 1500–1760: a social history*, London 1994

Lemire, B., 'Consumerism in pre-industrial and early industrial England: the trade in secondhand clothes', *Journal of British Studies* xxvii (1998), 1–24

Lynch, K., 'The family and the history of public life', *Journal of Interdisciplinary History* xxiv (1994), 665–84

MacDonald, M. and T. R. Murphy, *Sleepless souls: suicide in early modern England*, Oxford 1990

Macfarlane, A., *Witchcraft in Tudor and Stuart England: a regional and comparative study*, London 1970

—— 'Historical anthropology', *Cambridge Anthropology* iii (1977), 1–21

McIntosh, M. K., *A community transformed: the manor and liberty of Havering, 1500–1620*, Cambridge 1991

McLaughlin, E. C., 'Equality of souls, inequality of sexes: women in medieval theology', in R. Reuther (ed.), *Religion and sexism: images of women in the Jewish and Christian traditions*, New York 1974, 218–29

Maclean, I., *The Renaissance notion of woman: a study in the fortunes of scholasticism and medical science in European intellectual life*, Cambridge 1980

Macray Beier, L., *Sufferers and healers: the experience of illness in seventeenth-century England*, London 1987

Machin, R., 'The great rebuilding: a reassessment', *P&P* lxxvii (1977), 33–56

Maltby, J., *Prayer book and people*, Cambridge 1998

Marchant, R. A., *The Church under the law: justice and discipline in the diocese of York, 1540–1640*, Cambridge 1969

Marsh, C., '"Common Prayer", in England, 1560–1640: the view from the pew', *P&P* clxxi (2001), 66–92

—— 'Sacred space in England, 1560–1640: the view from the pew', *JEH* liii (2002), 286–311

—— 'Order and place in England, 1580–1640: the view from the pew', *Journal of British Studies* xliv (2005), 3–26

Massey, D., *Space, place and gender*, Cambridge 1994

Medick, H., 'The proto-industrial family economy: the structural function of household and family during the transition from peasant society to industrial capitalism', *Social History* iii (1976), 291–315

Meldrum, T., *Domestic service and gender, 1660–1750*, London 2000

Mendelson, S., 'The civility of women in seventeenth-century England', in Burke, Harrison and Slack, *Civil histories*, 111–26

―――― and P. Crawford, *Women in early modern England*, Oxford 1998

Mennell, S., *All manner of foods: eating and taste in England and France from the Middle Ages to the present*, Oxford 1985

Merritt, J. F., 'Puritans, Laudians and the phenomenon of church-building in Jacobean London', *HJ* xxxi (1998), 935–60

Mikalachki, J., 'Women's networks and the female vagrant: a hard case', in S. Frye and K. Robertson (eds), *Women's alliances in early modern England*, Oxford 1999, 52–69

Moore, H., *Space, text and gender: an anthropological study of the Marakwet of Kenya* Cambridge 1986

Morrill, J., 'The Church in England, 1642–1649', in his *The nature of the English Revolution*, London 1993, 148–75

Muldrew, C., *The economy of obligation: the culture of credit and social relations in early modern England*, Basingstoke 1998

Overton, M., J. Whittle, D. Dean and A. Hann, *Production and consumption in English households, 1600–1750*, Oxford 2004

Pahl, R. E., *Divisions of labour*, Oxford 1984

Paster, G., 'The unbearable coldness of female being: women's imperfections and the humoral economy', *English Literary Renaissance* xxviii (1998), 416–40

Pateman, C., *The sexual contract*, Stanford 1988

Peters, C., *Patterns of piety: women, gender and religion in late medieval and Reformation England*, Cambridge 2003

―――― *Women in early modern England, 1580–1640*, Basingstoke 2004

Phythian Adams, C., *Desolation of a city: Coventry and the urban crisis of the late Middle Ages*, Cambridge 1979

―――― 'Ceremony and the citizen: the communal year at Coventry, 1450–1550', in P. Clark and P. Slack (eds), *Crisis and order in English towns, 1500–1700*, London 1982, 57–85

―――― 'Milk and soot: the changing vocabulary of a popular ritual in Stuart and Hanoverian London', in D. Fraser and A. Sutcliffe (eds), *The pursuit of urban history*, London 1983, 83–104

Picard, L., *Restoration London*, London 1997

Pinchbeck, I., *Women workers in the industrial revolution*, London 1930

Pipkin, J. S., 'Space and the social order in Pepys' diary', *Urban Geography* xi (1990), 153–75

Pollock, L. A., ' "Teach her to live under obedience": the making of women in the upper ranks of early modern England', *C&C* iv (1989), 231–58

―――― 'Childbearing and female bonding in early modern England', *Social History* xxii (1997), 286–306

Porter R. and M. Teich (eds), *Sexual knowledge, sexual science: the history of attitudes to sexuality*; Cambridge 1994

Prendergast, S., 'Stoolball: the pursuit of vertigo?', *Women's Studies International Quarterly* i (1978), 15–26

Priestley, U., P. Corfield and H. Sutermeister, 'Rooms and room use in Norwich housing, 1580–1730', *Post-Medieval Archaeology* xvi (1982), 93–123

Prior, M., 'Women and the urban economy: Oxford, 1500–1800', in Prior, *Women in English society*, 93–117

———— (ed.), *Women in English society, 1500–1800*, London 1985

Purkiss, D., *The witch in history: early modern and twentieth-century representations*, London 1996

Quaife, G. R., *Wanton wenches and wayward wives: peasants and illicit sex in seventeenth-century England*, London 1979

Quinn, W. E., *A history of Braintree and Bocking*, Lavenham 1981

Reiter, R. R., 'Men and women in the south of France: public and private domains', in R. R. Reiter (ed.), *Towards an anthropology of women*, New York 1975, 21–49

Revel, J., 'The uses of civility', in Chartier, A *history of private life*, iii. 167–205

Ribeiro, A., *Dress and morality*, Oxford 2003

Richardson, C. (ed.), *Clothing culture, 1350–1650*, Aldershot 2004

Roberts, M., 'Sickles and scythes', *HWJ* vii (1979), 3–28

———— '"Words they are women and deeds they are men": images of work and gender in early modern England', in Charles and Duffin, *Women and work*, 122–80

———— 'Women and work in sixteenth-century towns', in P. J. Corfield and D. Keene (eds), *Work in towns, 850–1850*, Leicester 1990, 86–102

Rollinson, D., 'Trails of progress: the reorientation and intensification of traffic, 1600–1800', in his *The local origins of modern society: Gloucestershire, 1500–1800*, London 1992, 45–66

Roper, L., *The holy household: religion, morals and order in Reformation Augsburg*, Oxford 1989

———— *Oedipus and the devil: witchcraft, sexuality and religion in early modern Europe*, London 1994.

Roubin, L., 'Male space and female space within the Provençal community', in R. Forster and O. Ranum (eds), *Rural society in France: selections from the Annales, economies, sociétés, civilisations*, London 1977, 252–82

Rowlands, A., 'Witchcraft and old women in early modern Germany', *P&P* clxxiii (2001), 51–89

Rowlands, M., 'Recusant women, 1560–1640', in Prior, *Women in English society*, 149–80

Rublack, U., 'Pregnancy, childbirth and the female body in early modern Germany', *P&P* cl (1996), 84–110

Sabean, D., *Power in the blood: popular culture and village discourse in early modern Germany*, Cambridge 1984

Sarti, R., *Europe at home: family and material culture, 1500–1800*, London 2002

Schiebinger, L., *The mind has no sex? Women and the origins of modern science*, Cambridge, MA 1989

Scott, J. W., 'Gender: a useful category for historical analysis', *American Historical Review* xcii (1986), 1053–76

Shammas, C., 'The world women knew: women workers in the north of England during the late seventeenth century', in R. S. Dunn and M. M. Dunn (eds), *The world of William Penn*, Philadelphia 1986, 99–114

Sharpe, J. A., *Defamation and sexual slander in early modern England: the church courts at York* (Borthwick Papers lviii, 1980)

———— *Crime in seventeenth-century England: a county study*, Cambridge 1983, new edn 1985

———— *Crime in early modern England, 1550–1750*, London 1984

Sharpe, K., *The personal rule of Charles 1*, New Haven 1992

Sharpe, P., 'Literally spinsters: a new interpretation of local economy and demography in Colyton in the seventeenth and eighteenth centuries', *EcHR* xliv (1991), 46–65

———— *Adapting to capitalism: working women in the English economy, 1700–1850*, London 1996

Shawcross, H., *A history of Dagenham in the county of Essex*, London 1904

Sheils, W. and D. Wood (eds), *Women in the Church* (Studies in Church History xxvii, 1990)

Shepard, A., *Meanings of manhood in early modern England*, Oxford 2003

Shoemaker, R. B., *Prosecution and punishment: petty crime and the law in London and rural Middlesex, c. 1660–1725*, Cambridge 1991

———— *Gender in English society, 1650–1850: the emergence of separate spheres?* London 1998

———— 'Gendered spaces: patterns of mobility and perception of London's geography, 1660–1750', in J. Merritt (ed.), *Imagining early modern London: perceptions and portrayals of the city from Stow to Strype, 1598–1720*, Cambridge 2001, 144–65

Shorter, E., *A history of women's bodies*, London 1983

Skipp, V., *Crisis and development: an ecological case study of the Forest of Arden*, Cambridge 1978

Slack, P., *Poverty and policy in Tudor and Stuart England*, London 1988

Smail, J., *The origins of middle-class culture: Halifax, Yorkshire, 1660–1780*, New York 1994

Snell, K., *Annals of the labouring poor: social change and agrarian England, 1600–1900*, Cambridge 1985

Sommerville, M., *Sex and subjection: attitudes to women in early modern society*, London 1995

Spain, D., *Gendered spaces*, London 1992

Spicer, A., '"Accommodating of thame selfis to heir the worde": preaching, pews and reformed worship in Scotland, 1560–1638', *History* lxxxviii (2003), 405–22

Spufford, M., *The great reclothing of rural England: petty chapmen and their wares in the seventeenth century*, London 1984

Stallybrass, P., 'Patriarchal territories: the body enclosed', in M. W. Ferguson, M. Quilligan and N. J. Vickers (eds), *Rewriting the Renaissance*, Chicago 1987, 122–42

Stea, D., *Landscape*, London 1967

Steer, F.W., *Farm cottages and inventories of mid-Essex, 1635–1750*, Chelmsford 1950

Stone, L., *The family, sex and marriage in England, 1500–1800*, London 1977

Stretton, T., *Women waging law in Elizabethan England*, Cambridge 1998

Styles, J., 'Embezzlement, industry and the law in England, 1500–1800', in M. Berg, P. Hudson and M. Sonnenscher (eds), *Manufacture in town and country before the factory*, Cambridge 1983, 173–208

Thirsk, J., *Economic policy and projects: the development of a consumer society in early modern England*, Oxford 1978

———— (ed.), *The agrarian history of England and Wales*, IV: 1500–1640, Cambridge 1985

Thomas K., *Religion and the decline of magic*, London 1971

———— 'Cleanliness and godliness in early modern England', in A. Fletcher and P. Roberts (eds), *Religion, culture and society in early modern Britain: essays in honour of Patrick Collinson*, Cambridge 1994, 56–83

Thompson, P., 'Women in the fishing: the roots of power between the sexes', *Comparative Studies in Society and History* xxvii (1985), 3–32

Thwaites, W., 'Women in the market place: Oxfordshire, c.1690–1800', *Midland History* ix (1984), 23–42

Tilly, L. A. and J. A. Scott, *Women, work and family*, New York 1978

Tittler, R., *The Reformation and the towns in England*, Oxford 1998

Todd, B. J., 'The re-marrying widow: a stereotype reconsidered', in Prior, *Women in English society*, 54–92

Todd, M., *The culture of Protestantism in early modern Scotland*, London 2002

Tosh, J., *Men at home: domesticity and the Victorian middle class*, London 1999

Ulrich, L. T., *Goodwives: image and reality in the lives of women in northern New England, 1650–1750*, New York 1980

Underdown, D., *Revel, riot and rebellion: popular politics and culture, 1603–1660*, Oxford 1985

———— 'The taming of the scold: the enforcement of patriarchal authority in early modern England', in A. Fletcher and J. Stevenson (eds), *Order and disorder in early modern England*, Cambridge 1985, 116–36

Unwin, G., 'The history of the cloth industry in Suffolk', in R. H. Tawney (ed.), *Studies in economic history: the collected papers of George Unwin*, London, 1927

Valenze, D., 'The art of women and the business of men: women's work and the dairy industry. c.1740–1840', *P&P* cxxx (1991), 142–69

Vickery, A., 'Golden age to separate spheres? A review of the categories and chronology of English women's history', *HJ* xxxvi (1993), 383–414

———— *The gentleman's daughter: women's lives in Georgian England*, London 1998

Walker G., 'Women, theft and the world of stolen goods', in Kermode and Walker, *Women, crime and the courts*, 81–105

———— 'Expanding the boundaries of female honour in early modern England', *Transactions of the Royal Historical Society* 6th ser. vi (1996), 235–45

Walker, W., *Essex markets and fairs*, Chelmsford 1981

Wall, C., 'Gendering rooms: domestic architecture and literary arts', *Eighteenth Century Fiction* v (1993), 349–72

Wall, R., 'Women alone in English society', in *Annales de demographie historique*, London 1981, 303–17

Walsham, A., '"A glose of godliness": Philip Stubbes, Elizabethan Grub Street and the invention of Puritanism', in S. Wabuda and C. Litzenberger (eds), *Belief and practice in Reformation England: a tribute to Patrick Collinson from his students*, Aldershot 1998, 177–206

Walter, J., 'Confessional politics in pre-Civil War Essex: Prayer Book, profanation and petitions', *HJ* xliv (2001), 667–701

——— '"Abolishing superstition with sedition"? The politics of popular icono-clasm in England, 1640–1642', *P&P* clxxxiii (2004), 79–123

Warner, M., *From the beast to the blonde: on fairy tales and their tellers*, London 1994

Weatherill, L., 'A possession of one's own: women and consumer behaviour in England, 1660–1740', *Journal of British Studies* xxv (1986), 131–56

——— *Consumer behaviour and material culture, 1660–1715*, London 1988

Wiesner, M., *Women and gender in early modern Europe*, Cambridge 2000

Wildeblood, J. and P. Brinson, *The polite world: a guide to English manners and deportment from the thirteenth to the nineteenth century*, London 1965

Willen, D., 'Women in the public sphere in early modern England', *Sixteenth Century Journal* xix (1988), 559–75

Wilson, A., 'The ceremony of childbirth and its interpretation', in V. Fildes (ed.), *Women as mothers in pre-industrial England*, London 1990, 68–107

Wilson, S., *The magical universe: everyday ritual and magic in pre-modern Europe*, London 2000

Wood, A., 'The place of custom in plebeian political culture: England, 1550–1800', *Social History* xxi (1997), 46–60

——— *The politics of social conflict: the Peake country, 1520–1770*, Cambridge 1999

Wright, S., '"Churmaids, huswyfes and hucksters": the employment of women in Tudor and Stuart Salisbury', in Charles and Duffin, *Women and work*, 100–21

Wrightson, K., 'Ale-houses, order and Reformation in England, 1590–1660', in E. Yeo and S. Yeo (eds), *Popular culture and class conflict, 1590–1914: explorations in the history of labour and leisure*, Brighton 1981, 1–27

——— *English society, 1580–1640*, London 1982

——— 'The social order of early modern England: three approaches', in L. Bonfield, R. M. Smith and K. Wrightson (eds), *The world we have gained: histories of population and social structure*, Oxford 1986, 177–202

——— 'Estates, degrees and sorts: changing perceptions of society in Tudor and Stuart England', in P. Corfield (ed.), *Language, history and class*, Oxford 1991, 28–51

——— 'The politics of the parish in early modern England', in Fox, Griffiths, and Hindle (eds), *The experience of authority in early modern England*, Cambridge 1996, 10–46

——— and D. Levine, *Poverty and piety in an English village: Terling, 1525–1700*, Oxford 1995

Yentsch, A., 'The symbolic division of pottery: sex related attributes of English and Anglo-American household pots', in R. M. McGuire and R. Paynter (eds), *The archaeology of inequality*, Oxford 1991, 192–230

Unpublished dissertations

Burley, K. H., 'The economic development of Essex in the later seventeenth and early eighteenth centuries', PhD diss. London 1957

Carney, P. L., 'Social interactions in early modern England: Cheshire and Essex, 1560–1640', PhD diss. Boulder 2002

Cliftlands, W., 'The "well-affected" and the "country": politics and religion in English provincial society, c. 1640–1645', PhD diss. Essex 1987

Dillow, K., 'The social and ecclesiastical significance of church seating arrangements and pew disputes, 1500–1740', DPhil. diss. Oxford 1990

Gammon, J., 'Ravishment and ruin: the construction of stories of sexual violence in England, c. 1640–1820', PhD diss. Essex 2000

Issa, C., 'Obligation and choice: aspects of family and kinship in seventeenth century county Durham', PhD diss. St Andrews 1986

Johnson, C., 'A proto-industrial community study: Coggeshall in Essex c. 1500–1750', PhD diss. Essex 1990

Mackinnon, A. D., '"According to the custom of the place I now live in": life and land in seventeenth-century Earls Colne, Essex', PhD diss. Melbourne 1994

Melville, J. D., 'The use and organisation of domestic space in late seventeenth-century London', PhD diss. Cambridge 1999

Pennell, S., 'The material culture of food in early modern England, c. 1650–1750', DPhil. diss. Oxford 1997

Pilgrim, J. E., 'The cloth industry in Essex and Suffolk, 1558–1640', MA diss. London 1938

Wright, K., 'A looking glass for Christian morality? Three perspectives on Puritan clothing culture and identity in England, c. 1560–1620', MPhil. diss. Birmingham 2004

Index

Lightning Source UK Ltd.
Milton Keynes UK
08 January 2011

165318UK00001B/63/P